The Best of Food Digest

The Best of Food Digest

More than 500 Brand-Name
Recipes from America's Most Popular Magazine

Reader's Digest

The Reader's Digest Association, Inc.
Pleasantville, New York/Montreal

A Reader's Digest Book
Edited and produced by Roundtable Press, Inc.
Directors: Susan E. Meyer, Marsha Melnick
Editor: Maryanne Bannon
Design concept: Beth Tondreau, Beth Tondreau Design
Design and layout: Laura Smyth, smythtype

The credits and acknowledgments that appear on page 6 are hereby
made a part of this copyright page.

Library of Congress Cataloging in Publication Data
The best of food digest: more than 500 delicious brand name recipes
    from Reader's Digest, American's most popular magazine.
        p.   cm.
    ISBN 0-89577-970-6
    1. Cookery.   2. Brand name products.   I. Reader's Digest.
TX714.B423 1997
641.5—dc21   97-2683

Printed in Hong Kong

Contents

Grateful acknowledgment is made to the companies and organizations listed below for the use of their recipes in this book.

Alberto Culver USA
Bertolli USA
Best Foods, CPC International Inc.
Blue Diamond
Campbell Soup Company
Con Agra
Dairy Management, Inc.
Del Monte Foods
Dow Brands
Florida Department of Citrus
General Mills, Inc.
Heinz USA
Hershey Foods Corporation
Hillshire Farm & Kahn's
Hormel Foods
Hunt-Wesson, Inc.
Kellogg USA, Inc.

Kikkoman
Kraft Foods, Inc.
Land O Lakes, Inc.
Lawrey's Foods, Inc.
Lipton
Mars Inc.
Motts North America
Nabisco Inc.
National Cattlemen's Beef Association
National Pork Producers Council
Nestlé
Pillsbury
The Quaker Oats Company
Reckitt and Colman
Sunkist
Uncle Ben's, Inc.

Special thanks to Kathleen Perry the everyday gourmet

Original photography for the book by David Bishop and Dennis M. Gottlieb

Portions of this book are published with permission from Joshua Morris Publishing, Inc.

Recipes previously appeared in the Food Digest® cooking feature of *Reader's Digest*

Introduction

In celebrating the 75th anniversary of *Reader's Digest*, we looked into our archives and selected more than 500 recipes from *Food Digest*, our popular monthly feature on cooking. The result is a cookbook which is sure to become a staple in kitchens across America.

Food Digest started out as an occasional food feature, but it was so well received by our readers that we soon started to run it every month. And the pages continue to showcase fresh and prepared ingredients in recipes that have been put to the test in brand-name kitchens. These recipes are proven winners—delicious dishes that you can rely on.

The pages of this book are filled with mouth-watering recipes in an easy-to-follow format that makes cooking techniques and procedures simple. From meat and poultry, appetizers, soups and salads, to cookies and cakes, and breads and muffins, our unique cookbook will have you cooking with the best and having fun in the process.

Perhaps the most special thing about this cookbook is that the recipes are meant to be shared and are sure to become family favorites. All of the recipes use the quality brands you know, and are brought to you by the magazine millions of Americans have loved and trusted for over 75 years. ❖

Greg Coleman
Publisher,
Reader's Digest

Appetizers, Snacks, AND Dips

Orange Glazed Chicken Wings

MAKES 16 APPETIZERS

1 cup **Florida Orange Juice**
Grated zest from 1 small orange
2 cloves garlic, finely chopped
½ teaspoon dried thyme, crumbled
½ teaspoon dried rosemary, crumbled
2 tablespoons balsamic vinegar
2 teaspoons Dijon mustard
2 teaspoons firmly packed brown sugar
1 tablespoon cornstarch
2 pounds chicken wings, each wing halved at the
   second joint
Salt and pepper to taste

1. In a small saucepan, combine the orange juice, orange zest, garlic, herbs, vinegar, mustard, sugar, and cornstarch. Bring to a boil over moderate heat, whisking occasionally.

2. Simmer the mixture, stirring, until lightly thickened. Remove from the heat.

3. Heat the broiler.

4. Arrange the chicken wings on the broiler pan. Broil about 6 inches from the heat for 5 minutes on each side. Add seasoning, then liberally baste the wings with the glaze. Broil 3 minutes more on each side, or until cooked through.

5. Remove to a platter and serve.

COURTESY: FLORIDA DEPARTMENT OF CITRUS

Hawaiian Chicken Strips

MAKES 25 TO 30 APPETIZERS

4 cups **Rice Chex® brand cereal,** crushed to 1⅔ cups
½ cup flaked coconut
2 pinches cayenne (red) pepper
½ cup mayonnaise *or* salad dressing
1 tablespoon Dijon mustard
1 tablespoon honey
1 pound skinless, boneless chicken breasts,
   cut into 30 ½-inch-wide strips
1 fresh pineapple, cut into 60 1-inch chunks,
   or 2 cans (20 ounces *each*) pineapple chunks
2 red *or* green bell peppers, cut into ¾-inch pieces
30 10-inch bamboo skewers

1. Heat the oven to 400° F.

2. In a large plastic bag, combine the cereal, coconut, and cayenne pepper. Set aside.

3. In a medium bowl, combine the mayonnaise, mustard, and honey.

4. Stir the chicken strips into the mayonnaise mixture.

5. Place the strips in the bag with the cereal mixture, a few at a time, and shake until well coated.

6. Thread each strip onto a skewer with 2 chunks each of the pineapple and bell pepper.

7. Place the skewers on a rack in a shallow baking pan.

8. Bake 15 to 20 minutes or until the strips are no longer pink in the center.

9. Remove to a platter and serve.

NOTE

Skewers may be assembled a day before serving, covered, and refrigerated. Cooking time may need to be increased.

®Chex cereal brands are registered trademarks of General Mills, Inc.

❖

Sticky Wings

Sticky Wings

24 chicken wings (about 4 pounds)
¾ cup **Wish-Bone® Italian Dressing**
1 cup apricot *or* peach preserves
1 tablespoon hot pepper sauce *or* to taste (optional)

1. Cut the tips off the chicken wings and then cut them in half at the joint.

2. In a small bowl, whisk together the Italian dressing, preserves, and hot pepper sauce, if desired, for the marinade.

3. In a large, shallow, non-aluminum baking dish or a plastic bag, pour half the marinade over the chicken wings and toss to coat. Cover the dish or close the bag and marinate in the refrigerator for 3 to 24 hours, turning occasionally. Cover and refrigerate the remaining marinade.

4. Prepare the grill or broiler.

5. Remove the wings, discarding the marinade. Grill or broil the wings, turning once and brushing frequently with the reserved marinade until the wings are done.

6. Remove to a platter and serve.

Peppy Pizza Mini-Bagels

MAKES 20 APPETIZERS

10 mini-bagels, sliced in half
60 **HORMEL® pepperoni (slices)**
1 jar (15 ounces) pizza sauce
1 cup shredded mozzarella cheese

1. Heat the oven to 350° F.

2. Place 20 bagel halves, cut side up, on a baking sheet.

3. Place 1 pepperoni slice over the hole of each bagel. Over the pepperoni, spoon 1 tablespoon pizza sauce, 1 tablespoon cheese, and 2 more pepperoni slices.

4. Bake about 10 minutes or until the bagels are heated and the cheese has melted.

5. Remove to a platter and serve hot.

Sausage Rolls

MAKES 36 APPETIZERS

½ package (17¼ ounces) frozen puff pastry sheets (1 sheet)
8 ounces bulk pork sausage

1. Thaw the pastry sheet at room temperature for 20 minutes. Heat the oven to 400° F.

2. Unfold the pastry on a lightly floured surface. Roll into a 12×10-inch rectangle. Cut into 3 strips along the fold marks.

3. Divide the sausage into thirds. Roll each portion into a cylinder the length of the pastry. Place on the edge of each pastry strip. Starting at the long side, roll up. Press the edges to seal.

4. Cut each roll into twelve 1-inch slices. Place 1½ inches apart on the baking sheet. Bake 15 minutes or until golden.

5. Remove to a platter and serve hot.

Mini BLTs

MAKES 20 APPETIZERS

1 package (16 ounces) **Black Label® Bacon**
1 package (10 ounces) refrigerated biscuit dough
⅓ cup mayonnaise *or* salad dressing
4 plum tomatoes, thinly sliced
5 lettuce leaves, broken in small pieces

1. Cook the bacon according to package directions and drain.

2. Bake the biscuits according to package directions.

3. Split each biscuit in half. Spread the mayonnaise on the cut side of each biscuit half and place a piece of lettuce on it. Top with a tomato slice.

4. Cut each bacon slice in half. Cross halves over each tomato slice and fasten with a toothpick.

5. Remove to a platter and serve hot.

Hot Peppy Toasts

MAKES 12 TO 16 APPETIZERS

2 ounces **HORMEL® pepperoni (slices),** diced (½ cup)
½ cup mayonnaise
¼ cup finely chopped green onions
2 tablespoons grated Parmesan cheese
4 slices bread, cut into triangles or quarters

1. Heat the oven to 375° F.

2. Stir together the pepperoni, mayonnaise, green onions, and cheese.

3. Spread the mixture atop each bread triangle and place on a baking sheet.

4. Bake 10 to 12 minutes until the bread is lightly toasted.

5. Remove to a platter and serve hot.

Lit'l Smokies Crescent Wraps

2 packages (8 ounces *each*) refrigerated crescent roll dough
1 package (16 ounces) **Hillshire Farm® Lit'l Smokies,**
  any variety

1. Separate the dough into 8 triangles. Cut each lengthwise into 3 triangles.
2. Place 1 Lit'l Smokie across the wide end of each triangle. Roll toward the narrow end to wrap the Lit'l Smokie in the dough.
3. Place on an ungreased baking sheet, dough point down. Bake according to dough package directions.
4. Remove to a platter and serve hot or warm.

Lit'l Smokies Cornbread Wraps

1 package (11½ ounces) cornbread twist dough
1 package (16 ounces) **Hillshire Farm® Lit'l Smokies,**
  any variety

1. Separate the dough into 16 strips. Cut each strip crosswise into thirds.
2. Flatten the dough and wrap around the Lit'l Smokies. Press the ends together to seal.
3. Place on an ungreased baking sheet, seam side down. Bake according to dough package directions.
4. Remove to a platter and serve hot or warm.

Italian Roll-Ups

3½ ounces **HORMEL® hard salami, Genoa salami,** *or*
  giant slice pepperoni
1 package (5 ounces) string cheese
½ cup all-purpose flour
1 egg, beaten
⅓ cup milk
1 tablespoon vegetable oil

1. Cut the cheese to fit the meat. Roll together 1 meat slice and 1 cheese piece and secure with a wooden toothpick. Repeat with the remaining meat and cheese.
2. In a small bowl, stir together the remaining ingredients until well moistened.
3. Dip each roll-up in the batter.
4. Deep-fat fry at 375° F for 1 to 2 minutes or until golden. Do not overcook. Drain.
5. Remove to a platter and serve immediately.

For the best results when deep-fat frying, use a dual-purpose candy/deep-fat thermometer to make sure the oil is just the right temperature. Too low a temperature will cause the food to become greasy. If it's too high, the food will burn. For easy handling, choose a thermometer with a plastic handle or one that clips onto the pan.

Appetizer Rounds

For cheesy-onion topping:

⅓ cup mayonnaise *or* salad dressing
⅓ cup shredded Cheddar cheese
⅓ cup shredded mozzarella cheese
3 green onions (with tops), sliced

For rounds:

2 cups **Bisquick® Original** *or* **Reduced Fat baking mix**
¼ teaspoon garlic powder
½ cup boiling water*

1. In a small bowl, combine the topping ingredients and refrigerate.

2. Heat the oven to 400° F.

3. In a medium bowl, mix the baking mix, garlic powder, and water until a soft dough forms. Let stand about 10 minutes or until cool.

4. Turn onto a surface dusted with baking mix and shape into a ball. Knead 12 to 15 times or until smooth.

5. Roll the dough ⅛-inch thick. Cut with a 2-inch round cutter dipped in baking mix.

6. Place the rounds about 1 inch apart on a large ungreased baking sheet. Top each round with about ½ teaspoon topping.

7. Bake 10 to 12 minutes or until the topping is golden brown.

8. Immediately remove from the baking sheet. Serve hot.

NOTE

*If using **Reduced Fat baking mix,** increase boiling water to ⅔ cup.

Spicy Sausage Snacks

1 package (12 ounces) spicy ground pork sausage
2 cups **Bisquick® Original** *or* **Reduced Fat baking mix**
1½ cups shredded Cheddar cheese (6 ounces)
¾ cup finely chopped green onions
½ cup grated Parmesan cheese
¼ cup sour cream
½ teaspoon garlic powder
⅔ cup milk
1 egg

1. Heat the oven to 350° F.

2. Grease a 15½ × 10½-inch jelly-roll pan.

3. In a 10-inch skillet, cook the sausage, stirring frequently, until brown. Drain. Sausage pieces should be the size of small peas.

4. In a large bowl, mix the sausage and remaining ingredients, then spread in the pan.

5. Bake 20 to 25 minutes or until golden brown.

6. Cool 5 minutes, then cut into 1½-inch squares.

7. Remove to a platter and serve warm.

Spicy Sausage Snacks, Appetizer Rounds

Peppy Puffs

MAKES 24 APPETIZERS

¼ cup (½ stick) butter *or* margarine
½ cup water
½ cup all-purpose flour
2 eggs
½ cup **HORMEL® pepperoni (slices)** (2 ounces), diced

1. Heat the oven to 400° F.
2. In a small saucepan, over high heat, bring the butter and water to a rolling boil.
3. Add the flour and stir vigorously until the mixture forms a ball. Cook 1 minute, stirring, until the dough dries slightly and leaves a light film on the bottom of the pan.
4. Remove the pan from the heat. Using a hand mixer or a spoon, beat in 1 egg until completely absorbed. Add the second egg and continue beating until the dough is smooth and shiny. Stir in the pepperoni.
5. On an ungreased baking sheet, drop teaspoons of the mixture 2 inches apart. Bake 20 to 25 minutes until puffed and golden brown.
6. Remove to a platter and serve.

Antipasto

SERVES 8 TO 10

1 package (16 ounces) frozen mixed vegetables
4 ounces mozzarella cheese, cut in ½-inch cubes
¼ cup Italian salad dressing
3½ ounces **HORMEL® hard salami**
3½ ounces **HORMEL® Genoa salami**
3½ ounces **HORMEL® pepperoni (slices)**
Leaf lettuce

1. Cook the vegetables according to package directions. Drain under cold water.
2. In a large bowl, toss together the vegetables, cheese, and salad dressing.
3. Roll up each meat slice.
4. Spoon the vegetable mixture onto a lettuce-lined platter.
5. Arrange the meat around the vegetables.
6. Serve with a crusty bread.

Peppy Bruschetta

MAKES ABOUT 24 APPETIZERS

3½ ounces **HORMEL® pepperoni (slices),** chopped
1 loaf French bread, cut into ½-inch rounds and lightly toasted
2 tablespoons olive oil
2 cloves garlic, cut in half
2 cups seeded and diced plum tomatoes
1 cup chopped fresh basil
Salt and pepper (optional)

1. In a medium skillet, cook the pepperoni over medium heat until crisp, about 8 minutes. Remove the pepperoni and drain on paper towels.
2. Lightly brush one side of the toasted bread with the olive oil. Rub the cut side of the garlic over the olive oil.
3. In a medium bowl, stir together the pepperoni, tomatoes, and basil. Mound onto the toasts.
4. Remove to a platter and serve.

❖

Finger Sandwiches

1 pita round (6 to 8 inches)
2 tablespoons mayonnaise
⅛ teaspoon ground cumin
¼ teaspoon chopped jalapeño pepper
4 slices ripe tomatoes, halved
1 package (6 ounces) **Deli Select® Thin Sliced Premium Meat,** any variety
2 pitted olives, sliced (optional)
Alfalfa sprouts (optional)

1. Cut the pita round into 8 wedges and lightly toast.

2. In a small bowl, combine the mayonnaise, cumin, and jalapeño.

3. Spread each wedge with a dab of the mayonnaise mixture. Top with a half-slice of tomato and 2 slices of your favorite Deli Select®. If desired, garnish with a slice of olive and a few sprouts.

4. Remove to a serving dish and serve.

Vegetable Bundles

1 package (3 ounces) cream cheese, softened
1 tablespoon chopped chives
⅛ teaspoon lemon pepper
1 package (6 ounces) **Deli Select® Thin Sliced Premium Meat,** any variety
8 steamed asparagus tips
1 yellow *or* red bell pepper, trimmed, seeded, and sliced in thin strips
8 blanched green onion tops (green part only)

1. In a small bowl, combine the cream cheese, chives, and lemon pepper.

2. Spread ⅛ of the mixture over 2 folded slices of Deli Select.®

3. Place an asparagus tip and 2 strips of bell pepper in the center and wrap with the meat slices. Tie it all together with a blanched green onion.

4. Remove to a serving dish and serve.

Peppy Stuffed Celery

1 package (8 ounces) cream cheese, softened
1 tablespoon lemon juice
½ cup **HORMEL® pepperoni (slices),** chopped
2 tablespoons chopped chives
Celery stalks, cleaned

1. In a medium bowl, beat together the cream cheese and lemon juice until fluffy. Stir in the pepperoni and chives.

2. With a knife, spread the cheese mixture evenly into the celery stalks. Refrigerate until the cheese is firm, then cut the stalks into 3-inch pieces.

3. Remove to a serving dish and serve.

VARIATION

Spread the cheese mixture onto carrot slices, mushroom caps, bell pepper strips, or other vegetables.

Herbed Stuffed Eggs, Creamy Dijon Topped Potatoes

Herbed Stuffed Eggs

MAKES 24 APPETIZERS

12 hard-cooked eggs
½ cup garlic and herb cheese spread
¼ cup mayonnaise
¼ cup finely chopped green onions
2 tablespoons finely chopped pimientos
¼ cup **Grey Poupon® Dijon** *or* **Country Dijon Mustard**
Sliced green onions

1. Halve the eggs lengthwise. Scoop out the yolks into a large bowl. Set the egg white halves aside.
2. Mash the yolks and blend in the cheese spread, mayonnaise, green onions, pimientos, and mustard until smooth.
3. Spoon or pipe the yolk mixture into the egg white halves.
4. Garnish with the sliced green onions and serve.

Creamy Dijon Topped Potatoes

MAKES 36 APPETIZERS

1 package (8 ounces) cream cheese, softened
¼ cup **Grey Poupon® Dijon** *or* **Country Dijon Mustard**
1 teaspoon dried basil
⅓ cup finely chopped black olives
¼ cup finely chopped green onions
¼ cup finely chopped red bell pepper
18 small red-skin potatoes, roasted and cut in half lengthwise
Green onions tips

1. In a medium bowl, with an electric mixer at medium speed, beat the cream cheese, mustard, and basil until smooth.
2. Stir in the olives, green onions, and bell pepper.
3. Pipe or spoon 1 tablespoon mixture onto each potato half. Garnish with the green onion tips and serve.

Ham Mushrooms

1½ pounds medium white mushrooms
1 package (6 ounces) **Deli Select® Smoked Ham**
2 tablespoons vegetable oil
3 tablespoons chopped red bell pepper
¾ cup shredded Cheddar *or* Swiss cheese
¼ cup bread crumbs
2 tablespoons minced fresh parsley

1. Heat the oven to 400° F.
2. Wipe the mushrooms clean with a damp paper towel. Separate the stems from the caps and reserve.
3. Chop the stems and ham together.
4. In a medium skillet, heat the oil over medium heat. Briefly sauté the ham mixture with the bell pepper until the bell pepper is crisp-tender. Stir in the remaining ingredients.
5. Fill the caps with the mixture.
6. Bake on a baking sheet for 8 to 10 minutes.
7. Remove to a platter and serve warm.

Seasoned Potato Wedges with Chive Dip

⅓ cup all-purpose flour
⅓ cup grated fresh Parmesan cheese
1 teaspoon paprika
3 large baking potatoes, cleaned and each cut into 8 wedges
⅓ cup low-fat milk
¼ cup (½ stick) margarine, melted
1 carton (16 ounces) **LAND O LAKES® Light Sour Cream**
½ cup crumbled cooked bacon
2 tablespoons chopped fresh *or* dried chives
½ teaspoon garlic powder

1. Heat the oven to 400° F.
2. In a 9-inch pie pan, combine the flour, Parmesan cheese, and paprika. Mix well.
3. Dip the potatoes in the milk, then coat with the flour mixture. Place skin side down on a 15½ × 10½-inch jelly-roll pan or a small baking sheet with sides. Drizzle with the margarine.
4. Bake 45 to 50 minutes or until the potatoes are fork-tender and browned.
5. Meanwhile, in a medium bowl, stir together the sour cream, bacon, chives, and garlic powder.
6. Arrange the hot potato wedges in a fan around a small bowl with the dip and serve.

Cream Cheese Mushroom Puffs

MAKES ABOUT 48 APPETIZERS

3 tablespoons butter
1 pound mushrooms, cleaned and diced
1 small onion, finely chopped
24 ounces **Cream Cheese,** at room temperature
2 egg yolks
3 tablespoons minced fresh parsley
Salt and pepper to taste
48 party bread slices
Paprika

1. In a medium skillet, melt the butter. Sauté the mushrooms and onion over medium heat until golden, stirring occasionally. Drain.

2. Heat the broiler.

3. In a medium bowl, beat the cream cheese, egg yolks, parsley, and seasonings together until smooth. Stir in the mushroom mixture until combined.

4. Spread evenly on the bread and sprinkle with the paprika.

5. Broil 1 to 2 minutes or until lightly browned and puffed.

6. Remove to a platter and serve immediately.

COURTESY: DAIRY MANAGEMENT, INC.

Mushroom Mozzarella Bruschetta

MAKES 18 TO 20 APPETIZERS

1 can (10¾ ounces) condensed cream of mushroom soup
1 clove garlic, minced *or* ¼ teaspoon garlic powder
¼ teaspoon dried Italian seasoning
1 tablespoon grated Parmesan cheese
1 loaf Italian *or* French bread
¼ cup olive oil
¼ cup chopped green onions
¼ cup chopped red bell pepper
2 cups shredded mozzarella cheese

1. Heat the broiler.

2. Combine the soup, garlic, Italian seasoning, and Parmesan cheese until well blended. Set aside.

3. Cut the bread into 1-inch slices and place on a baking sheet.

4. Brush the bread with the oil and toast lightly under the broiler.

5. Heat the oven to 375° F.

6. Spread 1 tablespoon soup mixture evenly over each slice. Sprinkle with the green onions and bell peppers. Top with the mozzarella.

7. Bake 5 to 7 minutes or until the cheese is melted.

8. Remove to a platter and serve.

Party Tidbits

MAKES 36 APPETIZERS

1 cup all-purpose flour
1 cup grated Parmesan cheese
¼ teaspoon cayenne (red) pepper
½ cup (1 stick) **I Can't Believe It's Not Butter!**®
¼ cup water
1 teaspoon Worcestershire sauce
1 can (14 ounces) artichoke hearts, drained and finely chopped

1. Heat the oven to 375° F.

2. In a medium bowl, stir together the flour, cheese, and pepper.

3. Cut in I Can't Believe It's Not Butter!® until the mixture resembles coarse cornmeal.

4. In a small bowl, combine the water and Worcestershire sauce. Stir into the flour mixture until the dough forms a ball.

5. Fold in the artichokes and blend well.

6. On a lightly greased baking sheet, drop the dough by rounded teaspoons 1 inch apart.

7. With a fork, lightly flatten each tidbit.

8. Bake 20 to 25 minutes until browned.

9. Remove to a platter and serve warm.

Cheddar Cheese Puffs

MAKES 36 APPETIZERS

1 cup water
½ cup (1 stick) butter
1 cup all-purpose flour
4 eggs, beaten
1 cup **Cheddar Cheese,** grated and divided

1. Heat the oven to 425° F.

2. In a large saucepan, over medium heat, bring the water and butter to a boil.

3. Quickly add the flour, stirring until the mixture forms a ball. Remove from the heat.

4. Add the eggs, a little at a time, beating well after each addition. Add ½ cup cheese.

5. Drop the mixture by teaspoons onto a greased baking sheet, 1½ inches apart.

6. Top each puff with a pinch of the remaining cheese.

7. Bake approximately 20 minutes. Turn off the oven.

8. Pierce the sides of each puff in a few places and return to the turned-off oven for 5 minutes.

9. Remove to a platter and serve warm.

COURTESY: DAIRY MANAGEMENT, INC.

Onion-Butter Appetizers

½ cup (1 stick) margarine *or* butter, melted
¼ cup onion soup mix
2⅓ cups **Bisquick® Original** *or* **Reduced Fat baking mix**
½ teaspoon parsley flakes
⅔ cup cold water

1. Heat the oven to 450° F.

2. In a small bowl, combine the margarine and soup mix.

3. Pour half the mixture into a 9-inch square pan. Rotate the pan so the mixture covers the bottom.

4. In a medium bowl, blend together the baking mix, parsley, and water until a soft dough forms. Hand beat 30 seconds.

5. Drop by teaspoons onto the soup mixture.

6. Stir the remaining soup mixture and drizzle over the dough.

7. Bake 10 to 15 minutes or until light golden brown. Gently separate the appetizers.

8. Remove to a platter and serve warm.

❖ ❖ ❖ ❖ ❖ ❖ ❖ ❖ ❖ ❖ ❖ ❖ ❖ ❖ ❖ ❖

For a festive treat, place your favorite cheese or cheese spread on rings of red and green apples. Core the apples, slice them into ¼-inch rings, and dip in lemon juice to keep them from discoloring. Arrange alternating slices of red and green apples on a serving plate with the cheese.

Cheddar Cheese Straws

6 tablespoons (¾ stick) butter
1 cup all-purpose flour
1 cup grated **Cheddar Cheese** (4 ounces)
1 egg yolk
2 teaspoons water

1. Using a food processor, pastry blender, or two knives, cut the butter into the flour until finely distributed throughout.

2. Stir in the cheese.

3. In a small bowl, mix the egg yolk and water. Stir into the flour mixture.

4. Process or knead lightly to form a smooth dough.

5. Wrap the dough in plastic wrap and chill at least 1 hour before rolling it out.

6. Heat the oven to 375° F.

7. Roll out the dough to about ¼-inch thickness. Cut into ¼-inch-wide strips about 4 inches long. Place the strips on an ungreased baking sheet.

8. Bake 12 to 15 minutes until lightly browned.

9. Transfer to a platter and serve warm.

N O T E

After wrapping the dough in plastic wrap, it can be frozen, then thawed and baked later.

COURTESY: DAIRY MANAGEMENT, INC.

❖

Mozzarella Sticks

MAKES ABOUT 15 APPETIZERS

1 package (8 ounces) **Mozzarella Cheese**
2 eggs
1 tablespoon water
1 cup bread crumbs
2 teaspoons dried Italian seasoning
½ teaspoon garlic powder
⅓ cup unsifted all-purpose flour
4 teaspoons butter, melted
1 cup hot marinara sauce (optional)

1. Cut the cheese into 3×½×½-inch sticks and set aside.

2. In a shallow bowl, beat together the eggs and water.

3. In another bowl, combine the bread crumbs, Italian seasoning, and garlic powder.

4. Coat the cheese sticks with the flour, then the egg mixture, then the bread crumb mixture. Repeat the egg and bread crumb mixture coatings.

5. Place the coated sticks on a plate in a single layer. Cover with foil and chill 2 to 3 hours.

6. Heat the oven to 400° F.

7. Make sure the cheese sticks are very cold and the oven is adequately preheated before baking. Then, place the cheese sticks on a foil-lined baking sheet. Drizzle with the butter.

8. Bake 8 to 10 minutes or until crisp.

9. Remove to a plate and serve with marinara sauce.

COURTESY: DAIRY MANAGEMENT, INC.

Almond Pine Cone

MAKES 2 CONES

1¼ cups **Blue Diamond® Whole Natural Almonds**
1 package (8 ounces) cream cheese *or* Neufchâtel cheese, softened
½ cup sour cream
5 crisp bacon slices
1 tablespoon chopped green onion
½ teaspoon dill weed
½ teaspoon pepper

1. Heat the oven to 300° F.

2. Spread the almonds in a single layer on a shallow pan.

3. Bake 15 minutes, stirring often, until the almonds just begin to turn color. Set aside.

4. In a small bowl, combine the cream cheese and sour cream and mix well. Add the bacon, onion, dill weed, and pepper. Mix well.

5. Cover and chill overnight.

6. With your fingers, form the cheese mixture into the shape of two pine cones that lie on their sides.

7. Beginning at the narrow end, press in the fat end of the almonds at a slight angle in rows. Continue overlapping rows until all the cheese is covered.

8. Garnish with artificial pine sprigs. Refrigerate until ready to serve.

9. Serve with crackers.

Cream Cheese Country Artichoke Bake

MAKES ABOUT 2 CUPS

1 round loaf crusty bread (1 pound), unsliced
1 package (8 ounces) **Cream Cheese**
½ cup sour cream
2 jars (6 ounces *each*) marinated artichoke hearts, drained and chopped
1 jar (4 ounces) chopped pimientos, drained
1½ cups shredded Cheddar cheese
3 tablespoons grated Parmesan cheese
Salt and freshly ground pepper to taste

1. Cut a ½-inch slice horizontally from the top of the bread and set aside. Remove the center from the bread, leaving a ¾-inch-thick shell. (Make bread crumbs from the removed center and store for future use.)

2. In a large bowl, beat the cream cheese with the sour cream until smooth. Stir in the artichoke hearts, pimientos, Cheddar and Parmesan cheeses, salt, and pepper.

3. Heat the oven to 400° F.

4. Spoon the mixture into the bread shell. Place the reserved slice on top and wrap tightly in foil.

5. Bake 1½ hours.

6. Serve with thin slices of crusty French bread or raw vegetables.

NOTE

The dip can also be baked alone in a shallow 1-quart covered baking dish at 350° F for 30 minutes or until hot and bubbly.

COURTESY: DAIRY MANAGEMENT, INC.

Cucumber-Dill Dressing/Dip

MAKES 2 CUPS

1 medium cucumber, peeled, cut in half lengthwise, seeded, and finely chopped (1 cup)
1 large egg white
1 tablespoon vinegar
1 teaspoon Dijon mustard
½ teaspoon sugar (optional)
¼ teaspoon salt
2 tablespoons fresh dill
1 teaspoon lemon juice
½ clove garlic (optional)
1 cup **Low-fat Cottage Cheese** (8 ounces)

1. Prepare the cucumber and set aside.

2. In a blender, whip the egg white, vinegar, mustard, sugar, and salt 1 minute until light and frothy. Add the dill, lemon juice, and garlic, if using.

3. With the blender running, spoon in the cottage cheese and blend until smooth. Transfer the mixture to a bowl.

4. Squeeze excess water from the cucumber and stir the cucumber into the dressing.

5. Cover and refrigerate at least 1 hour before serving.

COURTESY: DAIRY MANAGEMENT, INC.

Artichoke Dip, Cucumber Dill Dressing

Artichoke Dip

MAKES ABOUT 2 CUPS

8 ounces canned artichoke hearts, drained and finely
    chopped
12 ounces **Cream Cheese,** softened
¼ cup (½ stick) butter, softened
2 tablespoons Parmesan cheese, grated
Small crackers

1. Heat the oven to 350° F.

2. In a medium bowl, mix together the artichokes, cream cheese, and butter.

3. Place the mixture in a shallow baking dish and sprinkle the Parmesan cheese on top.

4. Bake 20 minutes.

5. Serve on small crackers.

COURTESY: DAIRY MANAGEMENT, INC.

Extra Special Spinach Dip

MAKES 3 CUPS

1 envelope **Lipton® Recipe Secrets® Vegetable Soup Mix**
1 container (8 ounces) regular *or* light sour cream
1 cup regular *or* light mayonnaise
1 package (10 ounces) frozen chopped spinach, thawed and squeezed dry
1 can (8 ounces) water chestnuts, drained and chopped (optional)

1. In a medium bowl, combine all the ingredients.
2. Chill at least 2 hours.
3. Serve with your favorite dippers.

The Big Dipper

MAKES 4 CUPS

1 can (15 ounces) **HORMEL® Chili No Beans**
1 can (10 ounces) tomatoes and green chilies, reserving 1 tablespoon, drained
1½ cups cubed Monterey Jack cheese (about 8 ounces)
½ cup sliced green onions
½ teaspoon cayenne (red) pepper

1. In a medium saucepan, combine all the ingredients. Heat just until the cheese melts, stirring frequently.
2. Garnish the dip with the reserved tomatoes and additional cayenne pepper and green onions, if desired.
3. Serve warm with assorted raw vegetable dippers and toasted French bread slices.

Hot Spinach-Cheese Dip

MAKES 3½ CUPS

1 package (10 ounces) frozen chopped spinach, thawed and squeezed dry
1 package (8 ounces) **Cream Cheese,** at room temperature
1 cup shredded **Cheddar Cheese**
1 cup shredded **Monterey Jack Cheese**
1 cup sour cream
1 tablespoon minced onion
1 teaspoon Dijon mustard
1 clove garlic, minced
¼ teaspoon salt
¼ teaspoon pepper

1. In a large microwave-safe bowl, place all the ingredients.
2. Microwave on high for 2 minutes.
3. Stir, microwave 2 more minutes. Stir again.
4. Microwave 1 more minute or until the cheeses have melted and the mixture is hot. (Or, heat the oven to 350° F. In a large oven-proof bowl, mix all the ingredients. Bake 15 to 20 minutes, stirring twice, or until the cheeses have melted and the mixture is hot.)
5. Serve immediately.

COURTESY: DAIRY MANAGEMENT, INC.

❖

Macho Nacho

Macho Nacho

SERVES 12

1 can (15 ounces) **HORMEL® Chili No Beans**
1 bag (8 ounces) tortilla chips, any flavor
½ cup shredded cheese such as Cheddar,
 Monterey Jack, *or* American

1. Heat the chili according to package directions.
2. Arrange the chips on a microwave-safe dish or ovenproof pan.
 Spoon the chili over the chips and sprinkle with the cheese.
3. Heat in a microwave oven or broil until the cheese melts, about
 1 to 2 minutes.
4. Remove from the heat and serve.

Low-fat tortilla chips, wonderful with dips and spreads, are easy to make at home. All you need are corn tortillas and nonstick cooking spray. The secret to these tasty chips is that they are broiled, not fried.

Preheat the broiler, setting the rack 6 inches from the heat. Lightly coat the tortillas on both sides with non-stick cooking spray. Salt them lightly if you wish. Cut the rounds into 6 wedges and arrange them on a baking sheet. Broil 3 minutes or until crisp; there is no need to turn them over. When cool, they can be stored in an airtight container up to 2 weeks.

Cheddar Cheese Spread

MAKES 1 ½ CUPS

2 cups shredded **Sharp Cheddar Cheese** (8 ounces)
1 package (3 ounces) **Cream Cheese,** at room temperature
1 clove garlic, minced
1 teaspoon lemon juice
1 teaspoon Dijon mustard
1 teaspoon Worcestershire sauce
¼ teaspoon pepper
¼ cup milk

1. In a deep bowl, place the Cheddar and cream cheeses.
2. With an electric mixer, beat well for 2 minutes to soften the mixture. Add the garlic, lemon juice, mustard, Worcestershire, pepper, and milk. Continue beating until the mixture is well blended.
3. Mound the cheese mixture into a crock or serving bowl. Refrigerate 1 hour or more to allow the flavors to develop and blend.
4. To serve: Let the cheese soften at room temperature to spreading consistency.

COURTESY: DAIRY MANAGEMENT, INC.

Zesty Seafood Spread

MAKES ABOUT 2 CUPS

1 package (8 ounces) reduced-fat cream cheese, softened
¼ cup **Heinz® Chili Sauce**
1 teaspoon lemon juice
¼ to ½ teaspoon hot pepper sauce
1 cup chopped cooked seafood such as shrimp, crab, *or* sea legs
4 sliced green onions, including some tops
¼ cup finely chopped red bell pepper
¼ cup finely chopped celery
Crackers, bagel chips, *or* pita crisps

1. In a bowl, thoroughly combine the cream cheese, chili sauce, lemon juice, and hot pepper sauce.
2. Stir in the seafood, onions, bell pepper, and celery until well blended.
3. Transfer to a serving bowl.
4. Serve with crackers, bagel chips, or pita crisps.

When choosing crudités, keep in mind the kind of dip they're meant for. Bland or sweet-tasting vegetables—white mushrooms, zucchini strips, or carrot sticks—tend to go well with hot or sharp-tasting dips. Vegetables with a decided character—radishes, fennel, green onions, and Belgian endive—complement milder-tasting dips.

To crisp vegetables for dipping, place them in a bowl of water and ice cubes. Refrigerate at least 1 hour. Or, after cutting and rinsing, put the vegetables in plastic bags and seal the bags tightly. Place them in the refrigerator at least 2 hours or overnight.

Creamy Salsa Dip

MAKES 3½ CUPS

1 envelope **Lipton® Recipe Secrets® Onion** *or* **Savory Herb with Garlic Soup Mix**
1 container (16 ounces) sour cream
2 cups prepared salsa

1. In a medium bowl, combine all the ingredients.
2. Chill at least 2 hours.
3. Serve with tortilla chips or assorted fresh vegetables.

Hot and Spicy Chex® Brand Party Mix

MAKES 11 CUPS

¼ cup (½ stick) margarine *or* butter
1 tablespoon **Lea & Perrins® Worcestershire Sauce**
2 to 3 teaspoons **Tabasco® Brand Pepper Sauce**
1¼ teaspoon **Lawry's® Seasoned Salt**
2⅔ cups **Corn Chex® brand cereal**
2⅔ cups **Rice Chex® brand cereal**
2⅔ cups **Wheat Chex® brand cereal**
1 cup mixed nuts
1 cup pretzels
1 cup bite-size cheese crackers

1. Heat the oven to 250° F.
2. Melt the margarine in a large open roasting pan. Stir in the seasonings.
3. Gradually add the cereals, nuts, pretzels, and cheese crackers. Stir to coat evenly.
4. Bake 1 hour, stirring every 15 minutes. Spread on absorbent paper or paper towels to cool.
5. Store in an airtight container or serve.

®Chex cereal brands are registered trademarks of General Mills, Inc.

Chex® Brand Caramel Corn Mix

MAKES 9½ CUPS

4½ cups of your favorite **Chex® brand cereals**
4 cups popped popcorn
½ cup honey-roasted peanuts (optional)
¼ cup (½ stick) margarine *or* butter
6 tablespoons firmly packed brown sugar
2 tablespoons light corn syrup
¼ teaspoon vanilla extract

1. Combine the cereals, popcorn, and nuts, if using, in a large microwave-safe bowl. Set aside.
2. Combine the margarine, sugar, corn syrup, and vanilla in a microwave-safe bowl. Microwave on high for 2 minutes or until the mixture is boiling, stirring after 1 minute.*
3. Pour the syrup over the cereal mixture, stirring until all the pieces are evenly coated.
4. Microwave on high for 5 to 6 minutes, stirring thoroughly every minute. While stirring, make sure to scrape the sides and bottom of the bowl.
5. Spread on wax paper to cool, stirring occasionally to break up.
6. Store in an airtight container or serve.

NOTE

*Due to differences in microwave ovens, cooking time may need adjustment.

®Chex cereal brands are registered trademarks of General Mills, Inc.

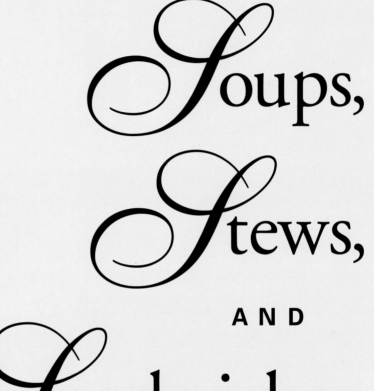

Soups, Stews, AND Sandwiches

Italian Smoked Sausage Bean Soup

SERVES 6

1 package (16 ounces) **Hillshire Farm® Smoked Sausage,** any variety, sliced
1 cup chopped onions
2 teaspoons olive oil
1 can (28 ounces) tomatoes, chopped
3½ cups hot water
1 cup pasta shells
2 cubes chicken bouillon
1 can (18 ounces) kidney beans, drained

1. In a large deep skillet or Dutch oven, over medium-high heat, brown the sausage and onions in the oil, about 5 minutes.
2. Add the tomatoes with their juice, water, pasta, and bouillon. Bring to a boil. Add the beans.
3. Reduce the heat, cover, and simmer until the pasta is tender, about 15 minutes.
4. Ladle into bowls and serve.

❖ ❖ ❖ ❖ ❖ ❖ ❖ ❖ ❖ ❖ ❖ ❖ ❖ ❖ ❖ ❖

To dice an onion, cut it in half from stem to root. Place the flat side of one half on the cutting board and steady it with your fingers at the root end. Make thin slices lengthwise, perpendicular to the cutting board. Cut crosswise to desired thickness. Repeat with the other half.

Spinach Pasta Soup

SERVES 4

1 package (1 pound) **Green Giant® Pasta Accents® Florentine Frozen Vegetables and Pasta**
1 can (10¾ ounces) condensed chicken broth
1⅓ cups milk
1⅓ cups water
1 cup diced cooked chicken (optional)
Seasoned croutons

1. In a large saucepan, combine all the ingredients *except* croutons.
2. Bring to a boil. Reduce the heat and simmer 8 to 10 minutes, stirring occasionally.
3. Ladle into bowls and garnish with the croutons. Serve.

Hearty Vegetable Soup

SERVES 8

3 cans (14½ ounces *each*) vegetable broth
½ teaspoon dried basil, crushed
2 cups shredded cabbage
2 medium zucchini, cut in half lengthwise and sliced
1 package (about 10 ounces) frozen cut green beans
3 medium carrots, sliced
2 stalks celery, sliced
¼ cup regular long-grain rice

1. In a large soup kettle, mix the broth, basil, and vegetables.
2. Over medium-high heat, bring to a boil. Stir in the rice.
3. Cover, reduce the heat to low, and cook 20 minutes or until the rice is done.
4. Ladle into bowls and serve.

Hearty Corn and Lima Bean Soup

SERVES 6

2 cans (13¾ ounces *each*) chicken broth
3 cups tomato juice
1 can (17 ounces) **Del Monte® Whole Kernel Golden Sweet Corn**
1 can (17 ounces) **Del Monte® Green Lima Beans**
1 cup diced cooked chicken
2 medium potatoes, pared and diced
1 medium onion, chopped
1 tablespoon Worcestershire sauce
1 teaspoon dried basil
¼ teaspoon pepper

1. In a large saucepan or soup pot, combine all the ingredients.
2. Bring to a boil and reduce the heat. Cover and simmer 30 minutes or until the potatoes are tender.
3. Ladle into soup bowls and serve.

Tomato Salsaria Soup

SERVES 2

1 can (10¾ ounces) condensed tomato soup
1 soup can water
¼ cup prepared salsa (medium hot)
¼ cup grated Cheddar cheese
½ cup crumbled tortilla chips
2 tablespoons sour cream

1. In a 1½-quart saucepan, stir the soup. Gradually add the water and salsa. Heat through over medium heat.
2. Ladle into bowls. Top with the cheese, tortilla chips, and sour cream. Serve.

Creamy Tomato Basil Soup

MAKES 6 CUPS

⅓ cup **Wesson® Oil**
1 medium onion, chopped
½ teaspoon minced garlic
¼ cup all-purpose flour
1½ pounds ripe tomatoes, peeled, seeded, and chopped
2 cans (14½ ounces *each*) chicken broth
½ cup half-and-half
¼ cup chopped fresh basil
1 teaspoon sugar
½ teaspoon salt
¼ teaspoon *each* dill weed and pepper

1. In a large saucepan, heat the oil. Over medium-low heat, sauté the onion and garlic until tender. Do not brown.
2. Stir in the flour and cook 1 minute.
3. Add the remaining ingredients. Stir until well blended.
4. Bring to a boil, reduce the heat, and simmer, uncovered, 20 minutes.
5. Pour in batches into a blender or food processor and purée until smooth.
6. Ladle into bowls and serve.

To peel tomatoes, half-fill a large saucepan with water and bring to a boil. Core the tomatoes. With a sharp, pointed knife, mark a shallow × on the bottom of each one. Drop into the water for 15 to 30 seconds. Using a slotted spoon, transfer to ice water, then peel the skin with the knife or your fingers, starting at the ×.

Pepperoni Pizza Soup

SERVES 2

1 can (10¾ ounces) condensed tomato soup
1 soup can water
⅓ cup sliced pepperoni
¼ teaspoon dried Italian seasoning
¼ cup shredded mozzarella cheese
½ cup croutons

1. In a 1½-quart saucepan, stir the soup. Gradually add the water. Add the pepperoni and Italian seasoning. Heat through over medium heat.

2. Ladle into bowls and top with the cheese and croutons. Serve.

Tomato Tortellini Soup

SERVES 2

1 can (10¾ ounces) condensed tomato soup
½ soup can water
½ soup can milk
⅓ teaspoon dried Italian seasoning
½ cup frozen cheese tortellini
2 tablespoons grated Parmesan cheese

1. In a 1½-quart saucepan, stir the soup. Gradually add the water and milk. Add the Italian seasoning. Heat to simmering over medium heat.

2. Add the tortellini. Simmer 10 minutes, stirring occasionally.

3. Ladle into bowls and garnish with the Parmesan cheese. Serve.

COURTESY: CAMPBELL SOUP COMPANY

Pepperoni Pizza Soup (top), Tomato Tortellini Soup

Sausage Stew

SERVES 6

¼ cup olive oil
1 medium white onion, quartered
2 garlic cloves, minced
1 cup chopped celery
1 teaspoon fennel seed
Salt and pepper to taste
1 tablespoon dried oregano
4 large carrots, peeled and roughly chopped
1 pound mushrooms, cleaned and cut in half
2 cans (12 ounces *each*) diced tomatoes with juice
12 small whole new potatoes
1 can (8 ounces) tomato sauce
1 package (16 ounces) **Hillshire Farm® Polska Kielbasa** *or* any variety, cut in ½-inch slices

1. In a large heavy pot, heat the oil. Sauté the onion, garlic, and celery with the fennel, salt, and pepper until soft.

2. Add the oregano, carrots, mushrooms, tomatoes with their juice, potatoes, and tomato sauce. Cover and cook over low heat for 30 minutes.

3. Add the sausage and simmer an additional 15 minutes or until the potatoes are tender.

4. Ladle into bowls and serve.

New Orleans Stew

SERVES 6

1 small onion, chopped
2 green bell peppers, trimmed, seeded, and chopped
3 celery stalks, chopped
2 tablespoons seafood seasoning
1 tablespoon ground marjoram
Salt and pepper to taste
1 to 1½ pounds **Hillshire Farm® Polska Kielbasa, Lite, Turkey,** *or* **Regular,** sliced into bite-size pieces
4 ears corn, fresh *or* thawed frozen, cut into 2-inch pieces
1 pound shrimp, raw, unshelled

1. Into a large pot, place the onion, bell peppers, and celery. Add enough water to cover plus the seasonings. Bring to a boil, reduce the heat, and simmer 10 minutes.

2. Add the kielbasa and corn and cook 5 to 10 minutes, stirring occasionally.

3. Add the shrimp and cook 3 minutes longer. Remove the pot from the heat and let stand 5 minutes.

4. Ladle into bowls and serve.

Burgundy Beef Stew

SERVES 4

1 can (24 ounces) **DINTY MOORE® Beef Stew**
1 cup frozen small whole onions, thawed
1 can (4 ounces) sliced mushrooms, drained
½ cup tomato sauce
1 tablespoon Worcestershire sauce
1 teaspoon **Lawry's® Seasoning Salt**

1. In a large saucepan, combine all the ingredients.

2. Cook over medium heat until simmering, stirring frequently. Reduce the heat and simmer 5 minutes. Serve.

Italian Sirloin Stew

1 boneless **Beef Sirloin Steak,** cut 1 inch thick
(about 1 pound)
1 large clove garlic, crushed
2 tablespoons olive oil, divided
2 medium onions, cut into ¼-inch slices
1 teaspoon dried basil
⅛ teaspoon cayenne (red) pepper
1 can (14½ ounces) whole tomatoes, undrained
1 cup ready-to-serve beef broth
2 medium zucchini, cut into ¼-inch slices
2 teaspoons cornstarch
2 tablespoons water
Grated Parmesan cheese (optional)

1. Cut the beefsteak into ¼-inch strips. Cut each strip into 1-inch pieces. Place in a large bowl. Add the garlic with 1 tablespoon oil and stir into the beef. Reserve.

2. In a large saucepan, sauté the onion over medium heat in the remaining oil for 3 minutes. Sprinkle with the basil and pepper and cook and stir 1 minute. Add the tomatoes, beef broth, and zucchini. Bring to a boil. Cover, reduce the heat, and simmer 15 minutes.

3. Meanwhile, heat a large nonstick skillet over medium-high heat. Add the beef. Cook and stir 1 to 2 minutes, then add to the sauce.

4. In a cup, dissolve the cornstarch in 2 tablespoons water. Stir into the stew and cook until slightly thickened, about 2 minutes. Ladle into bowls and sprinkle with grated cheese, if desired. Serve.

Hearty Beef Stew

4 slices bacon
2 pounds boneless beef chuck *or* round steak,
cut into 1-inch cubes
1 large garlic clove, minced
1 envelope **Lipton® Recipe Secrets® Onion Soup Mix**
2½ cups water
1 tablespoon red wine vinegar

1. In a Dutch oven or 6-quart saucepan, brown the bacon until crisp. Remove the bacon, drain, crumble, and set aside. Reserve 1 table-spoon drippings.

2. Brown the beef in two batches in the reserved drippings. Remove and set aside.

3. Add the garlic to the drippings and cook over medium heat, stir-ring frequently, 30 seconds.

4. Return the beef to the Dutch oven. Add the onion soup mix blended with the water. Bring to a boil over high heat. Reduce the heat to low and simmer, covered, stirring occasionally, 1¼ hours or until the beef is tender.

5. Skim the fat, if necessary. Stir in the vinegar and sprinkle with the bacon.

6. Ladle into bowls and serve.

Hearty Beef Stew

Corn Chowder with Fresh Herbs and Smoked Ham

SERVES 6

2 cans (14½ ounces *each*) chicken broth
½ cup finely chopped onion
1 medium carrot, finely chopped
1 bay leaf
1 sprig fresh thyme
1 sprig fresh tarragon
2 cans (16 ounces *each*) whole potatoes, drained, divided
2 cans (16 ounces *each*) whole kernel corn, drained, divided
½ cup half-and-half
1 can (2 ounces) pimientos, drained and diced
3 tablespoons chopped fresh parsley
Pepper to taste (optional)
1 cup julienne-cut smoked ham

1. In a 3-quart saucepan, combine the chicken broth, onion, and carrot.

2. Tie together the bay leaf and fresh herbs to make a bouquet garni and add to the saucepan. Bring to a boil. Reduce the heat and simmer 10 minutes. Remove the herbs.

3. Dice enough potatoes to make 1 cup and set aside. Add the remaining whole potatoes and 1 can corn to the saucepan.

4. In a blender, purée the mixture in batches until smooth and return to the saucepan.

5. Stir the diced potatoes, remaining corn, and half-and-half into the saucepan. Bring to a boil. Reduce the heat and simmer 5 minutes.

6. Stir in the pimientos and parsley. Season with pepper, if desired.

7. Ladle into bowls. Garnish with the ham and additional chopped parsley and serve.

COURTESY: U.S. STEEL CAN COUNCIL

Chili Bravo

SERVES 4

1 can (15 ounces) **HORMEL® Chili No Beans**
1 can (6 ounces) vegetable juice
½ cup chopped onion
3 cups frozen vegetables, thawed and drained
4 cups hot cooked rice

1. In a large saucepan, combine the chili, vegetable juice, and onion. Cook 5 minutes over medium heat.

2. Stir in the mixed vegetables. Cover and simmer an additional 4 minutes.

3. Serve over the hot rice.

Cajun Chili

SERVES 4

6 ounces hot sausage links, sliced
4 skinless, boneless chicken thighs, cut into cubes
1 onion, chopped
⅛ teaspoon cayenne (red) pepper
1 can (15 ounces) black-eyed peas *or* kidney beans, drained
1 can (14½ ounces) **Del Monte® Chili Style Chunky Tomatoes**
1 green bell pepper, chopped

1. In a large skillet, lightly brown the sausage over medium-high heat for 7 minutes. Add the chicken, onion, and cayenne. Cook until browned. Drain off excess fat.

2. Stir in the remaining ingredients. Cook over medium-high heat for 5 minutes, stirring occasionally.

3. Spoon into bowls and serve.

Hearty Vegetable Chili

Hearty Vegetable Chili

MAKES 4 CUPS

1 tablespoon **Wesson® Oil**
½ cup chopped onion
¼ cup chopped green bell pepper
1 can (15½ ounces) **Hunt's® Chili Beans**
1 can (15 ounces) **Hunt's® Ready Tomato Sauces
Chunky Chili**
1 can (8½ ounces) mixed vegetables, drained
1 cup shredded Cheddar cheese

1. In a large saucepan, in hot oil, sauté the onion and bell pepper until very tender.

2. Stir in the remaining ingredients *except* cheese. Simmer, stirring occasionally, 15 minutes.

3. Spoon into bowls and sprinkle with the cheese before serving.

Three-Bean Chili

Three-Bean Chili

SERVES 6

8 ounces chorizo *or* other spicy cooked sausage, sliced
1 onion, chopped
2 cloves garlic, crushed
1 can (14½ ounces) **Del Monte® Chili Style Chunky Tomatoes**
1 can (15 ounces) barbecue-style beans
1 can (15 ounces) black *or* pinto beans, drained
1 can (8¾ ounces) kidney beans, drained
Sour cream (optional)
Sliced green onions (optional)

1. In a large saucepan, cook the sausage, onion, and garlic until tender and drain. Add the tomatoes and beans. Cover and simmer 15 minutes or until heated through, stirring occasionally.

2. Spoon into bowls and garnish with sour cream and sliced green onions, if desired. Serve.

Chili Chicken

SERVES 6

2 cups cubed cooked chicken
1 can (15 ounces) tomato sauce
2 cans (15 ounces *each*) spicy chili beans, undrained
1 can (8 ounces) whole kernel corn, undrained

For dumplings:

1½ cups **Bisquick® Original** *or* **Reduced Fat baking mix**
½ cup cornmeal
⅔ cup milk
½ cup shredded Cheddar cheese (2 ounces)

1. In a 4-quart Dutch oven, mix together the chicken and tomato sauce. Heat to boiling and reduce the heat. Cover and simmer 5 minutes, stirring occasionally. Stir in the beans and corn. Heat to boiling and reduce the heat to low.

2. Mix the baking mix, cornmeal, and milk until a soft dough forms.

3. Drop by spoonfuls onto the hot chili.

4. Cook, uncovered, 10 minutes. Cover and cook 10 minutes longer.

5. Sprinkle with the cheese. Cover and cook about 3 minutes or until the cheese is melted.

6. Spoon into bowls and serve.

Chunky Chicken Chili

SERVES 4 TO 6

1 tablespoon vegetable oil
2 skinless, boneless chicken breast halves, cut into bite-size chunks
1 medium onion, chopped
1 can (15 ounces) pinto beans, drained
1 can (14½ ounces) **Del Monte® FreshCut™ Diced Tomatoes**
1 tablespoon chili powder
Salt and freshly ground pepper

1. In a large saucepan, heat the oil over medium heat. Add the chicken and onion and stir-fry until the chicken is no longer pink.

2. Add the beans, tomatoes, and chili powder. Reduce the heat to low, cover, and simmer 20 minutes.

3. Season with the salt and pepper. Spoon into bowls and serve.

Really Ready Chili

Really Ready Chili

SERVES 3 TO 4

8 ounces ground beef
1 can (15 ounces) **Hunt's® Ready Tomato Sauces Chunky Chili**
1 can (15½ ounces) **Hunt's® Kidney Beans**
Cheddar cheese (optional)

1. In a medium-size skillet, brown the ground beef over medium-high heat. Pour off fat.

2. Stir in the sauce and kidney beans. Simmer, uncovered, 10 minutes over low heat.

3. Remove from the heat and spoon into soup bowls. Sprinkle with Cheddar cheese, if desired. Serve.

Italian-Style Meatball Sandwiches

SERVES 4

1 pound ground beef
½ cup **Kretschmer® Original Toasted Wheat Germ**
¼ cup water
1 egg white, lightly beaten
2 teaspoons dried Italian seasoning
½ teaspoon garlic powder
½ teaspoon salt (optional)
1 jar (16 ounces) prepared spaghetti sauce, heated
4 Italian rolls (each 5 inches long), warmed
Shredded mozzarella cheese (optional)

1. In a large bowl, combine the ground beef, wheat germ, water, egg white, and seasonings. Mix lightly but thoroughly.
2. Shape into 1½- to 2-inch meatballs.
3. Heat the broiler.
4. Spray the rack of the broiler pan with nonstick cooking spray and arrange the meatballs on the rack. Broil 4 to 5 inches from the heat source, 5 to 8 minutes per side or until no longer pink (160° internal temperature).
5. Add the meatballs to the warm sauce. Spoon into the rolls. Sprinkle with cheese, if desired. Serve.

Mighty Hero

SERVES 8

1 round loaf sourdough bread (1 pound)
¼ cup balsamic vinegar
1 tablespoon olive oil
1 teaspoon dried oregano
1 teaspoon parsley flakes
¼ teaspoon pepper
2 cloves garlic, minced
1 cup sliced mushrooms
6 tomato slices, ¼ inch thick
2 red onion slices, ¼ inch thick, separated into rings
2 cups shredded zucchini
1 cup **Healthy Choice® Fat-Free Natural Shredded Mozzarella Cheese** (4 ounces)
4 ounces **Healthy Choice® Deli Thin** *or* **Regular Sliced Bologna**
4 ounces **Healthy Choice® Deli Thin Oven Roasted Turkey Breast**

1. Slice the bread in half horizontally. Remove the soft bread from each half, leaving ½-inch-thick shells, and set aside.
2. In a bowl, whisk together the vinegar, oil, herbs, pepper, and garlic. Add the mushrooms, tomato slices, and onion rings and toss well. Let stand 15 minutes.
3. Drain the mushroom mixture. Brush the liquid inside the bread shells.
4. In the bottom half of the bread, layer half *each* of the zucchini, mushroom mixture, and cheese. Top with the bologna. Repeat the layers. Top with the turkey and the top half of the loaf.
5. Wrap in plastic wrap and chill.
6. To serve, unwrap the loaf and cut into wedges.

Fajita Pitas

SERVES 4 TO 6

2 tablespoons **Wesson® Oil**
1 small onion, sliced
1 small green bell pepper, sliced
2 skinless, boneless chicken breasts, thinly sliced
1 can (15 ounces) salsa-style tomato sauce
Pita rounds *or* warmed flour tortillas

1. In a large skillet, in hot oil, stir-fry the onion, bell pepper, and chicken. When the chicken is cooked through, stir in the sauce.

2. Heat through.

3. Spoon into the pita rounds or warmed flour tortillas. Serve.

Souperburger Sandwiches

SERVES 6

1 pound ground beef
1 medium onion, chopped
1 can (10¾ ounces) condensed cream of mushroom soup
1 tablespoon prepared mustard
⅛ teaspoon pepper
6 hamburger rolls, split and toasted

1. In a large nonstick skillet, over medium-high heat, cook the beef and onion until the beef is browned, stirring to separate the meat. Pour off fat.

2. Stir in the soup, mustard, and pepper. Simmer over low heat until heated through.

3. Divide the meat mixture among the rolls. Serve.

COURTESY: CAMPBELL SOUP COMPANY

The All-American Hero

SERVES 6 TO 8

1 large loaf Italian bread (about 15 inches long)
Lettuce leaves
1 tomato, sliced
1½ pounds assorted cheeses and cold cuts, sliced
4 tablespoons **French's® Classic Yellow™ Mustard**

1. Cut the bread in half lengthwise.

2. Arrange the ingredients in the following order: bottom half of the bread, lettuce, tomato, cheese, assorted cold cuts, mustard, and top half of the bread.

3. Cut into slices and secure with toothpicks. Serve.

Chili Dog of the '90s

SERVES 8

1 package (14 ounces) **HORMEL® Fat Free Beef Franks**
1 can (15 ounces) **HORMEL® Vegetarian Chili**
8 hot dog buns

1. Prepare the franks and chili according to package directions.

2. Place the franks in the buns. Spoon the chili over the franks.

3. Serve.

The All-American Hero

Smoked Sausage Reuben with Honey Mustard Dill Sauce

SERVES 4

½ cup mayonnaise
¼ cup honey mustard
2 teaspoons snipped dill
4 slices dark rye bread
8 ounces Swiss cheese, sliced
⅓ head cabbage, shredded finely
1 package (16 ounces) **Hillshire Farm® Smoked Sausage,** any variety, sliced lengthwise

1. In a medium bowl, combine the mayonnaise, honey mustard, and dill to make the honey mustard dill sauce.
2. Place the bread slices side by side in a baking dish.
3. Spread each slice with approximately 1 tablespoon sauce or to taste.
4. Layer each slice with ¼ of the cheese, cabbage, and sausage.
5. Bake at 350° F for 10 minutes or until warmed through and the cheese has melted.
6. Serve open-face style.

Philly Cheese "Ham-Steak" Hoagie

SERVES 2

1 tablespoon vegetable oil
1 green bell pepper, cut into ¼-inch strips
1 medium onion, thinly sliced
1 cup **Cure 81® ham,** cut into ¼-inch strips
2 hoagie rolls, split and toasted
4 thin slices provolone *or* mozzarella cheese

1. Heat the oil in a medium skillet over medium heat. Sauté the bell pepper and onion, stirring often, until softened, 5 to 7 minutes.
2. Add the ham to the skillet and stir until the ham is hot, about 1 minute.
3. Line the inside of each hoagie roll with 2 slices of cheese. Divide the ham mixture and spread it evenly over the cheese.
4. Cut the rolls in half and serve.

Hot Peppy Italian Hero

SERVES 4

3½ ounces **HORMEL® pepperoni (slices)**
1 large green bell pepper, stemmed, seeded, and cut into ¼-inch strips
1 large red bell pepper, stemmed, seeded, and cut into ¼-inch strips
1 large onion, thinly sliced
1 tablespoon olive oil (optional)
1 clove garlic, minced
4 hero sandwich rolls, sliced lengthwise

1. In a large skillet, over medium heat, cook the pepperoni, stirring occasionally, until the drippings are rendered, about 5 minutes. Remove the pepperoni from the skillet to a small bowl.
2. Stir the bell peppers and onion into the drippings and cook, stirring often, until softened, about 8 minutes. Add the olive oil, if needed. Stir in the garlic and pepperoni and cook 1 minute.
3. Spoon the mixture into the sandwich rolls and serve.

Polynesian Ham Pockets

SERVES 4

¾ cup **Healthy Choice® Honey Ham,** chopped
1 can (8 ounces) unsweetened pineapple tidbits, drained
½ cup shredded Swiss cheese (2 ounces)
2 green onions, chopped
1 tablespoon plus 1 teaspoon reduced-calorie mayonnaise
½ teaspoon ground ginger
4 curly leaf lettuce leaves
2 whole wheat pita rounds (6 inches), cut in half crosswise
¼ cup alfalfa sprouts, divided

1. In a large bowl, combine the ham, pineapple, cheese, green onions, mayonnaise, and ginger and stir well. Cover and chill.
2. Tuck a lettuce leaf inside each pita half. Spoon ½ cup ham mixture into each pita half and top with some alfalfa sprouts.
3. Serve.

"Sloppy Jose" Sandwiches

SERVES 8

1 can (15 ounces) **HORMEL® Turkey Chili No Beans**
1 can (10¾ ounces) nacho cheese soup, undiluted
¼ cup sliced green onions
¼ cup light sour cream
8 sandwich *or* hot dog buns

1. In a medium microwave-safe bowl, stir together the turkey chili, soup, onions, and sour cream.
2. Microwave on high for 2 minutes. Stir, microwave 2 minutes more until very hot. (Or, in a medium saucepan, combine all the ingredients *except* buns. Cook over medium heat, stirring occasionally, until hot, about 10 minutes.)
3. Spoon into the buns and serve.

HONEY MUSTARD MAYONNAISE (Makes ½ cup)
2 tablespoons honey mustard
½ cup low- *or* no-fat mayonnaise

In a small bowl, combine the honey mustard and mayonnaise. Cover and refrigerate 1 hour for flavors to blend.

GARLIC HERB MAYONNAISE (Makes ½ cup)
1 small clove garlic, minced
1 tablespoon chopped parsley
½ cup low- *or* no-fat mayonnaise

In a small bowl, combine the garlic, parsley, and mayonnaise. Cover and refrigerate 1 hour for flavors to blend.

GREEN CHILI MAYONNAISE (Makes ½ cup)
1 tablespoon chopped green chilies
½ cup low- *or* no-fat mayonnaise

In a small bowl, combine the chilies and mayonnaise. Cover and refrigerate 1 hour for flavors to blend.

GREEN ONION MAYONNAISE (Makes ½ cup)
1 tablespoon finely chopped green onion *or* chives
½ cup low- *or* no-fat mayonnaise

In a small bowl, combine the green onion and mayonnaise. Cover and refrigerate 1 hour for flavors to blend.

Cheesy Hot Ham Sandwich Loaf

SERVES 8

1 loaf whole wheat bread, unsliced
6 tablespoons (¾ stick) butter, softened, divided
2 tablespoons snipped chives
2 tablespoons prepared mustard
16 slices **Swiss Cheese**
16 slices boiled ham
1 tablespoon poppy seeds

1. Heat the oven to 400° F.

2. Slice the bread in nine places, diagonally, from the top almost through to the bottom of the loaf (leaving a wedge of crust on either end that will not be used).

3. Combine 4 tablespoons butter, chives, and mustard. Spread (to the right) on one side of each bread slice.

4. Put the loaf on a 20×18-inch sheet of foil.

5. Place 2 cheese slices and 2 ham slices over the spread, alternately, ending with ham on each of the 8 slices (not including the 2 crust wedges).

6. Brush the entire loaf with 2 tablespoons melted butter and sprinkle the poppy seeds over the top.

7. Wrap the loaf tightly in foil.

8. Bake on an ungreased baking sheet for 30 minutes. Remove the foil and cut to separate the loaf into eight pieces. Serve as open-face sandwiches.

COURTESY: DAIRY MANAGEMENT, INC.

Chicken Teriyaki Pita Pockets

SERVES 6

6 skinless, boneless chicken breast halves (approximately 1½ pounds)
1 cup **Lawry's® Teriyaki Marinade with Pineapple Juice**
1 tablespoon margarine *or* butter
1 medium onion, thinly sliced
1 cup reduced-calorie mayonnaise
¼ cup finely chopped green onions
6 pita rounds
1 small head lettuce
2 medium tomatoes, sliced

1. Place the chicken breasts and marinade in a resealable plastic bag. Seal the bag and marinate 2 hours. Drain and discard the marinade.

2. Prepare the outdoor grill or broiler.

3. Grill or broil the chicken breasts for 7 minutes on each side. Thinly slice and set aside.

4. In a small skillet, over medium heat, melt the margarine. Sauté the onion until tender and set aside.

5. In a small bowl, combine the mayonnaise and green onions.

6. Cut the top off the pita rounds and open to form a pocket. Spread the inside of each pocket with the mayonnaise mixture. Place 1 lettuce leaf, 1 tomato slice, some onion, and several chicken slices in each pocket. Serve.

Perfect Picnic Pita

SERVES 6

2 cups thinly sliced spinach leaves
1 cup very thinly sliced red bell pepper
1 cup grated carrot
¼ cup thinly sliced green onions with tops
3 tablespoons plain nonfat yogurt
3 tablespoons commercial 91% fat-free ranch-style salad
  dressing
¼ teaspoon dill weed
¼ cup shredded reduced-fat mozzarella cheese (2 ounces)
3 whole wheat pita rounds (6 inches), cut in half crosswise
1 package (6 ounces) **Healthy Choice™ Deli Thin Sliced
  Turkey, Ham,** *or* **Bologna,** divided

1. In a medium bowl, combine the vegetables, yogurt, salad dressing, and dill weed and mix well. Cover and chill.
2. Just before serving, stir in the cheese.
3. Line each pita half with the meat slices.
4. Spoon the salad mixture evenly into the pita halves and serve immediately.

Tortilla Pinwheels

SERVES 4

Reynolds® Crystal Color® Plastic Wrap
4 flour *or* whole wheat tortillas (8 inches)
¼ cup soft pineapple cream cheese
12 deli-thin slices honey-baked ham
4 spinach leaves

1. Place a sheet of plastic wrap on a flat surface and set 1 tortilla on top of it.
2. Spread 1 tablespoon cream cheese over the tortilla evenly to the edges. Cutting the ham slices if necessary, arrange 3 of them on top of the cream cheese. Place 1 spinach leaf in the center of the tortilla. Roll up the tortilla, enclosing the filling. (Cream cheese around the edges will hold it together.)
3. Repeat with the remaining tortillas.
4. Roll each one in plastic wrap and twist the ends to seal.
5. Refrigerate until ready to serve.
6. To serve, remove the wrap. Cut each tortilla into 3 pinwheel sections and serve upright on a plate.

❖

Tortillas are thin unleavened breads used in Mexican cooking. Corn tortillas have a slightly more robust flavor than flour tortillas and go well with spicy sauces. Because corn tortillas are relatively sturdy, they can be fried and folded into half-moon shapes for tacos or they can be shredded and added to soups. Flour tortillas are softer and have a more delicate flavor.

Salads

Taco Salad

Taco Salad

1 pound ground beef
1 envelope dry onion soup mix
½ cup water
2 tablespoons chili powder
6 cups torn salad greens
Tortilla chips (about 3 cups)
1 medium tomato, chopped
1 cup shredded Cheddar cheese (4 ounces)
Green onions, sliced (optional)
Pickled jalapeño peppers, sliced (optional)
Sour cream (optional)
6 fresh cilantro sprigs (optional)

1. In a 10-inch skillet, over medium heat, cook the beef until browned and no longer pink, stirring to separate the meat. Spoon off fat.

2. Stir in the soup mix, water, and chili powder. Heat to boiling. Reduce the heat to low. Cook 10 minutes, stirring occasionally.

3. To serve: Arrange the lettuce on a platter. Spoon the hot meat mixture over the lettuce. Top with the chips, tomato, and cheese. Additional toppings may include sliced green onions and sliced, pickled jalapeño peppers with sour cream served on the side. Garnish with cilantro, if desired.

Pineapple Ham Salad

1 medium fresh pineapple
3 cups diced cooked ham, turkey, *or* chicken
1 package (6¼ ounces) long-grain and wild rice mix, prepared according to package directions
¾ cup chopped celery
2 tablespoons chopped green onions
2 tablespoons vegetable oil
¼ cup red *or* white wine vinegar
2 tablespoons **Grey Poupon® Dijon Mustard**
¼ teaspoon ground ginger

1. Cut the pineapple in half lengthwise, slicing through the top, keeping the green leaves intact. Scoop out the pineapple, dice, and set aside.

2. In a large non-metal bowl, combine the ham, cooked rice, 1 cup diced pineapple (save the remaining pineapple for another use), celery, and green onions. Set aside.

3. In a small bowl, using a wire whisk, beat the oil, vinegar, mustard, and ginger until smooth. Stir into the ham mixture until well coated.

4. Cover and chill several hours to blend the flavors.

5. Mound in the pineapple halves and serve.

Peppy Pasta Salad

SERVES 4 TO 6

  8 ounces penne *or* elbow macaroni
1½ cups **HORMEL®** pepperoni (slices)
  1 can (14 ounces) artichoke hearts, drained and chopped
  ½ cup pitted black olives, sliced
  ½ cup sliced green onions
  ½ cup creamy Italian salad dressing
Lettuce (optional)

1. Cook the pasta according to package directions. Slice the pepperoni into halves or strips.
2. In a large glass or plastic bowl, combine the pasta, pepperoni, artichoke hearts, olives, and green onions. Add the salad dressing, tossing to coat all the ingredients.
3. For hot pasta salad: Microwave 1 minute or until hot. Spoon onto serving plates. For cold pasta salad: Refrigerate the mixture until chilled. Mound the salad onto serving plates over lettuce, if desired.

Hot Italian Bean, Potato, and Ham Salad

SERVES 3 TO 4

  1 can (14½ ounces) **Del Monte® Sliced New Potatoes**
  1 can (14½ ounces) **Del Monte® Italian Beans,** drained
  1 cup diced boiled ham (4 ounces)
  ½ cup sliced green onions
  ½ cup creamy Italian salad dressing

1. Place the potatoes, including their liquid, and beans in a medium glass bowl. Cover and microwave 3 minutes, or heat in a covered saucepan.
2. Drain the potatoes and beans. Place in a large resealable plastic bag. Add the ham, onions, and dressing.
3. Seal the bag and toss the ingredients to mix and coat evenly. Let marinate at room temperature at least 10 minutes for the flavors to blend. To serve cold, refrigerate for several hours.
4. Serve hot, warm, or cold.

Tangy Tortellini Salad

SERVES 4 TO 6

  1 can (8 ounces) **Hunt's® Tomato Sauce**
  ½ cup **Wesson® Oil**
  ⅓ cup red wine vinegar
  ½ teaspoon seasoned salt
  ¼ teaspoon garlic powder
  ¼ teaspoon celery seed
  ¼ teaspoon pepper
  ¼ teaspoon dried oregano
  1 box (7 ounces) tortellini, cooked according to package directions, rinsed, and drained
  1 cup julienne-cut ham *or* salami
  1 cup julienne-cut red bell peppers
  1 can (3½ ounces) sliced ripe olives, drained
  ¼ cup chopped red onions
Lettuce leaves

1. In a medium bowl, whisk together the sauce, oil, vinegar, and seasonings. Cover and refrigerate the dressing until ready to use.
2. In a large bowl, mix the tortellini, ham, bell peppers, olives, and onions.
3. Arrange on the lettuce leaves and top with the dressing before serving.

Buffalo-Style Chicken Salad

SERVES 4

⅔ cup **Kretschmer® Original Toasted Wheat Germ**
1 teaspoon chili powder
1 teaspoon paprika
¼ teaspoon garlic powder
¼ teaspoon cayenne (red) pepper
1 egg white
2 tablespoons water
4 skinless, boneless chicken breast halves
6 cups mixed salad greens
1 cup celery *or* carrot sticks
½ cup fat-free blue cheese salad dressing

1. Lightly spray the rack of the broiler pan with nonstick cooking spray.

2. In a shallow dish, combine the wheat germ and seasonings.

3. In a separate dish, combine the egg white and water and beat until frothy.

4. Pound the chicken breasts to flatten for even cooking.

5. Dip the chicken into the egg-white mixture, then into the wheat-germ mixture, coating thoroughly. Place the chicken on the prepared broiler pan.

6. Broil 3 minutes. Turn and broil 2 to 4 minutes more or until the chicken is cooked through.

7. Cool slightly then slice into ½-inch strips. Arrange over the mixed greens with the celery or carrot sticks. Dribble the dressing on top and serve.

Garden Chicken Salad

SERVES 6

¾ cup **Best Foods® or Hellmann's® Low Fat Mayonnaise Dressing** *or* **Light Mayonnaise**
3 tablespoons low-fat milk
2 tablespoons chopped green onions
1 teaspoon grated lemon zest (optional)
2 tablespoons lemon juice
1 teaspoon sugar
¼ teaspoon pepper
6 cups cut-up fresh vegetables such as red bell peppers, carrots, cucumbers, celery, zucchini, *or* green beans
Lettuce leaves, rinsed and dried
1 pound skinless, boneless chicken breasts, grilled *or* broiled, sliced

1. In a small bowl, whisk together the mayonnaise, milk, green onions, lemon zest, lemon juice, sugar, and pepper to make the dressing.

2. In a large bowl, toss the vegetables with half the dressing. Arrange on a lettuce-lined platter.

3. Top with the chicken and serve with the remaining dressing.

*B*lanching broccoli, asparagus, carrots, cauliflower, and green beans briefly in boiling water brings out their color and flavor and makes them easier to digest. Cut the vegetables into salad-size pieces and plunge them into a pot of boiling water. Remove them when the water begins to boil again. Rinse them immediately under cold water to stop the cooking. Vegetables will be crisp-tender.

Chicken Caesar Salad

Chicken Caesar Salad

SERVES 4

¼ cup **Kikkoman Soy Sauce**
2 tablespoons lemon juice
2 tablespoons vegetable oil, divided
1 large clove garlic, pressed
4 skinless, boneless chicken breast halves
½ cup mayonnaise
½ teaspoon sugar
2 small heads romaine lettuce, torn into bite-size pieces
1 cup seasoned croutons
¼ cup shredded Parmesan cheese (2 ounces)

1. Blend the soy sauce, lemon juice, 1 tablespoon oil, and garlic. Remove and reserve 2 tablespoons mixture.

2. Brush both sides of the chicken with the remaining mixture.

3. Broil the chicken for 6 minutes on each side or until no longer pink in the center. Brush occasionally with the remaining soy sauce mixture. Let cool.

4. Meanwhile, gradually blend the mayonnaise, sugar, and remaining 1 tablespoon oil into the reserved 2 tablespoons soy sauce mixture. Cover and refrigerate to blend the flavors.

5. Just before serving, toss the lettuce, croutons, cheese, and dressing together. Divide among individual serving plates. Slice the chicken and arrange over the lettuce.

Fruity Chicken Rice Salad

¼ cup red wine vinegar
2 tablespoons honey
1 tablespoon vegetable oil
1 teaspoon sugar
¼ teaspoon salt
1¼ cups water
1½ cups **Minute® Instant Brown Rice**
½ cup diced carrots
½ cup raisins
2 cups diced cooked chicken
1 cup red *or* green seedless grapes
2 tablespoons chopped toasted almonds
1 tablespoon chopped fresh parsley

1. Mix the vinegar, honey, oil, sugar, and salt in a small bowl and set aside.

2. In a medium saucepan, bring the water, carrots, and raisins to a boil. Stir in the rice. Return to a boil. Cover, reduce the heat, and simmer 5 minutes.

3. Remove from the heat and stir. Cover and let stand 5 minutes.

4. Stir in the chicken, grapes, almonds, and parsley. Pour into a serving bowl. Add the honey dressing and toss.

5. Refrigerate at least 1 hour before serving.

Easy Summer Rice Salad

For dressing:

1 tablespoon reduced-sodium soy sauce
1 tablespoon sesame oil
¼ teaspoon shredded fresh ginger
4 tablespoons cider vinegar
3 tablespoons vegetable oil
2 tablespoons Dijon mustard
1 clove garlic, minced

For salad:

2¼ cups water
2¼ cups **UNCLE BEN'S® Brand Instant Rice**
1 package (10 ounces) frozen peas, thawed
½ cup sliced green onions with tops
1½ cups cooked light chicken meat, cut into ½-inch cubes
½ cup diced celery
2 tablespoons chopped green bell pepper
2 tablespoons chopped red bell pepper

1. In a screw-top jar, combine the soy sauce, sesame oil, ginger, vinegar, vegetable oil, mustard, and garlic and shake well.

2. In a large saucepan, bring the water to a boil. Stir in the rice, cover, remove from the heat, and set aside 5 minutes or until all the liquid is absorbed. Allow the rice to cool.

3. In a large bowl, combine the cooled rice, peas, onions, chicken, celery, and bell peppers and toss.

4. Pour the dressing over the rice mixture and toss.

5. Transfer to a serving dish. Cover and chill before serving.

Chunky Chicken Salad

SERVES 6 TO 8

8   ounces **Creamette® Rotini**
1   cup frozen corn, cooked and drained
1   medium red bell pepper, chopped
1   cup sliced mushrooms
½   cup sliced stuffed olives
½   cup sliced celery
¼   cup chopped onion
1   cup julienne strips Cheddar cheese
¾   cup Italian salad dressing
½   cup mayonnaise
⅛   teaspoon pepper
2   cans (5 ounces *each*) **HORMEL® Chunk Chicken,**
     drained and flaked

1. Prepare the rotini according to package directions and drain.

2. In a large bowl, combine the rotini, corn, bell pepper, mushrooms, olives, celery, onion, and cheese.

3. In a small bowl, blend the Italian dressing, mayonnaise, and pepper.

4. Add to the salad mixture and toss to coat. Gently stir in the chicken.

5. Serve immediately or cover and chill.

Grilled Chicken and Pasta Salad

SERVES 6 TO 8

1   package (16 ounces) bow-tie pasta, cooked and drained
1   jar (12 ounces) marinated artichoke hearts, drained
1   jar (7 ounces) roasted red peppers, drained and sliced
⅓   cup slivered black olives
1   cup **Ragú® Chunky Gardenstyle Super Vegetable Primavera Pasta Sauce**
½   cup olive oil
2   tablespoons wine vinegar
2   tablespoons minced fresh parsley
½   teaspoon salt
1   pound skinless, boneless chicken breasts
1   tablespoon toasted pignoli nuts

1. In a large bowl, thoroughly combine the pasta, artichoke hearts, roasted red peppers, olives, sauce, oil, vinegar, parsley, and salt. Cover and chill.

2. Broil or grill the chicken until thoroughly cooked.

3. Thinly slice the cooked chicken and serve warm over the pasta salad.

4. Garnish with the pignoli nuts.

*P*ignoli (also called piñon or pine nuts) are blanched small seeds with a sweetly resinous taste and plump chewiness. Because the nuts are inside the pine cone, their removal is a laborious process, making the nuts rather expensive. Italian pignoli have a delicate flavor, while the sharp pine flavor of the Chinese variety can overwhelm some foods. Pignoli have a high fat content and can turn rancid quickly. Store them in an airtight container up to 3 months in the refrigerator.

Light Chicken and Pasta Salad

Light Chicken and Pasta Salad

SERVES 6

1 cup **2% Low-fat Cottage Cheese** (½ pint)
⅓ cup fresh orange juice
1½ teaspoons white wine vinegar
¾ teaspoon dried basil, crushed
½ teaspoon salt
¼ teaspoon white pepper
¼ teaspoon grated orange zest
1 box (8 ounces) bow-tie pasta, cooked and drained

8 ounces diced cooked chicken breast (2 cups)
1 tomato, seeded and diced
2 tablespoons chopped fresh parsley

1. In a blender, purée the cottage cheese, orange juice, vinegar, basil, salt, and pepper until smooth. Stir in the orange zest.

2. Stir the cottage cheese mixture into the pasta. Stir in the chicken, tomato, and parsley.

3. Refrigerate at least 1 hour. Serve.

COURTESY: DAIRY MANAGEMENT, INC.

Turkey Macaroni Salad

SERVES 6

1½ cups elbow macaroni
1 package (10 ounces) frozen green peas
2 cups cooked turkey breast, cut into bite-size pieces
1 can (10½ ounces) **Healthy Choice® Recipe Creations™ Cream of Celery with Sautéed Onion & Garlic Condensed Soup**
½ cup **Healthy Choice® Fat-Free Shredded Cheddar Cheese**
½ cup reduced-fat sour cream
¼ cup sweet pickle relish
4 medium green onions, sliced
2 tablespoons nonfat milk
½ teaspoon garlic salt (optional)
3 cups lettuce torn into bite-size pieces

1. Cook and drain the macaroni according to package directions.

2. Rinse the frozen peas with cold water to separate and drain.

3. Mix the macaroni, peas, turkey, soup, cheese, sour cream, relish, green onions, milk, and garlic salt, if using.

4. Cover and refrigerate 2 to 4 hours to blend the flavors.

5. Serve on the lettuce.

Salad Greens with Turkey and Oranges

SERVES 6

For orange-vinaigrette dressing:

1 cup rice vinegar *or* other mild vinegar
1 to 2 cloves garlic, minced *or* mashed
2 tablespoons frozen orange juice concentrate
2 tablespoons olive oil
½ teaspoon freshly ground *or* coarsely ground pepper

For salad:

2 heads red leaf lettuce, torn into bite-size pieces
5 ounces cooked turkey cut into julienne strips
3 oranges, peeled and sectioned
1 small red onion, thinly sliced into rings

1. In a small bowl, combine the dressing ingredients and mix well.

2. In a large bowl, combine the salad ingredients.

3. Toss the salad with ⅓ cup dressing.

4. Serve with the remaining dressing on the side.

COURTESY: HORMEL®

❖

For a lively salad, combine two or three varieties of greens with complementary flavors. Arugula has a peppery bite that goes well with milder greens like Boston lettuce, which has soft, buttery-flavored leaves. Chicory, escarole, and Belgian endive share a zesty sharpness that stands up well to heartier dressings. The purple-red, slightly bitter leaves of radicchio add flavor and color to any salad. Hearty, succulent, and sweet-flavored romaine blends well with more astringent greens like peppery watercress.

Salade Niçoise with Tangy Dressing

SERVES 6

1 small bunch red leaf lettuce, washed and drained
1 can (12¼ ounces) solid white tuna in water, drained and flaked
1 pound *each* green beans and red-skin potatoes, cooked and sliced
½ cup *each* diced celery and sliced cucumber
2 small tomatoes, cut into wedges
⅓ cup **French's® Dijon Mustard**
2 tablespoons olive oil
2 tablespoons red wine vinegar
½ teaspoon dried basil
½ teaspoon garlic powder

1. On a large platter, arrange a layer of lettuce leaves.

2. Spoon the tuna into the center of the platter. Arrange the green beans, potatoes, celery, cucumber, and tomatoes around the tuna. Chill until ready to serve.

3. In a small bowl, whisk together the mustard, oil, vinegar, and seasonings. Spoon over the salad. Serve.

Pizza Rice Salad

SERVES 6

1½ cups water
1½ cups **Original Minute® Rice**
1 cup shredded mozzarella cheese
1 cup sliced pepperoni, halved
1 large tomato, chopped
1 green bell pepper, cut into strips
2 mushrooms, sliced
6 pitted ripe olives, sliced
1 cup prepared **GOOD SEASONS® Salad Dressing Mix**, divided

1. In a medium saucepan, bring the water to a boil. Stir in the rice. Cover and remove from the heat. Let stand 5 minutes, then cool.

2. In a large bowl, mix the rice with the cheese, pepperoni, tomato, bell pepper, mushrooms, and olives.

3. Stir in ½ cup dressing and toss to mix well. Chill.

4. Just before serving, toss with the remaining dressing or to taste.

❖

*Y*ou can refrigerate salad greens up to 5 days. Thoroughly wash and dry the greens as soon as you bring them home. Place the leaves, layered with some paper towels, in a large plastic bag and refrigerate until ready to use. Other salad items such as cucumbers, celery, and green onions will stay fresh longer if your refrigerator's vegetable bin is lined with paper towels or a clean linen towel to absorb extra moisture. Or keep several clean, dry sponges in the bin to absorb moisture.

Shrimp and Rice Salad

Shrimp and Rice Salad

SERVES 4 TO 6

- 2 cups long-grain rice
- 12 ounces medium shrimp, shelled and deveined
- 4 ounces snow peas, trimmed and sliced into 1-inch pieces
- 4 ounces asparagus, cut into 1-inch pieces
- 1 package (9 ounces) frozen artichoke hearts, thawed and halved *or* frozen peas, thawed
- ½ *each* yellow and red bell peppers, cut into strips
- 1 stalk celery, sliced
- 4 green onions, thinly sliced (white and green parts)
- ⅓ cup olive *or* canola oil
- 3 tablespoons lemon juice
- 1¼ tablespoons chopped fresh parsley
- 1 tablespoon reduced-sodium soy sauce

Salt and pepper to taste

1. Cook the rice according to package directions. Pour into a large bowl and cool.

2. Bring a medium saucepan of salted water to a boil. Add the shrimp and cook about 3 minutes. Using a slotted spoon, transfer the shrimp to the bowl with the rice.

3. Add the snow peas, asparagus, artichokes or peas, bell peppers, celery, and green onions.

4. In a small bowl, combine the oil, lemon juice, parsley, soy sauce, salt, and pepper and whisk together.

5. Pour the dressing over the shrimp mixture and gently toss to coat well. Serve.

Molly Garlic Pasta Salad

SERVES 8

- 8 ounces medium-size pasta shells
- 1 cup reduced-calorie, reduced-fat sour cream
- 1 cup plain nonfat yogurt
- 8 tablespoons **Molly McButter® Roasted Garlic Flavor Sprinkles**
- ½ teaspoon dried basil
- ¼ teaspoon crushed oregano
- ¼ teaspoon pepper *or* to taste
- 12 cherry tomatoes, halved
- 1 medium zucchini, cut in julienne strips (about 1½ cups)
- ⅔ cup orange, yellow, *or* red bell pepper, seeded and cut in julienne strips
- ½ cup sliced low-sodium pitted ripe olives
- ½ cup chopped red *or* white onion
- 4 teaspoons grated Parmesan cheese (optional)

1. Cook the pasta according to package directions, omitting oil and salt. Rinse under cold running water and drain well.

2. In a medium bowl, combine the sour cream, yogurt, Molly McButter® Roasted Garlic Flavor Sprinkles, basil, oregano, and pepper. Mix well.

3. Stir the dressing mixture into the pasta shells. Add the tomatoes, zucchini, pepper strips, olives, and onion and toss well.

4. Cover and refrigerate at least 2 hours before serving. Sprinkle with Parmesan cheese, if desired. Serve.

Italian Pasta and Vegetable Salad

SERVES 8

8 ounces rotelle *or* spiral pasta
1½ cups broccoli florets, cooked to taste
½ cup cubed Cheddar *or* mozzarella cheese
½ cup halved cherry tomatoes
½ cup chopped red bell pepper
⅓ cup sliced, pitted ripe olives (optional)
1 cup **Wish-Bone® Italian Dressing**

1. Cook the pasta according to package directions. Drain and rinse with cold water until cooled.
2. In a large bowl, combine the pasta, broccoli, cheese, tomatoes, bell pepper, and olives.
3. Add the dressing and toss well.
4. Serve chilled or at room temperature.

NOTE

You can prepare the salad a day ahead. Cover and refrigerate. Before serving, stir in ¼ cup additional Italian dressing.

Pasta and Grapefruit Primavera

SERVES 6

8 cups cooked spinach rotelle
1 medium **Florida Grapefruit,** sectioned and diced with pith and membrane removed
½ cup sliced carrots
½ cup chopped red onion
¾ cup snow peas, blanched and slivered
½ cup sliced red bell pepper
⅓ cup **Florida Grapefruit Juice**
2 tablespoons **Florida Orange Juice**
1 tablespoon fresh lemon juice
3 tablespoons chopped fresh cilantro
1 tablespoon reduced-sodium soy sauce
½ teaspoon prepared mustard
¼ cup vegetable oil
Pinch of sugar
Salt and pepper to taste
Dash red pepper flakes

1. In a large bowl, combine the rotelle, grapefruit, carrots, onion, snow peas, and bell pepper. Toss and set aside.
2. In a medium bowl, combine the remaining ingredients to make the vinaigrette.
3. Add the vinaigrette to the pasta mixture and toss. For the best flavor, chill 1 hour, then serve.

COURTESY: FLORIDA DEPARTMENT OF CITRUS

❖

Italian Pasta and Vegetable Salad

Southwest Pasta 'n' Bean Salad

SERVES 8

¼ cup lime juice
2 tablespoons **Mazola Right Blend®**
⅓ cup chopped fresh cilantro *or* parsley
1 to 2 tablespoons chopped jalapeño peppers
2 cloves garlic, minced
¾ teaspoon ground cumin
¾ teaspoon salt
1 can (15 to 19 ounces) black beans, rinsed and drained
1 can (15 to 19 ounces) kidney beans, rinsed and drained
7 ounces pasta ruffles (about 2½ cups), cooked, rinsed with cold water, and drained
1 small red onion, diced
1 small red bell pepper, diced
1 small yellow *or* green bell pepper, diced

1. In a large bowl, combine the lime juice, oil, cilantro, jalapeño peppers, garlic, cumin, and salt.
2. Add the beans, pasta ruffles, red onion, and bell peppers. Toss to coat. Cover and chill to blend the flavors. Serve.

❼ ◆ ◆ ◆ ◆ ◆ ◆ ◆ ◆ ◆ ◆ ◆

Make potato salad with "new" potatoes, thin-skinned red or white boiling potatoes. They hold their shape better than baking potatoes and do not fall apart when stirred. Add herbs and dressing to potatoes while they are still warm so they can absorb the flavors better.

Parmesan Pasta Salad

SERVES 4 TO 6

8 ounces spiral pasta, cooked
1 medium zucchini, coarsely chopped
1 cup frozen peas, thawed
1 small red bell pepper, sliced into thin strips
3 green onions, sliced
1 medium carrot, peeled and shaved into curls
1 cup **Lawry's® Classic Italian with Aged Parmesan Cheese Dressing**
Lettuce leaves

1. In a large bowl, combine all the ingredients *except* lettuce leaves.
2. Refrigerate several hours or overnight to blend the flavors.
3. Serve on lettuce-lined plates.

Peppy Bread Salad

SERVES 4

3 to 4 ounces **HORMEL® pepperoni (slices)**
4 cups torn lettuce *or* mixed green beans
4 cups torn crusty bread
1 cup shredded Cheddar, mozzarella, *or* other cheese
½ cup sliced black olives
½ cup Italian *or* Caesar salad dressing

1. In a large skillet, heat or sauté the pepperoni slices over medium heat until crisp, about 3 minutes. Drain.
2. Place the pepperoni in a large bowl with the lettuce, bread, cheese, olives, and dressing. Toss to evenly coat the mixture with the dressing.
3. Divide the salad among four plates and serve.

◆

Peppy Green Bean and Potato Salad

SERVES 8

3 pounds small red-skin potatoes, unpeeled and quartered

3 cups sliced green beans, fresh *or* frozen, cooked and drained

3½ to 4 ounces **HORMEL® pepperoni (slices),** cut in half

½ cup sliced green onions

½ cup sliced black olives

¾ cup Italian salad dressing

1. In a large pot with a lid, boil the potatoes in water until just tender. Drain and let cool slightly.

2. In a large resealable plastic bag, place the warm beans, pepperoni, green onions, olives, and dressing. Seal and shake the bag to mix the ingredients.

3. Add the warm potatoes to the bag. Reseal and shake until the potatoes are evenly coated with the dressing. Set aside to marinate at room temperature 1 hour. Shake the bag or stir occasionally. Refrigerate until serving time.

4. Serve warm, at room temperature, or chilled.

Corn and Black Bean Salad with Lime Dressing

SERVES 6

For dressing:

¾ teaspoon ground cumin

¼ cup fresh lime juice

2 tablespoons vegetable oil

1 tablespoon minced fresh jalapeño pepper *or* to taste (optional)

½ teaspoon salt (optional)

For salad:

1 can (11 ounces) corn kernels, drained

1 can (15 ounces) black beans, rinsed and drained

½ cup *each* diced (¼ inch) red and green bell peppers

½ cup diced (¼ inch) sweet onion

¼ cup chopped fresh parsley

Parsley sprigs

1. In a small skillet, over low heat, heat the cumin just until the skillet gets warm, about 1 minute. Turn off the heat. Add the lime juice, vegetable oil, jalapeño pepper, and salt. Whisk to blend.

2. In a large bowl, combine the corn, black beans, bell peppers, onion, and parsley. Add the lime dressing and toss to coat.

3. Spoon the salad onto a deep platter or into a shallow bowl. Garnish with the sprigs of fresh parsley and serve.

Potato Salad

MAKES ABOUT 10½ CUPS

1 cup **Best Foods®** *or* **Hellmann's® Low Fat Mayonnaise Dressing** *or* **Light Mayonnaise**

1 tablespoon white *or* apple cider vinegar

1 teaspoon salt

¼ teaspoon pepper

5 cups cubed cooked potatoes (about 6 medium)

1 cup diced celery (2 stalks)

⅓ cup chopped onion

1. In a large bowl, whisk together the mayonnaise, vinegar, salt, and pepper.

2. Add the remaining ingredients and mix well.

3. Cover and chill before serving.

Ranch Potato Salad Primavera

Ranch Potato Salad Primavera

MAKES 8 CUPS

4 cups red-skin potatoes, diced, cooked, and cooled
Salt and pepper to taste
1 cup cooked broccoli florets
1 small yellow zucchini, sliced
1 stalk celery, chopped
½ cup diced red bell pepper
2 green onions, chopped
1 bottle (8 ounces) fat-free ranch dressing

1. In a large bowl, sprinkle the potatoes with the salt and pepper.

2. Add the remaining ingredients and marinate in the refrigerator at least 2 hours.

3. Remove from the refrigerator and serve.

VARIATION

For a tasty pasta salad, substitute 4 cups pasta, cooked and cooled, for the potatoes.

COURTESY: WISH-BONE®

When a recipe calls for crumbled bacon or bacon drippings, cut the bacon into small pieces before cooking. Cook the bacon pieces over medium heat, stirring occasionally so the drippings don't burn before the bacon is crisp.

Spinach Salad with Hot Bacon Dressing

SERVES 2 AS A MAIN DISH SALAD
OR 4 AS A SIDE DISH
MAKES 1 CUP DRESSING

8 ounces fresh spinach, thick stems and veins from larger leaves removed, washed, and thoroughly dried
4 to 6 strips cooked bacon, crumbled; reserve drippings for dressing
¼ cup golden raisins (do not substitute dark raisins)
4 ounces mushrooms, sliced
1 cup seasoned croutons

For hot bacon dressing:

¼ cup bacon drippings
¼ cup red wine vinegar
¼ cup mayonnaise
¼ cup sugar

1. Tear the spinach leaves into bite-size pieces and place in a large bowl. (If possible, choose small, tender leaves.)

2. Add the bacon, raisins, mushrooms, and croutons to the spinach.

3. Toss and set aside.

4. In a small saucepan, add all the dressing ingredients and stir to combine thoroughly.

5. Over low heat, cook several minutes until very hot. (Or, combine the ingredients in a glass bowl. Microwave on high for 30 seconds or until very hot.)

6. Pour the dressing over the salad and toss to distribute evenly.

7. Serve immediately.

Marinated Vegetable Salad

1 can (14½ ounces) vegetable broth
1 tablespoon sugar
½ teaspoon dried thyme, crushed
¼ teaspoon garlic powder
⅛ teaspoon pepper
6½ cups cut-up fresh vegetables such as cauliflower, green beans, and carrots
¼ cup vinegar
2 tablespoons minced fresh parsley

1. In a 3-quart saucepan, combine the broth, sugar, thyme, garlic powder, and pepper. Add the vegetables. Cover. Over medium-high heat, heat to boiling. Stir. Cook 1 minute or until the vegetables are crisp-tender. Add the vinegar and parsley.

2. Spoon the mixture into a large shallow serving dish. Cover and refrigerate 12 hours or overnight.

3. Remove from the refrigerator and serve.

Cucumbers with Dill Sour Cream

MAKES 2 CUPS

4 medium cucumbers, peeled, seeded, and thinly sliced (4 cups)
2 teaspoons salt
1 cup sour cream *or* nonfat sour cream
1 small clove garlic, minced
2 tablespoons snipped dill *or* 2 teaspoons dried dill weed

1. Place the cucumbers in a colander. Sprinkle with the salt and toss to distribute the salt evenly. Set aside to drain at least 20 minutes to disgorge excess water. With hands, squeeze out the remaining water.

2. In a medium bowl, mix together the sour cream, garlic, and dill. Add the cucumbers and stir to coat.

3. Chill at least 1 hour to allow the flavors to develop and blend.

4. Remove from the refrigerator and serve.

COURTESY: HORMEL®

If you find cucumbers hard to digest, usually the seeds are the problem. Slice cucumbers lengthwise and scrape out the seeds with a spoon or your thumb. Select vegetables that are small, dark green, and firm. Larger, more mature cucumbers have larger seeds and can be bitter. Sprinkle a pinch of sugar to sweeten bitter cucumbers or try English cucumbers, which are virtually seedless.

Classic Salad Refresher

¾ cup **Lawry's® Classic Italian with Aged Parmesan Cheese Dressing**
½ teaspoon Dijon mustard
1 shallot, minced
½ teaspoon **Lawry's® Lemon Pepper**
7 cups romaine lettuce, torn into bite-size pieces
1 jar (14 ounces) hearts of palm, drained and cut into 1½-inch julienne strips
2 bunches watercress, well-trimmed
1 bunch radishes, thinly sliced

1. In a small bowl, combine the dressing, mustard, shallot, and pepper. Blend well and chill.

2. In a large bowl, combine the remaining ingredients. Pour the dressing over the lettuce mixture. Toss well and serve.

Classic Bibb Salad

SERVES 4 TO 6

4 heads bibb lettuce, cored, washed, patted dry, and torn into bite-size pieces (about 8 cups)
5 cherry tomatoes, cut in half
3 bacon slices, cooked crisp and crumbled
1 hard-cooked egg, chopped
1 teaspoon chopped fresh chives
3 sprigs watercress
1 bottle (8 ounces) **Lawry's® Classic White Wine Vinaigrette with Chardonnay Dressing**

1. Place the lettuce in a large bowl. Arrange the tomatoes near the edge of the bowl with the bacon and egg in the center. Sprinkle with the chives and garnish with the watercress.

2. When ready to serve, toss the salad with the dressing.

Citrus Slaw

MAKES 7 CUPS

1 cup **Best Foods® *or* Hellmann's® Low Fat Mayonnaise Dressing *or* Light Mayonnaise**
⅓ cup frozen orange juice concentrate, thawed
2 teaspoons sugar
¾ teaspoon salt
¼ teaspoon pepper
8 cups shredded red *or* green cabbage
2 cups shredded carrots
1 green bell pepper, seeded, quartered, and thinly sliced

1. In a large bowl, whisk together the mayonnaise, juice concentrate, sugar, salt, and pepper.

2. Add the cabbage, carrots, and bell pepper and toss to coat.

3. Cover and chill before serving.

For perfect hard-cooked eggs, put the eggs in a saucepan, preferably in a single layer, cover completely with cold water, and bring just to a boil over high heat (the eggs should barely jiggle). Adjust the heat to the lowest setting possible and simmer, uncovered, 15 minutes. Quickly transfer the eggs to a pan or bowl filled with cold water and leave them until cool. This gentle way of cooking helps keep the shells from cracking and the yolks from becoming rubbery. Dousing them in cold water makes the shells easier to peel.

Hawaiian Delight Salad

SERVES 6

5 cups bite-size mixed salad greens
1 can (20 ounces) pineapple chunks, drained
1 cup sliced celery
1 cup thinly sliced red onion, separated into rings
1 cup toasted pecans, walnuts, *or* macadamia nuts
½ cup honey-Dijon salad dressing

1. In a large bowl, combine the greens, pineapple, celery, onion rings, nuts, and salad dressing.

2. Toss until well blended and serve.

COURTESY: HORMEL®

California Waldorf Salad

SERVES 6

1 can (16 ounces) **Del Monte® Fruit Naturals® Chunky Mixed Fruit** *or* **Fruit Cocktail**
¼ cup vegetable oil
¼ cup white wine vinegar
1 tablespoon Dijon mustard
1 tablespoon honey
½ medium green apple, sliced
⅓ cup **Del Monte® Seedless Raisins**
½ red onion, thinly sliced
⅓ cup walnut halves, toasted
6 cups torn lettuce leaves

1. Drain the fruit, reserving ¼ cup juice.

2. In a small bowl, combine the juice, oil, vinegar, mustard, and honey.

3. Combine the remaining ingredients and toss with the dressing just before serving.

Luscious Beet and Orange Salad

SERVES 6

3 tablespoons **Mazola Right Blend®**
3 tablespoons cider vinegar
1 teaspoon sugar
¼ teaspoon ground cumin
1 can (16 ounces) sliced beets, drained
¼ cup chopped red onion
2 large oranges, peeled and sectioned
Lettuce leaves

1. In a medium bowl, combine the oil, vinegar, sugar, and cumin. Add the beets and onion and toss gently to coat.

2. Cover and chill to blend the flavors.

3. With a slotted spoon, remove the beets and onion from the marinade. Arrange with the oranges on a lettuce-lined platter. Drizzle with 3 tablespoons marinade and serve.

Toasting nuts intensifies their rich flavor. Preheat the oven to 350° F. Spread the nuts on an ungreased baking sheet and toast them in the oven, stirring every 3 minutes or so, until brown but not burned. Toast whole blanched or unblanched almonds about 20 minutes; pecan halves, walnut halves, and slivered almonds, about 15 minutes; sliced almonds and chopped nuts, about 10 minutes.

Healthy Harvest Salad

SERVES 4

1   can (16 ounces) **Del Monte® Fruit Naturals® Pear Halves**
½   cup plain nonfat yogurt
⅓   cup reduced-calorie Italian salad dressing
½   teaspoon peeled and minced ginger
4   cups torn romaine lettuce *or* spinach leaves
¼   cup toasted wheat germ
½   red bell pepper, chopped
½   cup chopped **Del Monte® Pitted Prunes**

1. Drain the pears, reserving 1 tablespoon juice.
2. In a small bowl, combine the reserved juice, yogurt, salad dressing, and ginger.
3. Toss half the dressing with the lettuce.
4. Place the lettuce on a serving dish and sprinkle with the wheat germ. Arrange the pears, pepper, and prunes over the lettuce.
5. Top with the remaining dressing and serve.

Grapefruit Salad with Orange-Oil Vinaigrette

SERVES 4

Zest from 1 **Florida Orange**
2   tablespoons olive oil
8   ounces watercress *or* mesclun salad mix
1   **Florida Grapefruit,** sectioned
1   cup diced jicama
¼   cup balsamic vinegar

1. In a small bowl, combine the orange zest and olive oil. Microwave 20 seconds to meld the flavors.
2. Wash the greens and dry very well. Place in a large bowl. Pour the oil mixture over the greens and toss to coat.
3. Arrange the grapefruit sections around the edge of a large serving plate. Mound the greens in the center of the plate. Sprinkle the jicama over the greens. Drizzle the vinegar over the salad and serve.

COURTESY: FLORIDA DEPARTMENT OF CITRUS

Lemon Apple-Bran Salad

SERVES 4

½   cup plain nonfat yogurt
1   teaspoon sugar
1   teaspoon lemon juice
1   tablespoon chopped fresh parsley
½   teaspoon salt (optional)
2   cups cored and chopped red apples (2 apples)
½   cup thinly sliced celery (1 stalk)
½   cup halved green grapes *or* ¼ cup raisins
½   cup **Kellogg's® All-Bran® Cereal**
Lettuce leaves (optional)

1. In a medium bowl, combine the yogurt, sugar, lemon juice, parsley, and salt.
2. Stir in the apples, celery, and grapes.
3. Cover and refrigerate until ready to serve.
4. Just before serving, stir in the cereal and spoon onto lettuce leaves, if desired.

Beef

AND

Veal

Family-Style Beef Brisket Dinner

SERVES 8

1 envelope **Lipton® Recipe Secrets® Onion Soup Mix**
¾ cup water
3 pounds brisket of beef
1 pound potatoes, cut into chunks
8 ounces carrots, peeled and cut into chunks

1. Heat the oven to 325° F.

2. In a 3-quart baking or roasting pan, add the onion soup mix blended with the water. Add the brisket, turning to coat with the soup mixture on all sides. Loosely cover with foil and roast 1 hour.

3. Add the potatoes and carrots. Toss to coat with the soup mixture.

4. Cover with foil and continue roasting 2 hours or until the brisket and vegetables are tender. If desired, thicken the gravy.

5. Slice and serve.

VARIATION

To create a different taste, try the recipe with **Lipton® Recipe Secrets® Savory Herb with Garlic Soup Mix,** or **Fiesta Herb with Red Pepper Soup Mix.**

Prime Rib with Mustard Sauce

SERVES 6
MAKES 1 CUP SAUCE

1 5- to 6-pound standing rib roast
1 clove garlic, minced
1 teaspoon salt
1 teaspoon paprika
½ cup mayonnaise
¼ cup **Grey Poupon® Dijon Mustard**
¼ cup prepared horseradish

1. Heat the oven to 475° F.

2. Rub the meat with the garlic and sprinkle with the salt and paprika.

3. Place the meat in an uncovered roasting pan, fat side up.

4. Cook 30 minutes or until browned.

5. Reduce the temperature to 325° F and cook until the meat is tender, allowing 30 minutes per pound for medium-well and 18 minutes per pound for rare meat.

6. Meanwhile, in a small bowl, combine the mayonnaise, mustard, and horseradish and mix well.

7. Serve the sauce with the roast.

❖

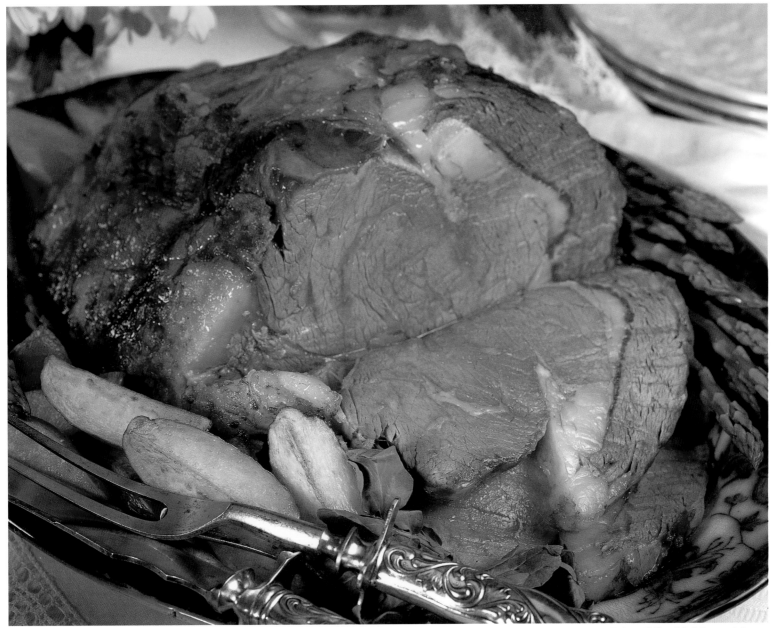

Prime Rib with Mustard Sauce

Grilled Italian Steak

Grilled Italian Steak

SERVES 8

¼ cup **Wish-Bone® Italian Dressing**
2 tablespoons grated Parmesan cheese
2 teaspoons dried basil, crushed
¼ teaspoon cracked black pepper
1 2- to 3-pound boneless sirloin *or* top round steak

1. In a large, shallow, non-aluminum baking dish, combine the Italian dressing, cheese, basil, and pepper. Add the steak and turn to coat. Cover and marinate in the refrigerator, turning occasionally, 3 to 24 hours.

2. Prepare the grill or broiler.

3. Remove the steak from the marinade, reserving the marinade. Grill or broil the steak, turning once, until done to taste. Remove to a platter.

4. Meanwhile, in a small saucepan, over medium heat, bring the reserved marinade to a boil and continue boiling 1 minute. Pour over the steak and serve.

Teriyaki-Tarragon Grilled Steak

SERVES 4

¼ cup **Kikkoman Teriyaki Marinade & Sauce**
½ teaspoon dry tarragon, crumbled
¼ teaspoon pepper
1 pound top round steak (about 1 inch thick)

1. Combine the teriyaki marinade sauce, tarragon, and pepper. Pour over the steak in a large resealable plastic bag. Press the air out of the bag and close the top securely.

2. Turn the bag over several times to coat both sides of the steak. Marinate 45 minutes, turning the bag over occasionally.

3. Remove the steak from the marinade and place on the grill 4 to 5 inches from the hot coals.

4. Cook 4 minutes on each side for rare, or to desired doneness. (Or, place the steak on the rack of the broiler pan. Broil 4 to 5 inches from the heat for 4 minutes on each side for rare, or to desired doneness.)

5. To serve: Cut across the grain into thin slices.

No one is quite sure when man discovered the delicious results of putting raw meat over a hot fire. While grilling may be the oldest cooking method, a few modern techniques can be very helpful. Grilling sears the surface of food more quickly than it cooks the inside. Cook thick cuts of meat at lower heat than thin cuts to avoid excessive charring. Use less charcoal for fatty meats such as hamburger and steak, more for lean cuts. Control cooking speed by taking full advantage of any adjustments available: Raise or lower the rack; if there's a lid, adjust its height. Push more charcoal under the food to raise the temperature; take more to the sides to lower it.

Grilled Steaks and Tomatoes with Basil-Garlic Bread

SERVES 4

3 tablespoons olive oil
1 teaspoon dried basil *or* 2 tablespoons finely chopped fresh basil
½ teaspoon garlic powder
2 **Beef T-Bone** *or* **Porterhouse Steaks,** cut 1 inch thick
Salt and pepper to taste (optional)
1 loaf French bread (8 ounces), cut in half lengthwise
2 tomatoes, cut into 6 slices, ¾ inch thick
2 tablespoons grated Parmesan cheese

1. Prepare the grill.

2. In a cup, combine the oil, basil, and garlic powder. Reserve.

3. Place the beef steaks on the grill rack over medium ash-covered coals. Grill 14 to 16 minutes for medium-rare to medium, turning once. Season with the salt and pepper, if desired.

4. Meanwhile, brush half the basil mixture evenly on the cut side of the bread halves. Brush the remaining mixture on one side of each tomato slice.

5. About 5 minutes before the steaks are done, place the bread, oil side down, and the tomatoes, oil side down, on the rack with the steaks. Grill 2 to 3 minutes. Turn the bread and tomatoes over and sprinkle with the Parmesan cheese. Continue grilling 1 to 3 minutes or until the bread is golden brown and the tomatoes are just heated through.

6. Cut the bread diagonally into slices.

7. Carve the steaks into thick slices and place on a platter with the tomatoes. Serve.

COURTESY: NATIONAL CATTLEMEN'S BEEF ASSOCIATION

Mexican Pepper Steak

SERVES 6

1 cup **Wish-Bone® Italian** *or* **Lite Italian Dressing**
1 cup prepared salsa
3 medium red, green, *and/or* yellow bell peppers, trimmed, seeded, and quartered
1 small red onion, peeled, cut into thick rings
1 8-ounce boneless sirloin *or* top loin steak, about 2 inches thick

1. In a large shallow baking dish, combine the Italian dressing, salsa, bell peppers, and onion rings. Add the steak and turn to coat. Cover and marinate in the refrigerator, turning occasionally, 3 to 24 hours.

2. Prepare the grill or broiler.

3. Remove the steak and vegetables, reserving the marinade.

4. Grill or broil the steak and vegetables, turning once, until the steak is done.

5. In a small saucepan, bring the reserved marinade to a boil and continue boiling 1 minute.

6. Serve the sauce with the steak and vegetables.

Mexican Pepper Steak

Savory Chuck Steaks

SERVES 4

½ cup steak sauce
2 tablespoons firmly packed brown sugar
2 tablespoons fresh lime juice
¼ teaspoon cayenne (red) pepper
4 **Boneless Beef Chuck Eye Steaks,** cut ¾ inch thick
Salt to taste (optional)

1. Prepare the grill.
2. In a small bowl, combine the steak sauce, brown sugar, lime juice, and cayenne pepper. Reserve 2 tablespoons marinade and set aside.
3. Place the beef steaks in a resealable plastic bag with the remaining marinade, turning to coat. Close the bag securely and marinate 10 minutes. Do not chill.
4. Pour off the marinade and discard.
5. Place the steaks on the grill rack over medium ash-covered coals. Grill 14 to 20 minutes for medium-rare to medium, turning once. Brush with the reserved marinade during the last 2 minutes of cooking. Season with salt, if desired.
6. Remove to a platter and serve.

COURTESY: NATIONAL CATTLEMEN'S BEEF ASSOCIATION

Beef Steaks with Tangy Corn Relish

SERVES 4

1 teaspoon vegetable oil
½ red *or* green bell pepper, trimmed, seeded, and cut into ½-inch pieces
1 can (8¾ ounces) whole kernel corn, undrained
1 tablespoon white vinegar
⅛ teaspoon cayenne (red) pepper
4 boneless **Beef Chuck Top Blade Steaks,** cut ½ inch thick
¼ teaspoon garlic salt
¼ cup sliced green onions

1. Heat the oil in a large nonstick skillet over medium heat and add the bell pepper. Cook and stir 3 minutes.
2. Stir in the corn, vinegar, and cayenne pepper. Continue cooking, uncovered, 2 to 3 minutes. Remove the relish from the skillet and keep warm.
3. Heat the same skillet over medium-high heat. Add the beef steaks and cook 3 to 5 minutes for medium-rare to medium, turning once. Season with the garlic salt.
4. Return the corn relish and add the green onions to the skillet. Cook 1 minute or until heated through. Serve.

COURTESY: NATIONAL CATTLEMEN'S BEEF ASSOCIATION

To determine the amount of charcoal needed, spread a single layer of briquettes in the grill pan to extend 1 inch beyond the food to be cooked. Then pile the coals in the center of the pan to start the fire. Self-lighting briquettes and jelly or wax-like charcoal starters are convenient, but if you prefer chemical-free methods, try an electric starter or chimney starter. And never use kerosene, gasoline, or alcohol to start a fire.

Orange Pepper Steaks

SERVES 4

2 teaspoons coarsely ground black pepper
4 **Beef Tenderloin Steaks,** cut 1 inch thick
½ cup orange marmalade
4 teaspoons cider vinegar
½ teaspoon ground ginger

1. Heat the broiler.

2. Press the pepper evenly into both sides of the beef steaks.

3. Place the steaks on the rack in the broiler pan so the surface of the meat is 2 to 3 inches from the heat.

4. In a small bowl, combine the marmalade, vinegar, and ginger.

5. Brush the tops of the steaks with half the marmalade mixture. Broil 13 to 16 minutes for medium-rare (145° F) to medium, turning once and brushing with the remaining marmalade mixture.

6. Remove to a platter and serve.

COURTESY: NATIONAL CATTLEMEN'S BEEF ASSOCIATION

Oriental Flank Steak

SERVES 6

½ cup **Wish-Bone® Italian** *or* **Robusto Italian** *or* **Lite Italian Dressing**
2 tablespoons soy sauce
2 tablespoons firmly packed brown sugar
½ teaspoon ground ginger (optional)
1 to 1½ pounds flank *or* top round steak

1. In a large, shallow, non-aluminum baking dish or resealable plastic bag, combine the Italian dressing, soy sauce, sugar, and ginger.

2. Add the steak and turn to coat. Cover the dish or close the bag and marinate in the refrigerator for 3 to 24 hours, turning occasionally.

3. Remove the steak, reserving the marinade. Grill or broil the steak, turning once, until the steak is done.

4. Meanwhile, in a small saucepan, bring the reserved marinade to a boil and continue boiling 1 minute. Pour over the steak and serve.

Marinating is a wonderful method of adding flavor to foods. Marinades usually contain an acid like lemon juice, wine, or vinegar and flavorings such as herbs and spices. Adding sugar, honey, or molasses to the marinade causes it to act like a sheer glaze, which can help to seal in moisture during cooking. The acidity of marinades is useful in tenderizing leaner cuts of meat but the acidic ingredients react with metal kitchenware, causing pitting and imparting an off-taste to the food. Resealable plastic bags are great for marinating. Clean-up is minimal and it's easy to distribute the marinade evenly. All you have to do is turn the bag over occasionally. **Important note:** *Because the mixture of meat juices and marinade ingredients is an ideal medium for bacteria, always marinate food in the refrigerator when the recipe calls for marinating food longer than a few minutes.*

Golden Glazed Flank Steak

Golden Glazed Flank Steak

SERVES 6 TO 8

1 envelope **Lipton® Recipe Secrets® Onion Soup Mix**

1 jar (12 ounces) apricot preserves

½ cup water

1 flank steak, cut into thin strips (about 2 pounds)

2 medium green, red, *or* yellow bell peppers, cut into thin vertical slices

Hot cooked rice

1. Heat the broiler

2. In a small bowl, combine the soup mix, apricot preserves, and water. Mix well.

3. In a large shallow baking pan, arrange the steak and bell peppers. Spoon the soup mixture evenly on top.

4. Broil, turning once, until the steak is done to taste.

5. Serve over the hot rice.

Spicy Glazed Short Ribs

SERVES 4

1½ teaspoons dry mustard
3 pounds beef short ribs, about 2½ inches long
½ cup **Kikkoman Teriyaki Baste & Glaze**
2 cloves garlic, pressed
¾ teaspoon crushed red pepper

1. Prepare the grill.
2. Combine the mustard with ½ teaspoon water to make a smooth paste. Cover and let stand 10 minutes.
3. Meanwhile, score the meaty side of the ribs, opposite the bone, ½ inch deep, ½ inch apart, lengthwise and crosswise.
4. Combine the baste and glaze, garlic, red pepper, and mustard mixture.
5. Place the ribs on the grill 5 to 7 inches from the hot coals. Brush thoroughly with the basting mixture.
6. Cook 15 minutes, or until the ribs are brown and crispy, turning over and brushing frequently with the remaining mixture.
7. Remove to a platter and serve.

Beef and Mushrooms Dijon

SERVES 4

1 pound boneless beef sirloin *or* top round steak, ¾ inch thick
2 tablespoons vegetable oil, divided
2 cups sliced mushrooms
1 medium onion, sliced
1 can (10¾ ounces) condensed cream of mushroom soup
½ cup water
2 tablespoons Dijon mustard
4 cups hot cooked rice

1. Slice the beef into very thin strips.
2. In a large skillet, over medium-high heat, heat half the oil. Cook the beef in two batches until browned, stirring often. Set the beef aside.
3. Add the remaining oil. Add the mushrooms and onion and cook over medium heat until tender.
4. Add the soup, water, and mustard. Heat to a boil. Return the beef to the pan. Heat through.
5. Serve over the hot rice.

To make slicing raw beef into thin strips easier, freeze it for 1 hour. Let the meat come to room temperature before sautéing or browning; it will absorb less fat, brown faster, and be less likely to stick. Before sautéing or browning, always pat the meat dry with paper towels. A moist surface slows browning.

Peppered Beef Kebabs

Peppered Beef Kebabs

SERVES 4

2 tablespoons vegetable oil

1 tablespoon *each* fresh lemon juice and water

2 teaspoons Dijon mustard

1 teaspoon honey

½ teaspoon dried oregano

¼ teaspoon pepper

1 pound **Boneless Beef Sirloin Steak,** cut 1 inch thick, then cut into 1¼-inch pieces

1 medium green, red, *or* yellow bell pepper, trimmed, seeded, and cut into 1-inch pieces

8 large mushrooms

Salt to taste (optional)

1. Heat the broiler.

2. In a large bowl, whisk together the oil, lemon juice, water, mustard, honey, oregano, and pepper. Add the beef, bell pepper, and mushrooms, tossing to coat.

3. Alternately thread pieces of beef, bell pepper, and mushrooms on each of four 12-inch skewers.

4. Place the kebabs on the rack in the broiler pan so the surface of the meat is 3 to 4 inches from the heat. Broil 8 to 10 minutes for medium-rare to medium, turning occasionally. Season with salt, if desired. (Or, prepare the grill and place the kebabs on the grill over medium ash-covered coals. Grill 9 to 12 minutes.) Serve.

COURTESY: NATIONAL CATTLEMEN'S BEEF ASSOCIATION

Mexican Beef Stir-Fry

SERVES 4

2 tablespoons vegetable oil
1 teaspoon ground cumin
1 teaspoon dried oregano
1 clove garlic, minced
1 red *or* green bell pepper, trimmed, seeded, and cut into thin strips
1 medium onion, cut into thin wedges
1 to 2 jalapeño peppers, thinly sliced (remove interior ribs and seeds if a milder flavor is desired)
1 pound **Beef Flank Steak,** cut into ⅛-inch-thick strips
3 cups thinly sliced lettuce

1. In a small bowl, combine the oil, cumin, oregano, and garlic. Reserve half.

2. In a large nonstick skillet, warm half the seasoned oil over medium-high heat. Add the bell pepper, onion, and jalapeño pepper and stir-fry 2 to 3 minutes or until crisp-tender. Remove and set aside.

3. In the same skillet, stir-fry the beef strips, half at a time, over medium-high heat in the remaining seasoned oil for 1 to 2 minutes or until the outside surface is no longer pink.

4. Return the vegetables to the skillet, toss with the beef, and heat through.

5. Serve the beef mixture over the lettuce.

COURTESY: NATIONAL CATTLEMEN'S BEEF ASSOCIATION

Orange Beef Stir-Fry

SERVES 6

2 **Florida Navel Oranges**
1¼ pounds top round steak, trimmed
½ cup **Florida Orange Juice,** divided
2 tablespoons reduced-sodium soy sauce
1 tablespoon plus 1 teaspoon cornstarch, divided
2 teaspoons firmly packed brown sugar, divided
½ cup reduced-sodium chicken broth
1 tablespoon Oriental sesame oil
1 teaspoon finely minced ginger
1 large clove garlic, minced
4 cups broccoli florets
4 medium green onions, cut into 2-inch pieces
1 can (8 ounces) sliced water chestnuts, rinsed and drained
3 tablespoons chopped cilantro

1. With a paring knife or zester, remove the orange rind in thin strips. Peel away and discard the white part of the rind. Section the oranges. Cut the steak along the grain into two 2-inch-wide strips. Then cut across the grain into ¼-inch slices.

2. In a medium bowl, whisk together 2 tablespoons orange juice, soy sauce, 1 tablespoon cornstarch, and 1 teaspoon brown sugar. Add the meat and toss to coat. In a mixing cup, combine the remaining orange juice, cornstarch, brown sugar, and broth.

3. In a large nonstick skillet, over medium-high heat, heat the oil until hot. Add the meat and stir-fry until browned but slightly rare, 3 to 4 minutes. Transfer to a bowl. Into the same skillet, add the chicken broth mixture, ginger, garlic, orange zest, broccoli, green onions, and water chestnuts. Stir-fry over high heat until the vegetables soften, 3 to 4 minutes. Lower the heat and add the cilantro and beef with its juices. Simmer, stirring until the sauce thickens, 2 to 3 minutes. Stir in the orange sections.

4. Remove from the heat and serve.

COURTESY: FLORIDA DEPARMENT OF CITRUS

French Beef au Gratin

French Beef au Gratin

SERVES 4

½ cup (1 stick) **I Can't Believe It's Not Butter!**®
4 cups thinly sliced Vidalia *or* white onions
1 pound beef tenderloin *or* sirloin, sliced into ½-inch cubes
3 tablespoons all-purpose flour
1 tablespoon firmly packed dark brown sugar
1 teaspoon ground cumin
1 teaspoon salt
½ teaspoon pepper
4 cups beef broth (1 quart)
2 cups cooked fettuccine
1 cup shredded mozzarella cheese (4 ounces)
½ cup grated Parmesan cheese

1. In a large heavy-bottomed pan, over medium heat, melt I Can't Believe It's Not Butter!® Add the onions and sauté, stirring often, until caramelized but not burned, 15 to 20 minutes.

2. With a slotted spoon, remove the onions to a medium bowl.

3. Add the beef to the pan and brown well on all sides. Return the onions and any juices to the pan.

4. In a small bowl, mix the flour, sugar, cumin, salt, and pepper. Add to the pan and stir 1 minute until bubbly.

5. Gradually add the broth, stirring to scrape any brown bits from the pan, and simmer 10 minutes.

6. Heat the broiler.

7. Place ½ cup fettuccine in each of four 16-ounce ovenproof bowls. Divide the beef mixture over the pasta.

8. In a medium bowl, stir the cheeses together and sprinkle evenly over the beef. Broil until the cheese is melted and lightly browned, about 5 minutes.

9. Remove from the broiler and serve.

Beef Stir-Fry

SERVES 4

1 pound boneless beef sirloin *or* top round steak, ¾ inch thick
2 tablespoons cornstarch
1 can (10½ ounces) condensed beef broth
2 tablespoons soy sauce
1 tablespoon orange juice
1 teaspoon hot pepper sauce
2 tablespoons vegetable oil, divided
1 bag (16 ounces) frozen Oriental vegetable combination, broccoli, carrots, water chestnuts, and red bell pepper
¼ teaspoon garlic powder
4 cups hot cooked rice

1. Slice the beef into very thin strips.

2. In a medium bowl, mix the cornstarch, broth, soy sauce, orange juice, and hot pepper sauce until smooth. Set aside.

3. In a large skillet, over medium-high heat, heat half the oil. Add the beef in two batches and stir-fry until browned. Set the beef aside.

4. Heat the remaining oil. Add the vegetables and garlic powder. Stir-fry over medium heat until crisp-tender.

5. Stir the cornstarch mixture and add to the vegetables. Cook until the mixture boils and thickens, stirring constantly.

6. Return the beef to the pan. Heat through.

7. Serve over the hot cooked rice.

Beef Stroganoff

SERVES 4

1 pound boneless beef sirloin *or* top round steak,
  ¾ inch thick
2 tablespoons vegetable oil, divided
1 medium onion, chopped
1 can (10¾ ounces) condensed cream of mushroom soup
½ cup sour cream *or* plain yogurt
½ teaspoon paprika
4 cups hot cooked medium egg noodles
Chopped fresh parsley

1. Slice the beef into very thin strips.
2. In a large skillet, heat half the oil over medium-high heat. Cook the beef in two batches until browned, stirring often. Set the beef aside.
3. Add the remaining oil to the skillet. Add the onion and cook over medium heat until tender. Pour off excess fat.
4. Stir in the soup, sour cream, and paprika. Heat to a soft boil.
5. Return the beef to the skillet and heat through.
6. Serve over the hot noodles, garnishing with the parsley.

Italian Beef Stir-Fry

SERVES 4

1 pound **Beef Round Tip Steaks,** cut ⅛ to ¼ inch thick
  or 1 pound **Beef Strips** for stir-fry
2 cloves garlic, crushed
1 tablespoon olive oil
Salt and pepper to taste (optional)
2 small zucchini, thinly sliced
1 cup cherry tomato halves
¼ cup reduced-calorie Italian salad dressing
2 cups hot cooked spaghetti
1 tablespoon grated Parmesan cheese

1. Stack the beef steaks. Cut lengthwise in half and then crosswise into 1-inch-wide strips.
2. In a large nonstick skillet, over medium-high heat, cook and stir the garlic in the oil for 1 minute.
3. Add the beef strips, half at a time, and stir-fry 1 to 2 minutes or until the outside surface is no longer pink. (Do not overcook). Season with salt and pepper, if desired. Remove with a slotted spoon and keep warm.
4. Add the zucchini to the same skillet and stir-fry 2 to 3 minutes or until crisp-tender.
5. Return the beef to the skillet with the tomato halves and dressing. Heat through.
6. Pour the beef mixture over the hot pasta and sprinkle with the Parmesan cheese. Serve.

COURTESY: NATIONAL CATTLEMEN'S BEEF ASSOCIATION

Italian Beef Stir-Fry

Foolproof Beef and Broccoli

Foolproof Beef and Broccoli

SERVES 4

12 ounces boneless beef sirloin steak, sliced across the grain into very thin strips
1 clove garlic, minced
1 tablespoon vegetable oil
1 medium onion, cut into wedges
1 can (10¾ ounces) condensed cream of broccoli soup
¼ cup water
1 tablespoon soy sauce
2 cups broccoli florets
Hot cooked noodles

1. In a skillet, over medium-high heat, cook the beef and garlic in hot oil until the beef is browned. Add the onion and cook 5 minutes, stirring often.
2. Stir in the soup, water, and soy sauce. Heat to boiling. Add the broccoli. Reduce the heat to low. Cover and cook 5 minutes or until the vegetables are crisp-tender.
3. Serve over the hot noodles.

Barbecue Beef Bake

SERVES 8

2 cups **Bisquick® Original** *or* **Reduced Fat baking mix**
¼ teaspoon paprika
½ cup water
1 cup barbecue sauce
½ cup chopped onion
¼ teaspoon pepper
8 ounces cooked roast beef, shredded

1. Heat the oven to 425° F. Grease a 12-inch pizza pan.
2. In a medium bowl, combine the baking mix, paprika, and water until a soft dough forms. Beat 30 seconds.
3. Shape into a ball. Pat or press the dough into the pan.
4. In a medium bowl, mix the barbecue sauce, onion, and pepper. Stir in the beef.
5. Spread the beef mixture over the dough. Bake 17 to 20 minutes or until the edge is brown.
6. Cut into wedges and serve warm.

Beefy Mac 'n' Corn

SERVES 5

1 pound ground beef
1 medium onion, chopped (about ½ cup)
1 can (10¾ ounces) condensed corn soup
1 cup spaghetti sauce
¼ cup water
⅛ teaspoon pepper
2 cups cooked elbow macaroni (1 cup dry)
Grated Parmesan cheese

1. In a 10-inch skillet, over medium-high heat, cook the beef and onion until the beef is browned and the onion is tender, stirring to separate the meat. Drain off fat.
2. Reduce the heat to low and stir in the soup, spaghetti sauce, water, pepper, and macaroni. Heat through, stirring occasionally.
3. Serve with the cheese.

❖ ❖ ❖ ❖ ❖ ❖ ❖ ❖ ❖ ❖ ❖ ❖ ❖ ❖

Have a ready supply of chopped bell peppers and onions by freezing ahead. Wash and seed the bell peppers, making sure to remove the membranes, which can be bitter, before chopping. Store in an airtight container up to 6 months. For the onions, remove the papery skin and chop them to the desired size. Freeze in an airtight container and use within 3 months.

Mexicorn Bake

SERVES 6

1 pound ground beef
1 medium green bell pepper, chopped
1 package (1¼ ounces) taco seasoning
¾ cup water
1 can (10¾ ounces) condensed corn soup
¼ cup milk
1 package (10 ounces) refrigerated biscuits
½ cup shredded Cheddar cheese (2 ounces)

1. Heat the oven to 400° F.
2. In a large skillet, over medium-high heat, cook the beef and bell pepper until the beef is browned, stirring to separate the meat. Drain off fat.
3. Add the taco seasoning and water. Simmer 5 minutes. Stir in the soup and milk.
4. Pour the mixture into a 2- to 3-quart casserole or baking dish. Bake 10 minutes or until the mixture begins to bubble.
5. Remove the dish from the oven and stir. Separate the biscuits and cut each in half. Place the biscuits, cut side down, over the hot meat mixture in spoke fashion around the edge of the casserole.
6. Sprinkle the cheese over the biscuits.
7. Bake 15 minutes or until the biscuits are golden brown.
8. Remove from the oven and serve.

Impossible Lasagna Pie

½ cup creamed cottage cheese
1 pound ground beef
1 cup shredded mozzarella cheese, divided
½ teaspoon salt
½ teaspoon dried oregano
1 can (6 ounces) tomato paste
½ cup **Bisquick® Original baking mix**
1 cup milk
2 eggs

1. Heat the oven to 400° F.

2. In a greased 9-inch pie plate, spread the cottage cheese.

3. In a large skillet, over medium heat, cook the ground beef until brown and drain. Stir in ½ cup mozzarella cheese, salt, oregano, and tomato paste.

4. Spoon the mixture evenly over the cottage cheese.

5. In a medium bowl, whisk together the remaining ingredients until blended and pour into the pie plate.

6. Bake 30 to 35 minutes or until a knife inserted in the center comes out clean. Sprinkle with the remaining cheese. Bake 1 to 2 minutes longer or until melted.

7. Remove from the oven and serve.

Saucy Meat Loaves with Parsley Rice

SERVES 8

¼ cup Dijon mustard
3 tablespoons honey
1½ pounds ground beef *or* turkey
¾ cup **Kretschmer® Original Toasted Wheat Germ**
½ cup chopped green onions
⅓ cup water
½ teaspoon salt (optional)
¼ teaspoon pepper
1 egg white, lightly beaten
1 tablespoon chopped fresh parsley
4 cups hot cooked rice

1. For the sauce: Combine the mustard and honey. Mix well and set aside.

2. Heat the oven to 350° F.

3. For the meat loaves: Combine the beef, wheat germ, green onions, water, salt, pepper, and egg white. Mix lightly, but thoroughly.

4. Shape the meat mixture into eight 3×2-inch loaves. Place in an 11×7-inch glass baking dish. Bake 30 to 35 minutes or until the meat is no longer pink and the juices run clear. Drain.

5. To serve: Spoon the sauce over the meat loaves. Stir the parsley into the rice. Serve the rice on the side.

NOTE

For added convenience, substitute prepared honey-mustard sauce, barbecue sauce, or salsa for the Dijon mustard and honey.

Southwestern Meat Loaf

SERVES 8

1 envelope **Lipton® Recipe Secrets® Onion Soup Mix**
2 pounds ground beef
2 cups corn flakes *or* bran flakes, crushed
1½ cups whole kernel corn, frozen, thawed *or* canned, drained
1 small green bell pepper, trimmed, seeded, and chopped
2 eggs
¾ cup water
⅓ cup ketchup

1. Heat the oven to 350° F.
2. In a large bowl, combine all the ingredients until completely blended.
3. In a 13×9-inch baking dish or roasting pan, shape the meat mixture into a loaf.
4. Bake 1 hour or until done. Let stand 10 minutes.
5. Slice and serve.

Monterey Burger Melt

SERVES 4

1 pound ground beef
1 can (11⅛ ounces) condensed Italian tomato soup
⅓ cup water
4 thick slices Monterey Jack cheese
4 hamburger buns, split and toasted

1. Shape the beef into 4 patties.
2. In a 10-inch skillet, over medium-high heat, cook the patties until just browned on both sides. Remove and set aside. Drain off fat.
3. In the same skillet, stir the soup and water. Heat to boiling.
4. Return the patties to the skillet. Reduce the heat to low. Cover and cook 10 minutes or until done, stirring occasionally.
5. Top the patties with the cheese. Heat 2 minutes more, uncovered, until the cheese is just melted.
6. Serve on the buns.

Ketchup, sometimes called catsup, the favorite American condiment, originated in China as a spicy pickled-fish sauce called ke-tsiap. British sailors carried it to the West where the recipe's ingredients were constantly evolving. Americans added tomatoes to the formula and omitted the fish, transforming the sauce into the basis of the now familiar thick and savory sauce.

Hamburger Update

Hamburger Update

SERVES 4

¼ cup plus 1 tablespoon plain nonfat yogurt
¼ cup crumbled feta cheese (1 ounce)
½ teaspoon ground cumin
1 pound low-fat ground beef
¼ cup minced green onions
¼ cup cilantro leaves, finely minced
1 large clove garlic, crushed
1 tablespoon grated fresh ginger
4 lettuce leaves
20 very thin slices peeled cucumber
4 onion rolls, split and toasted

1. In a small bowl, combine the yogurt, cheese, and cumin. Blend with a fork until the cheese is finely crumbled. Cover and chill at least 1 hour.

2. Combine the beef, green onions, cilantro, garlic, and ginger, mixing well. Shape into 4 patties.

3. Cook in a nonstick skillet or grill 3 inches from the heat for 6 to 7 minutes on each side or until the meat and juices are no longer pink. Drain on paper towels.

4. Place a lettuce leaf, 5 slices of cucumber, and a beef patty on each roll half. Top with 2 tablespoons yogurt mixture and the remaining half roll. Serve immediately.

COURTESY: HEALTHY CHOICE®

Fiesta Brunch Casserole

Fiesta Brunch Casserole

SERVES 4

4 flour tortillas (8 inches)
Butter-flavored nonstick cooking spray
1 can (15 ounces) **HORMEL® Chili No Beans**
3 medium russet potatoes, cooked, peeled, and diced (about 1 pound)
4 eggs
1 cup chopped tomato
½ cup chopped green onions
½ cup shredded Cheddar cheese
1 cup **Chi-Chi's® Salsa** (optional)

1. Heat the oven to 400° F.
2. Spray both sides of the tortillas with the cooking spray. Place 2 tortillas into each of two loaf pans, gently shaping each tortilla to create a "bowl."
3. In a medium saucepan, heat the chili. Stir in the potatoes and cook until thoroughly heated.
4. Divide the chili mixture among the tortillas.
5. With the back of a spoon, make an indentation in each chili mixture. Break an egg in each indentation.
6. Bake 10 minutes. Cover loosely with foil. Bake 5 to 10 minutes longer or until the eggs are done.
7. Gently lift out of the pans to serving plates.
8. Spoon on the tomato and onions. Sprinkle with the cheese. Serve with salsa, if desired.

Hearty Beef Pot Pie

SERVES 5

1 can (40 ounces) **DINTY MOORE® Beef Stew**
1 prepared 9-inch pie crust, refrigerated *or* frozen
1 tablespoon grated Parmesan cheese
½ teaspoon parsley flakes

1. Heat the oven to 375° F.
2. Spoon the stew into a 2-quart round casserole dish. Place the crust directly on top of the stew. Fold the edges under and flute.
3. Sprinkle with the cheese and parsley. Cut two or three slits in the crust.
4. Bake 35 to 40 minutes or until the crust is golden and the stew is heated through.
5. Spoon into bowls and serve.

Potato Nugget Casserole

SERVES 6

1 can (40 ounces) **DINTY MOORE® Beef Stew**
1 cup frozen mixed vegetables
1 tablespoon dried minced onion
1 package (16 ounces) frozen seasoned potato crowns

1. Heat the oven to 400° F.
2. Spoon the stew into a 12½×8-inch baking dish. Gently stir in the vegetables and onion. Arrange the potato crowns on top of the stew.
3. Bake 35 to 45 minutes or until heated through.
4. Spoon into bowls and serve.

Veal Scaloppine with Lemon and Capers

Veal Scaloppine with Lemon and Capers

SERVES 4

¼ cup all-purpose flour
¼ teaspoon pepper
8 veal scallops (about 1 pound)
3 tablespoons **I Can't Believe It's Not Butter!**®
½ cup beef broth
2 tablespoons lemon juice
2 tablespoons capers, drained

1. Combine the flour and pepper on a plate. Press the veal pieces into the mixture, coating them all over. Shake off any excess.

2. In a heavy 10-inch skillet, over moderately high heat, melt I Can't Believe It's Not Butter!® until the foam subsides, about 1 minute. Add the veal and brown quickly, about 1 minute on each side. Do not overcook. As each piece of veal is cooked, transfer it to a warm platter.

3. Add the broth to the skillet, scraping up any browned bits on the bottom. Cook until slightly reduced and thickened, about 1 minute. Stir in the lemon juice and capers. Reduce the heat to low.

4. Return the veal and any accumulated juices to the skillet. Heat through, turning them over once.

5. Arrange the veal pieces on the platter and spoon the sauce over them. Serve.

Veal Sausage and Pepper Polenta

SERVES 8

For polenta:

4 cups water
1 cup cornmeal
1 teaspoon salt

For topping:

1 pound veal sausage, thickly sliced
2 tablespoons olive oil
2 cloves garlic, minced
2 red *or* green bell peppers, trimmed, seeded, and diced
1 jar (27½ ounces) **Ragú® Light Pasta Sauce— Chunky Mushroom**

1. In a large saucepan, bring the water to a boil. Slowly mix in the cornmeal and salt, stirring constantly until the mixture boils. Reduce the heat to low and simmer 20 minutes, stirring frequently.

2. Evenly spread the polenta in a lightly greased, 13×9-inch baking pan. Cool completely.

3. In a large skillet, thoroughly brown the veal sausage in the olive oil. Remove and set aside.

4. In the same skillet, sauté the garlic and bell peppers until tender. Return the sausage to the skillet and add the pasta sauce. Simmer, covered, 20 minutes over low heat.

5. Heat the oven to 375° F.

6. Cut the polenta into 8 squares. Place in a large shallow baking pan. Spoon the sausage and pepper mixture evenly over the polenta.

7. Bake 20 minutes or until heated through. Serve.

Pork
AND
Lamb

Cinnamon-Rubbed Pork Tenderloin

SERVES 6

3 **Pork Tenderloins** (1 pound *each*)
¼ cup ground cinnamon
2 tablespoons chopped garlic
2 tablespoons fresh thyme, chopped *or* 2 teaspoons
   dried thyme
1 tablespoon kosher salt
1 tablespoon paprika
1 teaspoon ground allspice
½ teaspoon cayenne (red) pepper
3 to 4 tablespoons canola oil
Buttered spinach and mushrooms, roasted vegetables, *or*
   mashed potatoes (white or sweet)

1. Trim the tenderloins of any fat and cut each in half.
2. In a small bowl, thoroughly combine the cinnamon, garlic, thyme, salt, paprika, allspice, and cayenne pepper.
3. Rub the cinnamon mixture evenly over the pork. Place the pork in a resealable plastic bag or covered baking dish. Refrigerate and let marinate 3 hours or overnight before cooking.
4. In a large skillet, heat the oil over medium heat. Cook the pork 15 to 18 minutes, turning often to brown evenly.
5. To serve: Cut the pork on the bias into ½-inch slices. Arrange the pork slices over a bed of buttered spinach and mushrooms, roasted vegetables, or mashed potatoes.

COURTESY: CHEF DAVID WALZOG, THE JAMES BEARD FOUNDATION

Grilled Pork Roast with Pepper Jelly Glaze

SERVES 16

4 pounds **Pork Loin Roast,** rolled and tied

For marinade:

  1 cup apple juice
  1 cup cider vinegar
  1 cup hot pepper jelly

For glaze:

  ¾ cup pepper jelly
  ¼ cup cider vinegar

1. Place the pork in a large resealable plastic bag.
2. Heat the marinade ingredients together until the jelly melts. Cool slightly and pour over the pork. Seal the bag. Refrigerate 12 to 24 hours.
3. Prepare a covered grill with banked coals.
4. Remove the pork from the marinade, reserving the marinade. Insert a thermometer in the center of the roast.
5. When the coals are hot, place the pork over the drip pan. Cover the grill. Grill 1¼ hours or until the thermometer reads 150° F, basting occasionally with the marinade.
6. Combine the glaze ingredients. Coat the roast with the glaze for the last 10 minutes of grilling, bringing the roast to an internal temperature of 160° F.
7. Let the roast rest 10 to 15 minutes before removing the string and slicing. Serve.

COURTESY: NATIONAL PORK PRODUCERS COUNCIL

Grilled Pork Roast with Pepper Jelly Glaze

Pork Tenderloin with Raspberry Sauce Supreme

Pork Tenderloin
with Raspberry Sauce Supreme

SERVES 4

1 **Pork Tenderloin** (approximately 1 pound)
  cut into 8 crosswise pieces
Cayenne (red) pepper to taste
2 teaspoons butter
6 tablespoons red raspberry preserves
2 tablespoons red wine vinegar
1 tablespoon ketchup
½ teaspoon prepared horseradish
½ teaspoon soy sauce
1 clove garlic, minced
2 kiwi fruit, peeled and thinly sliced
Fresh raspberries (optional)

1. With the flat side of a wide knife, press each pork tenderloin slice to 1-inch thickness.

2. Lightly sprinkle both sides of each slice with the cayenne pepper.

3. Heat the butter in a nonstick skillet over medium-high heat. Add the pork slices and cook 3 to 4 minutes on each side.

4. Meanwhile, in a small saucepan, combine the preserves, vinegar, ketchup, horseradish, soy sauce, and garlic. Simmer over low heat for about 3 minutes, stirring occasionally. Keep warm.

5. Place the cooked pork on a warm serving plate. Spoon the sauce over and top each piece with a kiwi slice. Garnish the serving plate with remaining kiwi slices and, if desired, fresh raspberries.

COURTESY: NATIONAL PORK PRODUCERS COUNCIL

Harvest Pork Roast

SERVES 8

3½ to 4 pounds boneless pork shoulder roast (Boston butt), netted or tied
2 tablespoons vegetable oil
1 can (10¾ ounces) condensed cream of mushroom soup
1 envelope dry onion soup mix
1 teaspoon dried thyme leaves, crushed
1 bay leaf
1¼ cups water, divided
8 medium potatoes, quartered
8 medium carrots, peeled and cut into 2-inch pieces
2 tablespoons all-purpose flour

1. In an ovenproof 5-quart Dutch oven, over medium-high heat, cook the roast in hot oil until browned on all sides. Remove and set aside. Spoon off fat.

2. Heat the oven to 350° F.

3. In the same Dutch oven, combine the soups, thyme, bay leaf, and 1 cup water. Heat to boiling, stirring occasionally. Return the roast to the Dutch oven. Cover and bake 45 minutes.

4. Turn the roast and add the potatoes and carrots. Cover and cook 1¾ hours or until the roast and vegetables are fork-tender (170° F internal temperature).

5. Transfer the roast and vegetables to a platter. Remove the netting or string from the roast.

6. In a cup, stir together the flour and remaining water until smooth.

7. In the Dutch oven, over medium heat, heat the soup mixture to boiling. Gradually stir in the flour mixture. Cook until the mixture boils and thickens, stirring constantly (thin with additional water, if necessary). Remove the bay leaf before serving.

8. Serve the gravy with the roast.

Mediterranean Pork Made Easy

Mediterranean Pork Made Easy

SERVES 4

1 tablespoon olive oil

8 boneless pork medallions (small oval cutlets)

1 can (15 ounces) **Hunt's® Ready Tomato Sauces Chunky Garlic & Herb**

1 can (14 ounces) artichoke hearts, drained and quartered (not oil packed)

2 teaspoons chopped green olives

½ teaspoon sugar

1. In a large skillet, heat the oil over medium-high heat and brown the pork medallions on both sides. Drain.

2. Stir in the sauce, artichokes, olives, and sugar and simmer, uncovered, over low heat for 10 minutes or until the medallions are cooked through.

3. Transfer to warm plates and serve.

Twice-Cooked Pork

SERVES 8 TO 10

5 pounds **Boneless Pork Shoulder** *or* **Ribs,** trimmed of exterior fat
2 tablespoons olive oil
2 cachucha *or* jalapeño peppers, seeded and diced
½ cup chopped fresh cilantro
Juice of 4 limes
2 pounds boniato (white yams) *or* yams, cooked and mashed

For marinade:

½ cup chopped white onion
¼ cup distilled white vinegar
¼ cup fresh cilantro
2 tablespoons fresh thyme
2 tablespoons fresh oregano
2 tablespoons salt
1 tablespoon ground cumin
8 cloves garlic
3 bay leaves
Pepper to taste
4 cups water

1. Place the pork in a large resealable plastic bag or a pan with a lid. In a food processor or blender, place all the marinade ingredients *except* water. With the machine running, pour in the water to make a thin purée. Pour the marinade over the pork. Refrigerate 12 hours, turning the pork occasionally.
2. Heat the oven to 300° F.
3. Place the pork and marinade in a large ovenproof pot with a lid and bake 3 hours or until the pork is tender. Remove the pork from the pot and let cool slightly. Discard the marinade.
4. Using two forks, pull apart and shred the pork.
5. Heat the oil in a large skillet over medium-high heat. Add the shredded pork, peppers, and cilantro. Cook, stirring constantly, until the pork is crisp.
6. Just before serving, pour the lime juice over the pork. Arrange a scoop of the pork over a mound of boniato or yams.

COURTESY: CHEF DOUGLAS RODRIGUEZ, THE JAMES BEARD FOUNDATION

Pork Loin with Honey-Mustard Sauce

SERVES 6

1 cup apple juice
¼ cup honey
2 tablespoons Dijon mustard with seeds
2 tablespoons lemon juice
1 tablespoon fresh thyme *or* 1 teaspoon dried thyme
2 tablespoons olive oil, divided
4 **Pork Loin Chops,** 1-inch thick, trimmed
Salt and pepper (optional)
2 large red onions, thinly sliced (4 cups)

1. In a small saucepan, over high heat, boil the apple juice until reduced to ¼ cup.
2. In a small bowl, combine the honey, mustard, lemon juice, and thyme. Stir in the hot reduced apple juice. Set aside.
3. In a large skillet, heat 1 tablespoon oil over medium heat.
4. Season the chops with salt and pepper, if desired. Brown the chops 5 minutes on each side. Remove from the skillet.
5. Add the remaining oil and onions to the skillet. Cook the onions, stirring often, until soft and caramelized, about 15 minutes. Stir in the apple juice mixture.
6. Return the chops to the skillet. Cook 5 to 7 minutes, turning the pork and basting with the onion mixture several times.
7. Transfer to warm plates and serve.

COURTESY: CHEF SARAH STEGNER, THE JAMES BEARD FOUNDATION

Adobe Pork Loin

SERVES 4

3 cloves garlic, minced
1 teaspoon ground cloves
1 teaspoon ground coriander
1 teaspoon ground cumin
1 teaspoon coarsely ground pepper
2½ pounds boneless pork loin
1 can (15 ounces) **HORMEL**® **Chili No Beans**
1½ cups water
3 medium onions, cut into 1-inch pieces
Thin strips of lemon zest

1. Heat the oven to 350° F.

2. In a small bowl, combine the garlic, cloves, coriander, cumin, and pepper. Rub the mixture on the pork loin.

3. In a roasting pan, combine the chili and water. Place the pork loin on the chili mixture. Place the onions around the roast.

4. Cover and bake 1 hour. Uncover and baste. Continue baking, basting occasionally, 1 hour or until a meat thermometer inserted near the center reaches 165° F.

5. Serve the sliced pork with the chili and onions. Garnish with the lemon zest.

Super Pork Chops Pizzaiola

SERVES 6

6 loin *or* shoulder pork chops, ¾ inch thick, trimmed
2 tablespoons vegetable oil
1½ cups **Ragú® Chunky Gardenstyle Super Mushroom Pasta Sauce**
½ teaspoon dried rosemary
½ cup sliced ripe olives, drained
Salt and pepper to taste
2 tablespoons grated Parmesan cheese

1. In a large skillet, thoroughly brown the chops on both sides in hot oil. Drain. Add the sauce, rosemary, olives, salt, and pepper.
2. Simmer, covered, 30 minutes. Uncover and simmer 15 minutes or until the meat is tender.
3. Sprinkle with the cheese. Serve.

Roast Pork Chops with Sweet Potatoes, Apples, and Bitter Greens

SERVES 6

2 large sweet potatoes *or* yams, peeled
6 tablespoons (¾ stick) butter, melted, divided
2 baking apples, peeled and cored
6 **Pork Chops,** 1-inch thick
Salt and pepper to taste
2 tablespoons canola oil
10 ounces assorted bitter greens such as kale, chard, and collard greens

1. Heat the oven to 350° F.
2. Cut the sweet potatoes into quarters lengthwise. Slice into ⅛-inch slices and toss with 2 tablespoons melted butter.
3. Spread out the sweet potatoes on a baking sheet and bake until tender and slightly caramelized, about 20 minutes.
4. Quarter the apples. Sauté in a medium skillet in 2 tablespoons melted butter until tender. Set aside the apples and potatoes.
5. Heat the oven to 425° F.
6. Season the pork chops with the salt and pepper. In a large oven-proof skillet, heat the canola oil and sear the pork on both sides until golden brown. Place in the oven and roast 10 minutes.
8. Steam the greens in 2 tablespoons water and 2 tablespoons melted butter until slightly wilted. Toss together the sweet potatoes, apples, and greens. Season with the salt and pepper to taste. Mound the greens mixture in the center of each plate and lean a chop against the greens. Serve.

COURTESY: CHEF TRACI DES JARDINS, THE JAMES BEARD FOUNDATION

Onion-Glorified Pork Chops

SERVES 6

1 tablespoon vegetable oil
6 pork chops, ½-inch thick
1 medium onion, sliced
½ teaspoon dried thyme, crushed
1 can (10¾ ounces) condensed cream of celery soup
¼ cup water

1. In a large skillet, over medium-high heat, heat the oil. Cook the pork chops in two batches for 10 minutes or until browned on both sides. Set the chops aside.
2. Add the onion and thyme to the skillet. Cook over medium-low heat until crisp-tender.
3. Stir in the soup and water. Heat to a boil.
4. Return the chops to the skillet. Cover and cook over low heat for 5 minutes or until the chops are done. Serve.

Succulent BBQ Pork Chops

SERVES 4

⅓ cup **Kikkoman Teriyaki Baste & Glaze**
2 tablespoons plum jam
1 teaspoon firmly packed brown sugar
1 teaspoon grated fresh ginger
¼ teaspoon grated lemon zest
4 pork loin chops, about ¾ inch thick

1. Combine the baste and glaze, plum jam, brown sugar, ginger, and lemon zest. Remove and reserve ¼ cup mixture.
2. Place the pork chops on the grill 4 to 5 inches from the hot coals. Brush with the remaining baste and glaze mixture. Cook about 8 minutes, turning the chops over and brushing occasionally with the baste and glaze mixture.
3. Meanwhile, blend the reserved ¼ cup baste and glaze mixture with 1½ tablespoons water in a small microwave-safe serving bowl.
4. Cover and microwave on medium-high (70%) for 90 seconds, stirring every 30 seconds.
5. Serve the warm sauce with the chops.

Store-bought minced garlic is a great time-saver. Packed in oil and sold in jars, minced garlic can often be found in the deli or produce sections at the supermarket. One-half teaspoon of pre-minced garlic equals one clove of freshly minced garlic.

Pork Chops in Peach Sauce

SERVES 10

10 pork chops, ½ inch thick
1¼ teaspoons salt
½ teaspoon ground allspice
¼ teaspoon pepper
3 tablespoons vegetable oil
1 can (16 ounces) **Del Monte® Fruit Naturals® Yellow Cling Sliced Peaches,** drained, reserving ½ cup syrup
½ cup apricot preserves
1 teaspoon grated orange zest
2 cloves garlic, minced
Parsley (optional)

1. Season the meat with the salt, allspice, and pepper. In a large skillet, brown the meat on both sides in the oil. Place the meat in a 13×9-inch baking dish.
2. In a blender, combine the peaches, reserved syrup, preserves, orange zest, and garlic. Cover and blend until smooth. Pour over the meat.
3. Heat the oven to 350° F. Bake, uncovered, until the meat is tender, about 40 to 45 minutes, basting occasionally.
4. Remove the meat to a serving platter and spoon ½ cup sauce over the meat. Serve with the remaining sauce and garnish with parsley, if desired.

Glazed Pork Chops

SERVES 4

⅔ cup apricot *or* peach preserves
½ cup **Wish-Bone® Italian** *or* **Robusto Italian Dressing**
2 tablespoons Dijon mustard
4 pork chops, 1 inch thick (about 1½ pounds)

1. In a medium bowl, combine the preserves, dressing, and mustard.

2. In a large non-aluminum baking dish, arrange the chops in one layer. Pour ¾ cup apricot marinade over the chops, turning to coat.

3. Reserve the remaining marinade and refrigerate. Cover the pan and marinate in the refrigerator, turning occasionally, 3 to 24 hours.

4. Prepare the grill or broiler.

5. Remove the chops from the marinade, discarding the marinade.

6. Grill or broil the chops, turning once and brushing frequently with the reserved marinade, until the chops are done.

7. Remove to a platter and serve.

Pork Chop and Corn Stuffing Bake

Pork Chop and Corn Stuffing Bake

SERVES 4
MAKES 2¼ CUPS STUFFING

1 can (10¾ ounces) condensed corn soup
¼ cup finely chopped celery
¼ cup finely chopped onion
½ teaspoon paprika
1½ cups corn bread stuffing
4 boneless pork chops, ¾ inch thick (about 1 pound), well trimmed of fat
1 tablespoon firmly packed brown sugar
1 teaspoon prepared spicy brown mustard

1. In a medium bowl, combine the soup, celery, onion, paprika, and stuffing.

2. In a 9-inch greased pie plate, spoon the stuffing mixture. Arrange the chops over the mixture, pressing lightly into the stuffing.

3. In a cup, combine the sugar and mustard. Mix into a paste, then spread evenly over the chops.

4. Heat the oven to 400° F.

5. Bake 30 minutes or until the chops are no longer pink.

6. Transfer the chops to a serving platter.

7. Stir the stuffing and serve with the chops.

Spicy Pork Chop Bake

SERVES 6

6 pork chops, 1 inch thick (about 2½ pounds)
1 can (11⅛ ounces) condensed Italian tomato soup
2 tablespoons water
2 tablespoons vinegar
1 tablespoon firmly packed brown sugar
1 tablespoon Worcestershire sauce
¼ to ½ teaspoon hot pepper sauce *or* to taste

1. Heat the oven to 400° F.

2. In a 3-quart oblong baking dish, arrange the chops in a single layer.

3. Bake 20 minutes or until the chops begin to brown. Spoon off fat.

4. Meanwhile, in a small bowl, combine the soup, water, vinegar, brown sugar, Worcestershire sauce, and pepper sauce.

5. Spoon the soup mixture over the chops.

6. Bake 15 minutes or until the chops are no longer pink.

7. Stir the sauce before serving.

COURTESY: CAMPBELL SOUP COMPANY

Garden Pork Sauté

SERVES 4

2 tablespoons margarine *or* butter, divided
1 pound pork tenderloin, cut into ½-inch-thick slices, *or* 4 boneless pork chops, ¾ inch thick (about 1 pound)
1 cup broccoli florets
1 large carrot, trimmed, peeled, and thinly sliced (about ½ cup)
1 cup sliced mushrooms (about 3 ounces)
1 can (10¾ ounces) condensed cream of broccoli soup
⅓ cup milk
3 slices bacon, cooked crisp and crumbled (optional)
⅛ teaspoon pepper

1. In a 10-inch skillet, over medium-high heat, in 1 tablespoon hot margarine, cook the pork for 10 minutes or until browned on both sides. Remove and keep warm.

2. In the same skillet, over medium heat, add the remaining margarine and melt. Add the broccoli, carrot, and mushrooms and cook until tender and the liquid is evaporated, stirring often.

3. In a small bowl, combine the soup, milk, bacon, and pepper. Pour over the vegetables. Heat to boiling.

4. Return the pork to the skillet. Reduce the heat to low. Cover and cook 5 minutes or until the pork is tender and no longer pink, stirring occasionally.

5. Remove from the heat and serve.

Ham in Pastry

SERVES 8 TO 10

1 **Cure 81® half ham**
1 jar (10 ounces) orange marmalade
3 boxes (10 ounces *each*) single pie crust mix
1 egg, beaten

1. Put the ham in a shallow roasting pan. Add 1 cup water. Cover the pan with foil and place in a cold oven. Set at 325° F and heat 30 minutes.

2. Remove from the oven and pour off water.

3. Cool slightly and spread thickly with the marmalade.

4. Prepare the pie crust. Roll out the dough in a long rectangle, ⅜ inch thick.

5. Place the ham on one side of the dough. Fold the remaining pastry over the ham and trim. Seal the edges well.

6. Cover the seams and decorate with festive shapes cut from the trimmings. Attach with the beaten egg.

7. Brush the entire crust with the beaten egg. Replace the ham in the baking pan. Increase the heat to 375° F and bake 45 minutes. Cool 15 minutes and remove with a large spatula to a large platter. Serve.

Ham in Pastry

Apricot-Glazed Savory Ham

Apricot-Glazed Savory Ham

SERVES 8 TO 10

1 **Cure 81® half ham**
1 cup apricot preserves
¼ cup Dijon mustard
1 clove garlic, minced
1 tablespoon lemon juice (optional)
Whole cloves (optional)

1. Remove the wrapper from the ham. Place the ham in a shallow baking pan and add 1 cup water. Cover the pan securely with foil.

2. Place the ham in a cold oven set at 325° F.

3. Bake 20 to 25 minutes per pound or follow the directions on the label. If a meat thermometer is used, heat to an internal temperature of 135° F.

4. Meanwhile, in a small bowl, combine the preserves, mustard, garlic, and lemon juice, if using.

5. Thirty (30) minutes before done, remove the ham from the oven. Carefully pour the water from the pan.

6. Lightly score the top of the ham into diamonds and insert cloves, if desired. Spoon the glaze over the ham and return to the oven, uncovered, and continue baking for 30 minutes.

7. Transfer the glazed ham to a platter. Slice and serve.

❖ ❖ ❖ ❖ ❖ ❖ ❖ ❖ ❖ ❖ ❖ ❖ ❖ ❖ ❖

Let a ham rest out of the oven a few minutes before slicing, and it will carve more easily.

Grilled Ham with Savory Pineapple Sauce

SERVES 8 TO 10
MAKES 2½ CUPS SAUCE

1 **Cure 81® half ham**
1 can (20 ounces) crushed pineapple
2 tablespoons firmly packed brown sugar
2 tablespoons lemon juice
2 tablespoons Dijon mustard
2 tablespoons Worcestershire sauce
1 tablespoon cornstarch
1 clove garlic
½ teaspoon ground cinnamon

1. Prepare a charcoal or gas grill. Slice the ham into ½-inch steaks.

2. In a blender, place the pineapple, brown sugar, lemon juice, mustard, Worcestershire sauce, cornstarch, garlic, and cinnamon. Blend until smooth. Place the mixture in a small saucepan over high heat. Bring the mixture to a boil, stirring until thickened, 4 minutes. Set aside.

3. When the charcoal is covered with ash or the grill is heated, place the ham steaks on the grill. Heat 5 to 10 minutes or until hot, turning occasionally.

4. Spoon the sauce over the ham and serve.

VARIATION

For chunky pineapple sauce, place all the ingredients directly in the saucepan without first blending in a blender. Cook until thickened.

Broiled Ham Kebabs

SERVES 6

3 carrots, cut into 2-inch pieces
12 pearl onions, peeled
24 **Cure 81® ham** 1-inch cubes
1 fresh pineapple, cut into 1-inch chunks *or* 1 can
   (20 ounces) pineapple chunks
2 medium green bell peppers, cut into 2-inch pieces
1 cup orange marmalade
⅓ cup Dijon mustard
2 tablespoons firmly packed brown sugar
Hot cooked rice (optional)

1. In a medium saucepan, cook the carrots and onions in boiling water about 5 minutes or until barely tender. Drain.

2. On each of six 12-inch metal skewers, alternately thread the ham, pineapple, carrot, bell pepper, and onion.

3. Arrange the skewers in a shallow baking or broiler pan.

4. In a small bowl, combine the marmalade, mustard, and sugar. Mix well.

5. Brush the kebabs with the sauce.

6. Heat the broiler.

7. Broil 4 inches from the heat source for 10 to 15 minutes, turning and brushing frequently with the sauce.

8. Continue broiling until the kebabs are lightly browned.

9. Serve the kebabs with the remaining sauce and, if desired, with hot rice.

Ham and Grannies with Mustard Sauce

SERVES 6

2 tablespoons butter *or* oil, divided
6 slices **Cure 81® ham,** ¼ inch thick, cut in half
   (1 pound)
¼ cup finely chopped onion
1 cup apple juice
3 Granny Smith apples, peeled, cored, and
   cut into 8 wedges *each*
1 cup sour cream
2 tablespoons Dijon mustard

1. In a large skillet with a lid, heat 1 tablespoon butter over medium-high heat until very hot. Sear the ham slices for 1 minute on each side. Remove to a platter.

2. Add the second tablespoon butter to the skillet and add the onion. Cook, stirring, until the onion is softened, 2 minutes. Pour in the apple juice and bring to a boil, scraping the bottom of the skillet with a wooden spoon until all the brown particles are loosened.

3. Add the apple wedges to the skillet. Cover with the lid and simmer until the apples are just tender, 5 minutes. With a slotted spoon, remove the apples to a platter.

4. Stir together the sour cream and mustard and whisk into the liquid in the skillet. Over high heat, cook, stirring until the sauce reduces slightly and thickens, 5 minutes.

5. Return the ham and apples to the skillet to coat with the sauce and reheat.

6. Arrange the ham and apples on the platter. Spoon the sauce over the ham and apples. Serve.

Ham and Cheese Pie

SERVES 6

1½ cups shredded wheat cereal, crumbled
3 tablespoons butter *or* margarine, melted
2 cups grated Cheddar cheese, divided
1½ cups **Cure 81® ham,** cut into ½-inch cubes
½ cup sliced green onions
3 eggs, well beaten
1½ cups half-and-half
2 tablespoons chopped fresh parsley (optional)

1. Heat the oven to 375° F.

2. In a medium bowl, mix together the shredded wheat and butter. Press onto the bottom and sides of a 9-inch pie plate.

3. Sprinkle 1 cup Cheddar cheese over the cereal crust. Sprinkle the ham and onion over the cheese.

4. In a medium bowl, beat together the eggs and half-and-half and pour into the crust. Sprinkle with the remaining cheese and parsley.

5. Bake 30 to 40 minutes until set and a knife inserted in the center comes out clean.

6. Let stand 10 minutes before cutting into wedges. Serve.

Sauces and glazes deliciously enhance the rich flavor of cured ham.
The following glazes make enough for a 4-pound half ham; just double the quantities for a whole ham.

RAISIN CARAMEL SAUCE (Makes 2 cups)
1 cup firmly packed brown sugar
2 tablespoons butter *or* margarine
2 tablespoons corn syrup
1 cup evaporated milk
1 cup golden raisins
2 tablespoons honey mustard

In a saucepan, over medium heat, stir the sugar, butter, and corn syrup until the sugar is melted. Add the milk and bring to a boil over high heat, stirring to dissolve the sugar. Lower the heat and continue to boil for 3 to 4 minutes until the sauce begins to thicken. Remove from the heat. Stir in the raisins and mustard. Let cool slightly. Serve with **Cure 81® ham**.

CHERRY GLAZE (Makes 1½ cups)
1 teaspoon whole cloves
1 cup cherry preserves
1 cup honey

Remove the ham from the oven and stud with cloves. In a small bowl, combine preserves and honey. Spoon over the **Cure 81® ham** surface during the last 30 minutes of baking.

SAUCY FRUIT GLAZE (Makes 1 cup)
½ cup apricot preserves
½ cup pineapple preserves
2 teaspoons prepared horseradish mustard

In a small bowl, combine all the ingredients. Spoon over the **Cure 81® ham** surface during the last 30 minutes of baking.

Old Country Quiche

Old Country Quiche

1 teaspoon unsalted butter *or* margarine
1 small yellow onion, chopped
2 cups shredded Swiss cheese
6 slices lean bacon, cooked and crumbled
2 tablespoons all-purpose flour
1 9-inch unbaked pie crust
3 large eggs
1 cup low-fat milk
¼ teaspoon salt *or* to taste
⅛ teaspoon ground nutmeg

1. Heat the oven to 400° F.
2. In a 6-inch nonstick skillet, melt the butter over moderately high heat. Add the onion and sauté 5 minutes or until soft, then transfer to a medium bowl.
3. Toss with the cheese, bacon, and flour. Spread in the pie crust.
4. In the same bowl, whisk the eggs with the milk, salt, and nutmeg. Pour over the pie mixture and bake, uncovered, 35 minutes or until the center is set.
5. Let sit 10 minutes. Cut into wedges and serve.

Festive Ham, Bell Pepper, and Parmesan Quiche

SERVES 6

1 9-inch deep dish pie crust
1 tablespoon olive oil
1 small red bell pepper, cored, seeded, and diced
1 small green bell pepper, cored, seeded, and diced
1 small onion, diced
1 large clove garlic, minced
1½ cups diced **Cure 81® ham**
1 cup grated Parmesan cheese
2 eggs, beaten
1 cup half-and-half

1. With a fork, prick the bottom and the sides of the pie crust thoroughly.
2. Heat the oven to 375° F. Prebake the crust according to package or recipe directions until lightly browned. Set aside to cool.
3. In a medium skillet, heat the oil over medium heat. Cook the bell peppers and onion until softened, 3 to 5 minutes. Stir in the garlic and remove from the heat.
4. Add the ham and cheese and mix thoroughly. Spread the mixture evenly in the pie crust.
5. In a small bowl, combine the eggs and half-and-half. Pour over the bell pepper mixture.
6. Bake 30 to 40 minutes until the quiche puffs and a knife inserted in the center comes out clean. Remove the quiche from the oven and let stand 10 minutes.
7. Cut into wedges and serve.

Denver Brunch Bake

SERVES 6

2 eggs
2 cups **Bisquick® Original baking mix**
1½ cups chopped fully cooked smoked ham
1½ cups shredded Cheddar cheese, divided
⅓ cup chopped onion
⅓ cup chopped green bell pepper
⅓ cup milk
2 tablespoons vegetable oil

1. Heat the oven to 375° F.

2. Beat the eggs slightly and stir in the remaining ingredients *except* ¾ cup cheese.

3. Spread evenly in a greased 9-inch square pan.

4. Bake 25 to 30 minutes or until the top is light brown.

5. Sprinkle with the remaining cheese. Bake 1 to 2 minutes longer or just until the cheese is melted.

6. Cut into squares and serve.

Ham and Corn "Spoonbread" Bake

SERVES 6

2 eggs, beaten
1 cup sour cream
¼ cup (½ stick) butter *or* margarine, melted
2 cups diced cooked ham
1 can (8½ ounces) **Del Monte® FreshCut™ Golden Sweet Cream Style Corn**
1 can (11 ounces) **Del Monte® FreshCut™ Summer Crisp® Vacuum Packed Whole Kernel Sweet Corn,** drained
1 package (8½ ounces) corn muffin mix

1. Heat the oven to 400° F.

2. In a large bowl, combine the eggs, sour cream, and butter.

3. Stir in the ham, corn, and muffin mix and mix thoroughly.

4. Pour into a greased 8-inch square baking dish. Bake 30 to 35 minutes until a knife inserted in the center comes out clean.

5. Spoon onto plates and serve.

Ham and Swiss on Rye Strata

SERVES 12

6 cups rye bread (½-inch cubes), divided
2 cups shredded Swiss cheese, divided
2 cups diced **Cure 81® ham**
½ cup sliced green onions
6 eggs, lightly beaten
2 cups milk
1 tablespoon Dijon mustard

1. Into a greased 13×9-inch baking dish, place 4 cups bread cubes in an even layer.

2. Over the bread cubes, layer 1 cup cheese, ham, green onions, remaining cheese, and remaining bread cubes.

3. In a medium bowl, combine the eggs, milk, and mustard and pour the mixture evenly over the bread cubes. With a fork, gently press the layers together.

4. Cover with plastic wrap or foil and refrigerate at least 2 hours or overnight.

5. Remove the strata from the refrigerator 1 hour before baking. Heat the oven to 350° F. Bake the strata, uncovered, 40 to 50 minutes until a knife inserted in the center comes out clean.

6. Let sit 10 minutes, then cut into squares. Serve.

Sunny Ham and Eggs

SERVES 4

1 package (15 ounces) frozen hash brown potatoes, thawed
⅓ cup (5 tablespoons plus 1 teaspoon) butter *or* margarine, melted
1½ cups shredded Swiss cheese
1½ cups diced **Cure 81® ham**
1½ cups shredded Monterey Jack cheese
1 cup mushrooms, sliced *or* 1 can (4 ounces), drained
½ cup milk
3 eggs
½ teaspoon seasoned salt
¼ teaspoon paprika
1 tablespoon chopped fresh parsley

1. Cut and trim the thawed potato patties to fit into a greased 9-inch deep dish pie pan. With your fingers, press firmly to form a solid crust.

2. Brush with the butter and bake at 425° F for 25 minutes.

3. Remove from the oven; reduce the oven temperature to 350° F.

4. Into the potato crust, layer the Swiss cheese, ham, Monterey Jack cheese, then mushrooms.

5. In a small bowl, whisk the milk, eggs, and seasoned salt. Slowly pour over the pie filling. Sprinkle with the paprika and parsley.

6. Bake 30 to 40 minutes or until the center is set.

7. Remove and let stand 10 minutes before cutting into wedges.

Ham-Cornbread "Pizza"

SERVES 8

2 tablespoons butter *or* margarine
1 medium sweet onion, thinly sliced
2 cups diced **Cure 81® ham**
1 cup shredded mozzarella cheese, divided
1 cup shredded Cheddar cheese, divided
½ cup sour cream
1 package (8½ ounces) corn muffin mix

1. Heat the oven to 400° F.

2. In a medium skillet, over medium heat, melt the butter. Add the onion and cook, stirring often, until soft, about 5 minutes.

3. In a medium bowl, combine the onion, ham, half the mozzarella, half the Cheddar, and the sour cream. Set aside.

4. Prepare the corn muffin mix according to package directions, except spread the batter in a thin layer in a greased 13×9-inch baking pan.

5. Spoon the ham mixture evenly over the batter. Top with the remaining mozzarella and Cheddar.

6. Bake 15 to 20 minutes.

7. Cut into squares and serve.

Cheddar, Swiss, and other hard cheeses can be shredded more easily if they are first chilled in the freezer for 15 minutes. If you often use shredded cheese, shred more than you need, divide into recipe-size portions, and label and date the bags. Store them in the refrigerator or freezer.

Smoked Sausage and Vegetable Grill

SERVES 4

¼ cup olive oil
2 tablespoons lemon juice
1 small garlic clove, minced
1 tablespoon minced fresh parsley
1 teaspoon fresh rosemary *or* ¼ teaspoon dried rosemary
¼ teaspoon salt
Freshly ground pepper to taste
1 medium eggplant, cut into 1-inch slices
2 small zucchini, halved lengthwise
2 small yellow summer squash, halved lengthwise
2 medium onions, peeled, halved, and partially cooked
1 large red bell pepper, seeded and cut into quarters
1 large yellow *or* green bell pepper, seeded and cut into quarters
1 pound **Hillshire Farm® Smoked Sausage,** any variety, cut into 3-inch pieces

1. Prepare the grill or broiler.

2. In a medium bowl, combine the oil, juice, garlic, herbs, salt, and pepper to make the herb glaze.

3. Sprinkle the eggplant with additional salt and let stand 30 minutes. Rinse and pat dry.

4. Brush one side of all the vegetables with the herb glaze. Place the vegetables, glaze side down, on a medium-hot grill or broiler and brush the other side. Place the thicker vegetables over the hottest area of the grill or broiler. Turn when the eggplant is brown and the bell pepper is blistered, about 6 minutes.

5. Add the sausage to the grill or broiler and heat through, turning frequently. When the vegetables are tender, serve.

Sausage, Peppers, and Potatoes

SERVES 4

1 tablespoon vegetable oil
1 pound sweet Italian *or* turkey sausage, cut into 1-inch slices
2 large red *or* green bell peppers *or* 1 large red and 1 large green bell pepper, trimmed, seeded, and cut into ½-inch strips
1 pound all-purpose potatoes, peeled and diced (about 3 cups)
1 envelope **Lipton® Recipe Secrets® Onion Soup Mix**
1½ cups water

1. In a large skillet, heat the oil over medium heat and brown the sausage. Remove the sausage and set aside. Reserve the drippings.

2. Add the bell peppers to the reserved drippings and cook 2 minutes, stirring frequently.

3. Add the potatoes and onion soup mix blended with the water. Bring to a boil over high heat. Reduce the heat to low and simmer, covered, 10 minutes.

4. Return the sausage to the skillet and simmer, covered, an additional 5 minutes or until the sausage is cooked thoroughly and the potatoes are tender.

5. Transfer to warm plates and serve.

Sausage, Peppers, and Potatoes

Sweet Smoked Sausage

SERVES 6

1 small head green cabbage, quartered, cored, and roughly chopped
2 medium carrots, cut into ¼-inch slices
1 large red onion, thinly sliced
½ cup apple jelly
2 tablespoons apple cider vinegar
1 pound **Hillshire Farm® Polska Kielbasa,** cut into 1-inch slices
Rye bread (optional)

1. Combine the vegetables in a large bowl and set aside.
2. In a small pan, warm the apple jelly and vinegar over low heat until smooth. Pour the mixture over the vegetables and toss.
3. Transfer to a 13×9-inch glass baking pan. Place in a 400° F oven and bake 30 minutes, stirring occasionally.
4. Meanwhile, in a large skillet, over medium-high heat, sauté the sliced sausage until lightly browned.
5. When the vegetables are tender, arrange the drained sausage on top and bake 10 minutes longer.
6. Remove from the oven and stir. Serve with rye bread, if desired.

❖ ❖ ❖ ❖ ❖ ❖ ❖ ❖ ❖ ❖ ❖

Risotto is usually made with Arborio, an Italian rice that absorbs liquid easily, giving the dish its distinctive creamy consistency. You can also use white basmati or long-grain rice. With these types, the consistency will be slightly drier.

Risotto with Sausage and Mushrooms

SERVES 8

1 pound sweet *or* hot Italian sausages, pierced with a fork
12 ounces mushrooms, sliced
1 small onion, finely chopped
3 tablespoons butter
1 tablespoon olive oil
2 cups Arborio *or* short-grained rice
1 can (46 ounces) chicken broth
1½ cups **Ragú® Chunky Gardenstyle Super Mushroom Pasta Sauce**
⅓ cup grated Parmesan cheese
Salt and pepper to taste

1. In a medium saucepan, cook the sausages for 15 minutes in just enough water to cover, then drain thoroughly. Slice the sausages into 1-inch pieces and set aside.
2. In a large saucepan or stockpot, sauté the mushrooms and onion in the butter and olive oil until tender. Add the rice and sauté lightly for 3 minutes.
3. Meanwhile, in another large saucepan, combine the chicken broth and pasta sauce and heat until simmering. Add about 1 cup heated broth to the rice mixture. Cook over medium heat, stirring until the liquid has been absorbed. Continue cooking and stirring the rice, adding broth gradually after each addition has been absorbed. Cook about 20 minutes in total or until the rice is tender.
4. Add the cooked sausage and cook 5 minutes longer. The rice should be moist and creamy. Add the Parmesan cheese. Season with the salt and pepper and serve.

❖

Spicy Sausage Pizza Pie

Spicy Sausage Pizza Pie

SERVES 8

1 pound pork sausage
1 can (8 ounces) pizza sauce
½ teaspoon dried oregano
2 cups **Bisquick® Original** *or* **Reduced Fat baking mix**
¼ cup processed cheese spread, at room temperature
¼ cup hot water
Green bell pepper rings (optional)
1 cup shredded mozzarella cheese (4 ounces)

1. Heat the oven to 375° F.

2. In a 10-inch skillet, cook the sausage until brown and drain. Stir in the pizza sauce and oregano.

3. In a medium bowl, stir the baking mix, cheese spread, and water until a dough forms. Turn onto a surface dusted with baking mix. Knead 5 times. Roll into a 14-inch circle and place on a large greased baking sheet.

4. Spread the sausage mixture over the crust to within 3 inches of the edge. Fold the edge over the mixture. Top with the bell pepper rings, if desired, and sprinkle with the cheese.

5. Bake 23 to 25 minutes or until the cheese is melted. Serve.

Lamb Chops with Zucchini and Peppers

Lamb Chops with Zucchini and Peppers

SERVES 4

1 tablespoon olive oil
8 lamb chops, 1 inch thick, trimmed of excess fat
1 medium zucchini, trimmed and cut diagonally into ¾-inch-thick slices (about 1½ cups)
1 *each* red *and* yellow bell peppers, trimmed, seeded, and cut into ½-inch-wide slices
1 clove garlic, minced
½ teaspoon dried oregano, crumbled
Salt and freshly ground pepper

1. In a large heavy skillet, heat the oil over medium-high heat. Add the lamb and sauté 5 minutes on each side for rare or longer to desired doneness. Remove to a serving dish and keep warm.

2. Reduce the heat to medium and add the zucchini, bell peppers, garlic, and oregano. Toss to coat and cook 5 to 7 minutes or until crisp-tender, tossing frequently. Season with the salt and pepper.

3. Arrange the vegetables around the lamb. Serve immediately.

Jamaican Fruit Lamb Chops

SERVES 4

8 medium loin lamb chops, trimmed
1 can (16 ounces) **Del Monte® Lite Sliced Peaches** *or* **Apricot Halves**
2 teaspoons instant coffee crystals
2 tablespoons chopped fresh parsley
Pinch pepper

1. In a large skillet, brown the meat. Remove and keep warm.

2. Drain the fruit, reserving the liquid in the skillet. Add the coffee crystals. Cook over high heat for 5 minutes to reduce and thicken the liquid.

3. Return the meat to the skillet. Simmer 8 to 10 minutes, turning frequently.

4. Add the fruit, parsley, and pepper. Cover, heat through, about 5 minutes, and serve.

The spice pepper comes from the berry of the **piper nigrum.** *To obtain black peppercorns, the fruit is picked when green, then fermented and dried in the sun until either dark brown or black. If the berries are freeze-dried or packed in brine or vinegar rather then fermented and dried, green peppercorns are the result. For white peppercorns, the fruit is picked ripe, the husk is removed, and the berry is dried until white. The most pungent is black pepper; the taste of green peppercorns is milder than that of either black or white pepper.*

Black and white peppercorns retain their flavor for a fairly long time if stored in a cool dark place. Once opened, green peppercorns should be refrigerated. Since ground pepper loses its freshness quickly, a pepper mill is useful in any kitchen. The best mills have metal mechanisms.

Poultry

Everyday Broccoli Cheese Chicken

SERVES 4

1 tablespoon margarine *or* butter
4 skinless, boneless chicken breast halves (about 1 pound)
1 can (10¾ ounces) condensed broccoli cheese soup
⅓ cup water *or* milk
2 cups broccoli florets
⅛ teaspoon pepper

1. In a 10-inch skillet, heat the margarine over medium heat. Cook the chicken 10 minutes or until browned on both sides. Spoon off fat.

2. Stir in the remaining ingredients. Heat to boiling. Reduce the heat to low. Cover and cook 10 minutes or until the chicken is no longer pink and the broccoli is done, stirring occasionally.

3. Transfer to warm plates and serve.

An easy way to dress up rice is to add ¼ cup diced dried fruit to each cup of rice when the cooking water comes to a boil. Cook as directed and serve with butter. Raisins, currants, diced dates, figs, and apricots are all good to use. Check your supermarket for convenient packages of pre-chopped dried fruit or bags of dried-fruit-bit mixtures.

Everyday Broccoli Cheese Chicken (top), Skillet Herb-Roasted Chicken

Skillet Herb-Roasted Chicken

SERVES 4

¼ teaspoon ground sage
¼ teaspoon dried thyme, crushed
4 skinless, boneless chicken breast halves *or* 8 skinless, boneless chicken thighs
1 can (10¾ ounces) condensed reduced-fat cream of chicken soup
½ cup water
4 cups hot cooked rice

1. On a sheet of wax paper, mix the sage and thyme. Sprinkle the chicken with the seasoning mixture.
2. Spray a large skillet with nonstick cooking spray and heat over medium heat 1 minute. Cook the chicken 15 minutes or until the chicken is done. Remove the chicken and keep warm.
3. Stir in the soup and water. Reduce the heat to low. Heat through.
4. Serve the sauce over the chicken with the rice.

Citrus Skillet Chicken and Rice

SERVES 4

4 skinless, boneless chicken breast halves
1 can (14½ ounces) chicken broth
½ cup orange juice
1 medium onion, chopped
1 cup regular long-grain rice
3 tablespoons chopped fresh parsley

1. In a medium nonstick skillet, over medium heat, cook the chicken 10 minutes or until browned. Remove the chicken and set aside.

2. Stir in the broth, orange juice, and onion. Heat to a boil. Stir in the rice. Cover and cook over low heat for 10 minutes.
3. Return the chicken to the pan. Cover and cook 10 minutes more or until the rice is done.
4. Remove the chicken to a platter. Stir the parsley into the rice mixture. Serve.

COURTESY: CAMPBELL'S® SOUPS

Autumn Chicken with Peppers and Mushrooms

SERVES 4

2 tablespoons olive oil
4 skinless, boneless chicken breast halves, slightly flattened
2 cups sliced mushrooms
2 green bell peppers, trimmed, seeded, and sliced into thin strips
1 can (14½ ounces) **Del Monte® Fresh Cut™ Diced Tomatoes, Garlic & Onion**

1. In a large nonstick skillet, heat the oil over medium-high heat. Add the chicken and sauté on both sides until lightly browned. Remove from the pan and set aside.
2. Add the mushrooms and bell peppers and stir-fry 5 minutes.
3. Stir in the tomatoes. Return the chicken to the skillet and cover with the sauce. Reduce the heat to low and cook, partially covered, 20 minutes.
4. Transfer to warm plates and serve.

Chicken with Mushrooms and Spinach

SERVES 4

2 tablespoons olive *or* vegetable oil

1 pound skinless, boneless chicken breast halves, pounded thin

8 ounces fresh spinach leaves, rinsed and drained *or* 1 package (10 ounces) frozen leaf spinach, thawed and squeezed dry

1½ cups sliced mushrooms

1 envelope **Lipton® Recipe Secrets® Savory Herb with Garlic Soup Mix** *or* **Golden Herb with Lemon Soup Mix** *or* **Golden Onion Soup Mix**

1 cup water

1. In a skillet, heat 1 tablespoon oil and cook the chicken until done. Remove and keep warm.

2. In the same skillet, heat the remaining oil and cook the spinach and mushrooms. Stir 3 minutes.

3. Stir in the savory herb with garlic soup mix blended with the water. Bring to a boil. Continue boiling, stirring, 1 minute or until the sauce thickens.

4. Serve the chicken over the vegetable mixture.

Honey Mustard Chicken

SERVES 4

2 tablespoons cornstarch
1 can (14½ ounces) chicken broth
1 tablespoon honey
1 tablespoon Dijon mustard
4 skinless, boneless chicken breast halves
1 large carrot, cut into 2-inch matchstick-thin strips
1 medium onion, halved and sliced
4 cups hot cooked rice

1. In a medium bowl, mix the cornstarch, broth, honey, and mustard until smooth. Set aside.
2. In a large nonstick skillet, over medium-high heat, cook the chicken 10 minutes or until browned. Remove and set the chicken aside.
3. Stir the cornstarch mixture and add to the skillet. Cook until the mixture boils and thickens, stirring constantly.
4. Return the chicken to the pan. Add the carrot and onion. Cover and cook over low heat for 5 minutes or until the chicken is done and the carrot strips are tender.
5. Serve with the rice.

Savory Skillet Chicken and Rice

SERVES 4

1 tablespoon margarine *or* butter
1 pound skinless, boneless chicken breasts, cut up
1 can (10¾ ounces) condensed cream of mushroom soup
1 cup milk
1 tablespoon onion flakes
¼ teaspoon dried thyme, crushed
⅛ teaspoon pepper
2 cups frozen cut green beans
2 cups instant rice

1. In a large skillet, over medium-high heat, heat the margarine. Add the chicken and cook until browned, stirring often. Remove and set aside.
2. Add the soup, milk, onion, thyme, pepper, and beans and stir to combine. Heat to a boil.
3. Return the chicken to the pan. Cover and cook over low heat for 5 minutes or until the chicken is done.
4. Add the rice. Cover and remove from the heat. Let stand 5 minutes. Fluff with a fork and serve with the chicken.

To prepare rice ahead, boil it for about ¾ of the normal cooking time: 15 minutes for white rice, 30 minutes for brown. Drain it in a colander and cover it to prevent drying. To reheat, set the covered colander in a large saucepan or kettle containing about 1 inch of boiling water. Steam the rice to the perfect degree of doneness—5 to 7 minutes for white rice, 10 to 12 minutes for brown rice—fluffing occasionally with a fork to allow the steam to penetrate.

Chicken Cacciatore

SERVES 6

1 medium green bell pepper, chopped
1 medium onion, sliced
1 clove garlic, minced
2 tablespoons olive oil, divided
1½ pounds skinless, boneless chicken breast halves
1 jar (27½ ounces) **Ragú® Light Pasta Sauce—Chunky Mushroom**
½ cup sliced black olives (optional)
1 teaspoon dried basil
¼ teaspoon salt
Pinch dried oregano
Pinch pepper
1 package (12 ounces) ruffle *or* twist pasta, cooked and drained

1. In a large skillet, over medium heat, sauté the bell pepper, onion, and garlic in 1 tablespoon olive oil until tender. Remove and set aside.
2. In the same skillet, heat the remaining oil and brown the chicken on both sides. Drain.
3. Return the vegetables to the skillet. Add the pasta sauce, olives, basil, salt, oregano, and pepper. Heat to boiling.
4. Cover and simmer gently over low heat for 20 minutes or until the chicken is thoroughly cooked.
5. Serve the chicken and pasta topped with the sauce.

Cider Mill Chicken with Apples

SERVES 6

½ cup (1 stick) **I Can't Believe It's Not Butter!®**
2 tart cooking apples, peeled, cored, and thickly sliced
1 teaspoon apple pie spice *or* ½ teaspoon *each* ground cinnamon and ground nutmeg
6 skinless, boneless chicken breast halves
1 teaspoon lemon pepper
1 teaspoon curry powder
½ cup apple cider
2 tablespoons apple cider vinegar
¼ cup golden raisins
½ cup plain nonfat yogurt

1. In a large skillet, melt I Can't Believe It's Not Butter!® over medium-high heat. Add the apples in one layer and sprinkle with the apple pie spice. Sauté until tender, stirring occasionally. Remove with a slotted spoon and reserve.
2. Add the chicken breasts in one layer. Sprinkle with the lemon pepper and curry powder. Sauté, turning often, until the chicken just begins to brown. Add the apple cider, vinegar, and raisins. Bring to a boil, reduce the heat to low, cover, and simmer 10 minutes.
3. With a slotted spoon, remove the chicken from the skillet and arrange with the apples on a serving platter. Keep warm.
4. Remove the skillet from the heat and let cool for a minute. Beat in the yogurt until smooth. (This will help avoid curdling.) Pour over the chicken and apples. Serve.

Cider Mill Chicken with Apples

Cream Cheese and Spinach Stuffed Chicken Rolls

Cream Cheese and Spinach Stuffed Chicken Rolls

SERVES 6

6 skinless, boneless chicken breast halves
1 package (8 ounces) **Cream Cheese**
½ cup chopped cooked spinach, drained
1 small clove garlic, minced
⅛ teaspoon ground nutmeg
Salt and freshly ground pepper to taste
1 large egg, beaten with 1 teaspoon water
½ cup unseasoned dry bread crumbs
3 tablespoons butter, melted

1. Heat the oven to 375° F.

2. Flatten the chicken between sheets of plastic wrap to a uniform ¼-inch thickness.

3. In a large bowl, beat the cream cheese with the spinach, garlic, nutmeg, salt, and pepper until combined.

4. Spoon an equal amount of the mixture across the narrow end of each breast. Roll jelly-roll style and secure with toothpicks. Dip in the egg, then roll in the crumbs, and shake off excess.

5. In a baking dish, arrange the chicken in one layer, seam side down. Drizzle with the butter. Bake 25 to 30 minutes until golden.

6. Remove to a platter and serve.

COURTESY: DAIRY MANAGEMENT, INC.

Chicken Crunch with Lemon Parsley Sauce

SERVES 4

1 can (10¾ ounces) condensed cream of chicken soup, divided
½ cup milk, divided
4 skinless, boneless chicken breast halves
2 tablespoons all-purpose flour
1½ cups herb seasoned stuffing, finely crushed
2 tablespoons margarine *or* butter, melted
½ teaspoon lemon juice
1 teaspoon chopped fresh parsley *or* ¼ teaspoon parsley flakes

1. Heat the oven to 400° F.

2. In a medium bowl, mix ⅓ cup soup and ¼ cup milk. Lightly coat the chicken with the flour. Dip into the soup mixture. Coat with the stuffing.

3. Place the chicken on a baking sheet. Drizzle with the melted margarine. Bake 20 minutes or until the chicken is no longer pink.

4. In a small saucepan, mix the remaining soup, remaining milk, lemon juice, and parsley. Over medium heat, heat through.

5. Serve with the chicken.

Easy Chicken and Rice Dinner

Easy Chicken and Rice Dinner

SERVES 2

1 **Reynolds® Oven Bag,** small size, 10×16-inches
1 tablespoon all-purpose flour
1 can (10½ ounces) condensed chicken broth
1 cup instant rice
1 small yellow squash, trimmed and sliced
½ red bell pepper, seeded and diced
Seasoned salt
Lemon pepper
2 skinless, boneless chicken breast halves

1. Heat the oven to 350° F.

2. Shake the flour in the oven bag and place the bag in a 13×9-inch baking pan.

3. Add the chicken broth, rice, squash, and bell pepper to the oven bag. Holding the top of the bag closed, gently squeeze the bag to mix the ingredients.

4. Generously sprinkle the chicken with the seasoned salt and lemon pepper. Arrange the chicken over the rice mixture in an even layer in the oven bag.

5. Close the bag with a nylon tie and cut six ½-inch slits in the top.

6. Bake until the chicken is tender, about 30 to 35 minutes.

7. Stir the rice before serving.

Southwestern Chicken

SERVES 2

½ cup **Kretschmer® Original Toasted Wheat Germ**
1 teaspoon chili powder
1 teaspoon ground cumin
1 teaspoon instant minced onion
¼ teaspoon garlic powder
¼ teaspoon salt (optional)
⅛ teaspoon cayenne (red) pepper
1 tablespoon water
1 egg white
2 skinless, boneless chicken breast halves
Prepared salsa (optional)

1. Heat the oven to 400° F. Lightly spray an 8-inch square baking dish with nonstick cooking spray.

2. In a shallow bowl, combine the wheat germ and seasonings. Set aside.

3. In another shallow bowl, beat the water and egg white until frothy.

4. Dip the chicken into the egg white mixture and then into the wheat germ mixture. Repeat, coating the chicken thoroughly.

5. Place the chicken in the prepared pan. Bake 20 to 22 minutes or until done.

6. Transfer the chicken to warm plates and serve with salsa, if desired.

Wrapped Garlic Chicken

SERVES 4

4 skinless, boneless chicken breast halves
4 large sheets foil
½ teaspoon salt (optional)
1 cup sliced mushrooms, divided
1 can (10½ ounces) **Healthy Choice® Recipe Creations™ Cream of Roasted Garlic Condensed Soup,** divided
4 sprigs fresh rosemary *or* 1 teaspoon dried rosemary, divided

1. Heat the oven to 425° F.

2. Place one chicken breast in the center of each sheet of foil. Sprinkle with salt, if desired.

3. Divide the remaining ingredients into four equal portions. Top each chicken breast half with one portion apiece.

4. Fold the foil in half over the chicken and seal all the edges with double-fold seals. Bake 20 minutes or until the chicken is no longer pink in the center.

5. Carefully open the packets and serve.

Chicken-Vegetable Kebabs

SERVES 4

¾ cup **Wish-Bone® Italian Dressing**
1 pound skinless, boneless chicken breasts, cubed
1 large zucchini *or* yellow squash, cut into ½-inch slices
1 large red, green, *or* yellow bell pepper, seeded, cut into chunks

1. In a large shallow baking dish or a resealable plastic bag, place the Italian dressing, chicken, and vegetables. Turn to coat. Cover the baking dish or close the bag and marinate in the refrigerator, turning occasionally, up to 3 hours. Remove the chicken and vegetables, reserving the marinade.

2. Heat the broiler or prepare the grill.

3. On skewers, alternately thread chicken and vegetables. If using wooden skewers, soak them in water before using. Grill or broil, turning and basting frequently with the reserved marinade, until the chicken is done. Do not brush with the marinade during the last 5 minutes of cooking.

4. Remove to a platter and serve.

Salmonella, a type of bacteria that causes food poisoning, is sometimes found in poultry. Heat kills the bacteria; just make sure that the meat is cooked until no longer pink. If you use a thermometer when roasting poultry, place it in the thickest part between the breast and a thigh and not touching the bone. Cook the bird to 180° F.

There is some danger of salmonella being transferred from raw poultry to your hands or a work surface and then onto other foods. If the newly contaminated food is one that is served uncooked, the bacteria will not be killed. After handling poultry, thoroughly wash your hands, the work surface, sink, and utensils with hot water and detergent.

Chinese-Style Skewered Chicken

SERVES 4

1 can (8 ounces) **Hunt's® Tomato Sauce**
¼ cup firmly packed light brown sugar
¼ cup **La Choy® Soy Sauce**
1 tablespoon minced fresh ginger
1 teaspoon minced garlic
2 pounds skinless, boneless chicken breasts *or* thighs,
   cut into 1-inch cubes
2 medium green bell peppers, cubed
2 medium onions, cubed
1 tablespoon olive oil
Hot cooked rice
8 10-inch bamboo skewers

1. In a bowl, mix the tomato sauce, sugar, soy sauce, ginger, and garlic. Stir in the chicken. Cover and refrigerate 2 to 8 hours.

2. Heat the broiler.

3. Skewer the chicken and broil 7 to 10 minutes or until lightly browned. Turn and broil 7 minutes longer or to desired doneness.

4. Meanwhile, in a medium skillet, sauté the bell peppers and onions in the olive oil for 5 minutes.

5. Serve the chicken and vegetables over the rice.

Chinese-Style Skewered Chicken

Grilled Summer Chicken and Vegetables

Grilled Summer Chicken and Vegetables

SERVES 4

1 cup **Wish-Bone® Italian** *or* **Robusto Italian** *or*
  Lite Italian Dressing, divided
4 chicken breast halves (about 2 pounds)
4 ears fresh corn *or* frozen ears of corn, thawed
2 large ripe tomatoes, halved crosswise

1. In a shallow dish, pour ½ cup dressing over the chicken. In another dish, pour the remaining dressing over the corn and tomatoes. Marinate both, covered, in the refrigerator at least 3 hours or overnight, turning occasionally.

2. Remove the chicken and vegetables, reserving the marinades.

3. Grill or broil the chicken and corn for 20 minutes or until the chicken is done, turning and basting with the marinades.

4. Arrange the tomatoes, cut side up, on the grill or broiler pan. Grill or broil 10 minutes, basting frequently.

5. Transfer to warm plates and serve.

Honey Garlic Grilled Chicken

SERVES 4

2 tablespoons **Mazola Right Blend®**
2 tablespoons chopped fresh cilantro *or* parsley
1 tablespoon honey
1 tablespoon lime juice
2 large cloves garlic, minced
1 teaspoon salt
½ teaspoon pepper
4 skinless, boneless chicken breast halves (about 1 pound)

1. In a shallow baking dish, combine the oil, cilantro, honey, lime juice, garlic, salt, and pepper.
2. Add the chicken breasts, turning to coat.
3. Cover and let stand at room temperature no longer than 30 minutes, turning once.
4. Grill or broil 6 inches from the heat for 10 minutes or until cooked through.
5. Remove to a platter and serve.

Teriyaki Grilled Chicken Thighs

SERVES 4

⅓ cup **Kikkoman Teriyaki Marinade & Sauce**
3 green onions and tops, chopped
2 teaspoons paprika
1 teaspoon vinegar
8 boneless chicken thighs

1. Combine the teriyaki marinade sauce, green onions, paprika, and vinegar. Pour over the thighs in a large resealable plastic bag.
2. Press the air out of the bag and close the top securely.
3. Turn the bag over several times to coat all the thighs well.
4. Refrigerate 2 hours. Turn the bag over occasionally.

5. Place the thighs on the grill 4 to 5 inches from the hot coals.
6. Cook 15 to 18 minutes, or until the chicken is no longer pink in the center, turning over frequently. Serve.

Grilled Chicken Breast with Citrus Salsa

SERVES 4

½ cup **Florida Orange Juice**
2 teaspoons sesame oil
1 teaspoon jalapeño pepper, seeded and chopped
1 teaspoon chopped garlic
1 teaspoon chopped shallots
4 skinless, boneless chicken breasts

For citrus salsa:

3 green onions, thinly sliced on the bias
1 medium tomato, halved, seeded, and diced
1 **Florida Orange,** sectioned and diced
1 **Florida Blood Orange,** sectioned and diced
½ **Florida Grapefruit,** sectioned and diced
1 tablespoon fresh basil, minced
1 tablespoon fresh mint, minced
1 teaspoon jalapeño pepper, seeded and minced
Salt and pepper to taste

1. In a large bowl, blend the juice, sesame oil, jalapeño pepper, garlic, and shallots. Marinate the chicken in the mixture for 2 hours.
2. For salsa: In a medium bowl, mix the onions, tomato, oranges, grapefruit, basil, mint, jalapeño pepper, salt, and pepper. Set aside.
3. Grill the chicken breasts, then place them on a serving dish.
4. Spoon the salsa over the chicken and serve.

COURTESY: FLORIDA DEPARTMENT OF CITRUS

❖

Ginger Chicken Asparagus

Ginger Chicken Asparagus

SERVES 4

2 tablespoons vegetable oil, divided
1 pound skinless, boneless chicken breasts,
 cut into 1-inch pieces
12 ounces fresh asparagus spears (12 to 15), trimmed and cut
 into 1-inch pieces *or* 1 package (10 ounces) frozen
 asparagus cuts, thawed
4 green onions, cut diagonally into 1-inch pieces
 (about 1 cup)
2 medium carrots, diagonally sliced (about 1 cup)
¼ teaspoon ground ginger
1 can (10¾ ounces) condensed cream of asparagus soup
¼ cup water
1 tablespoon soy sauce
Hot cooked rice

1. In a 10-inch skillet or wok, over medium-high heat, in 1 table-spoon hot oil, stir-fry half the chicken until browned. Remove and set aside. Stir-fry the remaining chicken.

2. In the same skillet or wok, in the remaining 1 tablespoon oil, stir-fry the asparagus, onions, carrots, and ginger for 3 minutes or until crisp-tender.

3. Stir in the soup, water, and soy sauce. Heat to boiling. Stir in the reserved chicken.

4. Reduce the heat to low. Heat through, stirring occasionally.

5. Serve over the rice with additional soy sauce, if desired.

Thai Chicken with Peanut Sauce

SERVES 4

For chicken:
1 pound skinless, boneless chicken breasts, cut
 into 1-inch strips
1½ cups **Kretschmer® Original Toasted Wheat Germ**
1 teaspoon curry powder
1 teaspoon ground ginger
½ teaspoon garlic powder
¼ teaspoon cayenne (red) pepper
3 egg whites
2 tablespoons water

For peanut sauce:
2 tablespoons reduced-fat peanut butter
2 tablespoons reduced-sodium soy sauce
1 tablespoon water
2 teaspoons firmly packed brown sugar
2 teaspoons lime juice
¼ teaspoon ground ginger.

1. Heat the oven to 400° F.

2. In a shallow dish, combine the wheat germ and seasonings and mix well. In another shallow dish, beat the egg whites and water.

3. Dip the chicken strips into the egg white mixture, then into the wheat germ mixture. Dip and coat the chicken again, coating thoroughly. Place on a baking sheet sprayed with nonstick cooking spray. Lightly spray the chicken with nonstick cooking spray.

4. Bake 15 to 18 minutes or until the chicken is no longer pink.

5. For sauce: In a small bowl, whisk together all the ingredients until smooth.

6. Serve the chicken with the sauce.

Chicken Primavera

Chicken Primavera

 1 tablespoon vegetable oil
12 ounces skinless, boneless chicken breasts, cut into strips
 1 small onion, chopped
 1 cup broccoli florets
 1 cup frozen green peas, thawed
 1 carrot, cut into julienne strips
 1 can (13¾ ounces) chicken broth
 ½ teaspoon dried basil
Pinch pepper
1½ cup **Minute® Instant Brown Rice**
 ⅓ cup grated Parmesan cheese

1. In a large skillet, over medium-high heat, cook and stir the chicken in hot oil until browned. Add the onion, broccoli, peas, and carrot. Cook and stir until the vegetables are crisp-tender.

2. Add the broth, basil, and pepper and bring to a broil. Stir in the rice. Return to a boil. Reduce the heat, cover, and simmer 5 minutes. Stir in the cheese.

3. Remove from the heat. Cover and let stand 5 minutes.

4. Transfer to a platter and serve.

*B*rown long-grain rice is not polished as long-grain white rice is and therefore retains the bran that gives it a tan color and nutlike flavor. Compared to white rice, it is higher in fiber and some B vitamins. Oil in the bran layer of brown rice gives it a shorter shelf life than white rice—about 6 months.

Springtime Quiche

For crust:

- 1 cup all-purpose flour
- ¼ teaspoon salt
- ⅓ cup (5 tablespoons plus 1 teaspoon) **LAND O LAKES® Butter**
- 2 tablespoons chopped fresh chives
- 2 tablespoons cold water

For filling:

- 2 cups **LAND O LAKES® Cheddar Cheese, Shredded** (8 ounces)
- 1 cup shredded cooked chicken
- 6 slices crisply cooked bacon, cut into 1-inch pieces
- 4 ounces fresh asparagus
- 1½ cups half-and-half *or* milk
- 4 eggs, slightly beaten
- ¼ teaspoon salt
- ⅛ teaspoon pepper

1. Heat the oven to 400° F. In a medium bowl, combine the flour and salt. Cut in the butter until crumbly. Stir in the chives and water (the mixture will be crumbly). Shape into a ball.

2. On a lightly floured surface, roll the dough into a 12-inch circle, ⅛ inch thick. Fold into quarters. Unfold and ease into a 10-inch quiche pan, pressing firmly against the bottom and sides. Crimp or flute the crust.

3. Spread the cheese over the bottom of the crust and top with the chicken. Sprinkle the bacon over the chicken.

4. Place the asparagus spears in a spoke pattern on top of the bacon. In a small bowl, stir together all the remaining filling ingredients. Pour over the chicken mixture.

5. Bake 40 to 45 minutes or until golden and set in the center. Let stand 10 minutes. Serve.

Chicken-Mushroom Risotto

- 2 tablespoons margarine *or* butter, divided
- 12 ounces skinless, boneless chicken breasts, cut into cubes
- 1 small onion, finely chopped (about ¼ cup)
- 1 medium carrot *or* 1 small red bell pepper, finely chopped (about ⅓ cup)
- 1 cup regular long-grain rice
- 1 can (14½ ounces) chicken broth
- 1 can (10¾ ounces) condensed cream of mushroom soup
- ⅛ teaspoon pepper
- ½ cup frozen peas

1. In a 3-quart saucepan, over medium-high heat, in 1 tablespoon hot margarine, cook the chicken until browned, stirring often. Remove and set aside.

2. In the same saucepan, add the remaining margarine. Reduce the heat to medium and cook the onion, carrot, and rice until the rice is browned, stirring constantly.

3. Stir in the broth, soup, and pepper. Heat to boiling. Reduce the heat to low. Cover and cook 15 minutes, stirring occasionally.

4. Add the peas and reserved chicken. Cover and cook 5 minutes or until the chicken is no longer pink, the rice is tender, and the liquid is absorbed, stirring occasionally.

5. Transfer to warm plates and serve.

Hearty Chicken Bake

Hearty Chicken Bake

SERVES 4

3 cups hot mashed potatoes

1 cup shredded Cheddar cheese, divided

1 can (4½ ounces) **French's® French Fried Onions,** divided

1½ cups cubed cooked chicken

1 package (10 ounces) frozen mixed vegetables, thawed and drained

1 can (10¾ ounces) condensed cream of chicken soup

¼ cup milk

½ teaspoon **Durkee® Ground Mustard**

¼ teaspoon **Durkee® Ground Black Pepper**

¼ teaspoon garlic powder

1. Heat the oven to 375° F.

2. In a medium bowl, combine the potatoes, half the cheese, and half the onions. Mix thoroughly. Spoon into a greased 1½-quart casserole, spreading across the bottom and up the sides to form a shell.

3. In a large bowl, combine the chicken, mixed vegetables, soup, milk, and seasonings. Pour into the potato shell.

4. Bake, uncovered, 30 minutes or until heated through. Top with the remaining cheese and onions and bake, uncovered, 3 minutes or until the onions are golden brown.

5. Let stand 5 minutes before serving.

Midnight Garden Chicken Casserole

SERVES 4 TO 6

1 can (14½ ounces) **Del Monte® FreshCut™ Cut Green Beans**, drained
1 can (15¼ ounces) **Del Monte® FreshCut™ Golden Sweet Whole Kernel Corn**, drained
1 can (10¾ ounces) condensed cream of mushroom soup
2 cups diced cooked chicken
1 cup cooked rice
¾ cup milk
1 can (2¾ ounces) french-fried onion rings

1. Heat the oven to 350° F.

2. In a large bowl, combine the beans, corn, soup, chicken, rice, and milk.

3. Pour into a 2-quart baking dish and bake 20 minutes.

4. Top with the onion rings and bake 10 minutes or until golden brown.

5. Remove from the oven and serve.

Easy Chicken and Biscuits

SERVES 4

1 can (10¾ ounces) condensed cream of broccoli soup
1 can (10¾ ounces) condensed cream of potato soup
⅔ cup milk
½ teaspoon poultry seasoning
⅛ teaspoon pepper
2 cups cubed cooked chicken *or* turkey
2 cups frozen mixed vegetables
1 package (4½ ounces) refrigerated biscuits

1. Heat the oven to 400° F.

2. In a shallow 2-quart baking dish, mix the soups, milk, poultry seasoning, pepper, chicken, and vegetables.

3. Bake 25 minutes or until hot. Stir.

4. Arrange the biscuits over the chicken mixture. Bake 10 minutes or until the biscuits are golden.

5. Spoon onto warm plates and serve.

COURTESY: CAMPBELL SOUP COMPANY

If you need cooked chicken for a recipe, poach it on the stove or in the microwave. For 2 cups of cooked chicken, you will need two 6-ounce skinless and boneless breasts. To cook the chicken conventionally, place the breasts in a large skillet with 1⅓ cups water or broth. Bring to a boil, then reduce the heat and simmer, covered, 12 to 14 minutes, or until the chicken is tender and cooked through. To microwave the chicken, wrap each breast in a double length of paper towels, then moisten with water and place them on a microwave-safe plate. Cook on high 4 to 5 minutes. Let the chicken stand 3 minutes before cutting.

Garlic and Lemon Roast Chicken

Garlic and Lemon Roast Chicken

SERVES 4

1 small onion, finely chopped
1 envelope **Lipton® Recipe Secrets® Savory Herb with Garlic Soup Mix**
2 tablespoons olive oil
2 tablespoons lemon juice
2½ to 3 pounds chicken, cut into serving pieces

1. In a large resealable plastic bag or a non-metal baking dish, combine the onion, soup mix, oil, and juice. Add the chicken, turning to coat evenly. Marinate in the refrigerator for 2 hours.

2. Heat the oven to 350° F.

3. Transfer the chicken and marinade to a 13×9-inch baking or roasting pan or leave in the baking dish. Bake the chicken, uncovered, basting occasionally, 40 minutes or until done.

4. Transfer to warm plates and serve.

VARIATION

For Lemon Roast Chicken, use **Lipton® Recipe Secrets® Golden Herb with Lemon Soup Mix** and omit the lemon juice.

Tortilla Crunch Chicken

SERVES 4 TO 6

1 envelope **Lipton® Recipe Secrets® Fiesta Herb with Red Pepper Soup Mix** *or* **Onion Soup Mix**
1 cup finely crushed plain tortilla chips (about 3 ounces)
2½ to 3 pounds chicken, cut into serving pieces (with or without skin) *or* 6 skinless, boneless chicken breast halves (about 1½ pounds)
1 egg
2 tablespoons water
2 tablespoons margarine *or* butter, melted
Fresh *or* prepared salsa (optional)

1. Heat the oven to 400° F.

2. In a medium bowl, combine the soup mix and tortilla chips. Dip the chicken in the egg beaten with the water, then the tortilla mixture, coating well.

3. In a 13×9-inch baking or roasting pan sprayed with nonstick cooking spray, arrange the chicken and drizzle with the margarine.

4. For chicken pieces: Bake, uncovered, 40 minutes or until the chicken is done.

5. For chicken breast halves: Bake, uncovered, 15 minutes or until the chicken is done.

6. Serve the chicken with your favorite fresh or prepared salsa, if desired.

Oven-Barbecued Chicken Wings

SERVES 6

⅔ cup **Lawry's® Mesquite Marinade with Lime Juice**
1½ teaspoons hot pepper sauce *or* to taste
3 pounds chicken wings, split and wing tips discarded
1 cup cornmeal
½ cup grated Parmesan cheese
1 tablespoon minced fresh parsley
½ teaspoon **Lawry's® Seasoned Salt**
¼ teaspoon **Lawry's® Seasoned Pepper**
2 tablespoons vegetable oil

1. In a large bowl, whisk the marinade and hot pepper sauce together.

2. Pierce and slash each piece of chicken, then add to the marinade mixture, stirring to coat. Cover and marinate 1 hour.

3. In another large bowl, combine the cornmeal, cheese, parsley, salt, and pepper and mix well.

4. With a slotted spoon, remove the wings from the marinade, allowing excess to drip off. Coat the wings with the cornmeal mixture, shaking off excess. Arrange the wings in one layer on a lightly oiled baking sheet.

5. Heat the oven to 425° F.

6. Drizzle the oil over the chicken and bake 35 minutes until crisp and golden.

7. Cool the wings on paper towels. Transfer to a platter and serve.

Apricot-Dijon Glazed Chicken

SERVES 4
MAKES ⅓ CUP SAUCE

¼ cup **Grey Poupon® Dijon Mustard**
2 tablespoons apricot preserves, melted
½ teaspoon grated fresh ginger
1 pound chicken parts

1. Heat the grill or broiler.
2. In a small bowl, combine the mustard, apricot preserves, and ginger.
3. Grill or broil the chicken, turning and brushing frequently with the glaze while cooking.
4. Remove to a platter and serve.

Ready Mexican Chicken

SERVES 4

2 pounds chicken pieces
¼ teaspoon salt
½ teaspoon pepper
½ cup all-purpose flour
2 tablespoons vegetable oil
1 can (15 ounces) Mexican-style chunky tomato sauce
Hot cooked rice (optional)

1. In a medium bowl, sprinkle the chicken pieces with the salt and pepper. Add the flour and toss to coat.
2. In a large skillet, heat the oil over medium-high heat. Add the chicken and brown on both sides. Pour off excess oil and add the sauce.
3. Cover and simmer 30 to 40 minutes until the chicken is cooked through. If desired, serve over cooked rice.

COURTESY: HUNT'S®

Lemon Tarragon Chicken

SERVES 4

½ cup all-purpose flour
1 teaspoon dried tarragon, crumbled
1¼ teaspoons salt, divided
2½ to 3 pounds chicken, cut up
4 tablespoons **I Can't Believe It's Not Butter!®**
⅓ cup lemon juice
1 tablespoon grated yellow onion
1 clove garlic, minced
⅛ teaspoon black pepper

1. Heat the oven to 400° F.
2. Combine the flour, tarragon, and 1 teaspoon salt in a bag. Add the chicken a few pieces at a time. Shake the bag to coat the chicken with the flour mixture.
3. Remove the chicken from the bag and shake off any excess coating.
4. In a 13×9-inch baking dish, melt I Can't Believe it's Not Butter!® in the oven and coat the chicken on all sides. Then, turn the chicken skin side up.
5. In a small bowl, mix the lemon juice, onion, garlic, pepper, and remaining salt.
6. Drizzle the mixture evenly over the chicken. Bake, uncovered, 40 minutes.
7. Transfer to a warm platter and serve.

Oven-Roasted Chicken and Vegetables

SERVES 4

2½ to 3 pounds chicken, cut into serving pieces
2½ pounds assorted fresh vegetables such as zucchini, yellow squash, red *or* green bell peppers, yellow *or* red onions, carrots, and mushrooms, sliced
2 tablespoons olive *or* vegetable oil
1 envelope **Lipton® Recipe Secrets® Savory Herb with Garlic Soup Mix**

1. Heat the oven to 450° F.
2. In a large roasting pan, combine all the ingredients until evenly coated.
3. Bake, uncovered, basting occasionally, 50 minutes or until the chicken is done and the vegetables are tender.
4. Transfer to a platter and serve.

Savory Marinated Chicken

SERVES 4

1 can (10½ ounces) condensed chicken broth
3 tablespoons lemon juice
1 teaspoon dried basil, crushed
1 teaspoon dried thyme, crushed
⅛ teaspoon pepper
2 pounds chicken parts

1. In a non-metal dish, mix the broth, lemon juice, herbs, and pepper. Add the chicken and toss. Refrigerate 30 minutes.
2. Broil or grill the chicken on a rack 6 inches from the heat for 30 minutes or until no longer pink, turning and brushing often with the sauce.
3. Remove to a platter and serve.

For safety's sake poultry should be kept cold until you are ready to cook it. Do not leave poultry in the car while you do other errands. Also avoid letting it sit on a countertop to marinate; salmonella and other bacteria multiply rapidly at room temperature.

When you refrigerate poultry, store it in the meat compartment if there is one; this is the coldest area. It should be left in the store wrapper and, if necessary, set inside a plastic bag or on a plate to collect any juices. It will keep this way up to 3 days. Poultry that is to be frozen, in addition to the store wrap, should be covered with heavy-duty foil or freezer wrap or put in a freezer bag to prevent freezer burn. It will keep up to 9 months at 0° F.

Make-It-Easy Chicken

SERVES 4

1 **Reynolds® Oven Bag,** large size, 14×20 inches
2 tablespoons all-purpose flour
1 envelope golden onion soup mix
1 cup water
1 teaspoon dried basil, divided
3 carrots, cut in 1-inch pieces
2 red-skin potatoes, cut in small wedges
1 green bell pepper, cut in cubes
6 chicken pieces, skin removed
Seasoned salt and paprika to taste

1. Preheat the oven to 350° F.

2. Shake the flour in the oven bag. Place the bag in a 13×9-inch baking pan.

3. Add the onion soup mix, water, and ½ teaspoon basil to the oven bag. Squeeze the bag to blend in the flour.

4. Add the carrots, potatoes, and bell pepper to the oven bag. Turn over the bag to coat the ingredients with the sauce.

5. Sprinkle the chicken with the remaining basil, seasoned salt, and paprika. Arrange the chicken in an even layer in the oven bag with the vegetables around the chicken.

6. Close the oven bag with a nylon tie and cut six ½-inch slits in the top. Bake until the chicken is tender, 55 to 60 minutes.

7. Cut the bag open, stir the sauce, and serve.

Peachy Honey Mustard Chicken

SERVES 4

1 tablespoon vegetable oil
2½ pounds broiler-fryer chicken, cut up, skin removed, if desired
1 can (16 ounces) **Del Monte® Fruit Naturals® Lite Yellow Cling Sliced Peaches,** drained, liquid reserved
3 tablespoons Dijon mustard
1 tablespoon honey
¼ cup sliced green onions

1. Heat the oil in a 12-inch skillet. Add the chicken and brown on both sides over high heat. Drain off fat.

2. In a small bowl, blend the reserved peach liquid with the mustard and honey. Pour over the chicken. Cover, reduce the heat, and simmer 10 minutes or until the chicken is cooked through.

3. With a slotted spoon, remove the chicken to a serving plate.

4. Add the peaches and green onions to the skillet. Boil over high heat to thicken slightly, about 5 minutes.

5. Spoon the sauce and peaches over the chicken and serve.

Two-At-Once Roast Turkey Breast

SERVES 8 TO 14

1 **Reynolds® Oven Bag,** turkey-size, 19×23-inches
1 tablespoon all-purpose flour
2 medium onions, cut in eighths
4 stalks celery, sliced
2 bone-in turkey breasts, 4 to 7 pounds *each*
1 tablespoon vegetable oil
Seasoned salt
Pepper

1. Heat the oven to 350° F.
2. Shake the flour in the oven bag. Place the oven bag in a large roasting pan at least 2 inches deep. Add the vegetables.
3. Brush the turkey breasts with the oil and sprinkle with the seasoned salt and pepper, to taste. Place the turkey breasts in the oven bag on top of the vegetables. Close the oven bag with a nylon tie and cut six ½-inch slits in the top. Insert a meat thermometer through a slit in the bag into the thickest part of the turkey breast, not touching bone.
4. Bake 1½ to 2 hours or until the thermometer reads 170° F.
5. Let stand 10 minutes before carving. Slice and serve.

Ham and Cheese Turkey Rolls

SERVES 4

4 thin slices cooked ham (½ ounce *each*)
4 thin slices Swiss cheese (½ ounce *each*)
4 boneless turkey cutlets (about 1 pound)
2 tablespoons vegetable oil
1 can (10¾ ounces) condensed cream of broccoli soup
⅓ cup milk
2 medium green onions, sliced (¼ cup)
⅛ teaspoon dried thyme, crushed
Chopped fresh parsley

1. Place a ham slice and cheese slice on each cutlet. Roll up the turkey from the narrow end, jelly-roll fashion. Tuck in the ham and cheese, if necessary, and secure with wooden toothpicks.
2. In a 10-inch skillet, over medium-high heat, in hot oil, cook the turkey for 5 minutes or until browned on all sides. Spoon off fat.
3. In a small bowl, combine the soup, milk, onions, and thyme. Pour over the turkey. Heat to boiling. Reduce the heat to low. Cover and cook 10 minutes or until the turkey is tender and no longer pink, stirring occasionally.
4. Garnish with the parsley and serve.

*B*efore cooking poultry, pat it dry with paper towels. Drying is necessary because spices adhere better to a dry surface. It is especially important to remove surface moisture if you are going to sauté poultry. Otherwise the meat will steam rather than brown.

Holiday Cornbread Turkey Bake

SERVES 6

1 package (16 ounces) cornbread mix
1 can (10½ ounces) **Healthy Choice® Recipe Creations™ Cream of Roasted Chicken with Herbs Condensed Soup**
½ cup minced green onions
½ cup nonfat milk
¼ cup fat-free egg substitute
1½ cups cooked turkey breast, cut into bite-size pieces
1 cup whole-berry cranberry sauce

1. Heat the oven to 400° F.

2. In a medium bowl, combine the cornbread mix, soup, green onions, milk, and egg substitute and mix well.

3. In a 9-inch springform pan sprayed with nonstick cooking spray, spread half the cornbread mixture on the bottom.

4. Sprinkle the turkey pieces on top and cover with the cranberry sauce. Spread the remaining batter evenly over the turkey mixture.

5. Bake 35 to 40 minutes.

6. Release the sides from the pan. Cut into wedges and serve.

Before adding dried herbs to a recipe, rub them between the palms of your hands or crush them with your fingertips to release their flavor. To crush seeds, rock the bowl of a spoon over them slowly. One (1) teaspoon of dried herbs equals 1 table-spoon of fresh.

Cajun Turkey Vegetable Loaf

SERVES 10

2 pounds ground turkey breast (99% lean)
1 package (10 ounces) frozen chopped spinach, thawed and well drained
½ cup finely chopped onion
½ cup chopped red *or* green bell pepper
½ cup shredded carrots
½ cup **Kretschmer® Original Toasted Wheat Germ**
3 egg whites, slightly beaten
2 tablespoons water
2 teaspoons ground cumin
2 teaspoons dried oregano
1 teaspoon dried thyme
1 teaspoon paprika
1 teaspoon salt (optional)
⅛ teaspoon crushed red pepper flakes

1. Heat the oven to 350° F.

2. Lightly spray a 13×9-inch baking dish with nonstick cooking spray or grease lightly.

3. In a large bowl, combine all the ingredients and mix lightly but thoroughly. Place in the prepared baking dish and shape into a 9×6-inch loaf.

4. Bake 1 hour or until the juices run clear.

5. Let stand 10 minutes and serve.

Turkey Tetrazzini

SERVES 4

MAKES 4 CUPS

1　can (10¾ ounces) condensed cream of mushroom soup
½　cup water
½　cup grated Parmesan cheese
2　cups cooked spaghetti (about 4 ounces dry)
1½　cups diced cooked turkey *or* chicken
2　tablespoons chopped fresh parsley *or* 1 teaspoon
　　parsley flakes
2　tablespoons chopped pimiento (optional)

1. In a 2-quart saucepan, over medium heat, combine the soup, water, and cheese. Heat to boiling, stirring occasionally.

2. Stir in the spaghetti, turkey, parsley, and pimiento. Heat through, stirring occasionally.

3. Transfer to plates and serve.

COURTESY: CAMPBELL SOUP COMPANY

For a quick glaze for chicken or turkey, brush the pieces with a mixture of prepared barbecue sauce and 1 or 2 tablespoons of orange juice. Prepared teriyaki sauce makes the quickest marinade for chicken or turkey. For best results in the shortest time, cut the boned meat into pieces to soak in enough marinade to coat, then stir-fry.

Turkey Tetrazzini

Turkey Pot Pie

1 can (10¾ ounces) condensed cream of celery soup
1 can (10¾ ounces) condensed cream of potato soup
1 cup milk
¼ teaspoon dried thyme, crushed
¼ teaspoon pepper
4 cups cooked cut-up vegetables such as a combination of broccoli florets, cauliflower florets, and sliced carrots; *or* broccoli florets and sliced carrots; *or* broccoli florets, sliced carrots, and peas
2 cups cubed cooked turkey *or* chicken
1 package (7½ *or* 10 ounces) refrigerated buttermilk biscuits

1. Heat the oven to 400° F.

2. In a 3-quart shallow baking dish, mix the soups, milk, thyme, pepper, vegetables, and chicken.

3. Bake 15 minutes or until hot. Stir.

4. Arrange the biscuits over the chicken mixture. Bake 15 minutes or until the biscuits are golden. Serve.

❖ ❖ ❖ ❖ ❖ ❖ ❖ ❖ ❖ ❖ ❖ ❖ ❖ ❖

When you stir-fry, stir the food quickly and constantly until it is cooked on all sides and is the desired degree of doneness. Foods are added to the wok in a certain order. Such flavoring ingredients as garlic and ginger go in first, then the items that take the longest to cook; quickly cooked foods are added last.

Hawaiian Turkey Smoked Sausage Stir-Fry

1 can (15 ounces) pineapple chunks
½ cup orange juice
2 tablespoons soy sauce
1 tablespoon cornstarch
¼ cup water
1 to 1½ pounds **Hillshire Farm® Turkey Smoked Sausage,** thickly sliced
1 can (6 ounces) mandarin oranges, drained
6 ounces snow peas (optional)
6 green onions, trimmed and sliced
1 bag (10 ounces) frozen Oriental vegetable mix (broccoli, red pepper, bamboo shoots, and mushrooms), thawed
1½ cups brown rice, cooked according to package directions, kept covered, and warm

1. Into a small bowl, drain the pineapple chunks. Set the fruit aside. Combine the orange juice and soy sauce with the pineapple juice.

2. In another small bowl, combine the cornstarch and water. Mix well.

3. In a wok or large skillet, stir-fry the sausage slices over medium heat until lightly browned.

4. Add the pineapple, mandarin oranges, and vegetables. Cook 4 minutes, stirring constantly.

5. Combine the reserved juices with the cornstarch mixture. Pour over the sausage mixture and stir until the liquid thickens.

6. Serve immediately over the rice.

❖

Turkey Smoked Sausage with Summer Salsa

SERVES 4 TO 6

1 pound **Hillshire Farm® Turkey Smoked Sausage** or **Polska Kielbasa**

For summer salsa:

3 green onions, chopped
1½ cups corn cut fresh off the cob *or* frozen, thawed
1 jalapeño *or* other chile pepper, seeded and chopped (optional)
⅓ cup chopped red bell pepper
⅓ cup chopped green bell pepper
⅓ cup chopped fresh cilantro
Juice of ½ lime
¼ teaspoon salt

1. Prepare the grill.
2. Slice the sausage lengthwise and set aside.
3. In a medium bowl, combine all the salsa ingredients. Let stand 15 minutes to blend the flavors.
4. Meanwhile, grill the sausage over medium heat for 5 to 8 minutes or until heated through.
5. Serve the sausage on a bun, in a tortilla, or by itself.
6. Garnish with the summer salsa.

Chili Cheesy-Rice Pie

SERVES 6

4 cups cooked rice
1 can (10¾ ounces) nacho cheese soup, undiluted
2 cans (15 ounces *each*) **HORMEL® Turkey Chili with Beans**
½ cup light sour cream (optional)
¼ cup sliced green onions (optional)

1. Heat the oven to 350° F.
2. In a medium bowl, stir together the rice and soup.
3. Transfer the rice mixture to a greased 9-inch pie plate. Press the rice evenly over the bottom and up the sides to form a "pie crust."
4. Pour the turkey chili into the rice crust. Bake, uncovered, 25 to 30 minutes or until very hot.
5. Remove from the oven and let sit 5 minutes before cutting.
6. Top each serving with sour cream and a sprinkling of green onions, if desired, and serve.

Turkey Divan

SERVES 4

1 can (15 ounces) **DINTY MOORE® Turkey Stew**
½ cup mayonnaise
1 teaspoon lemon juice
⅛ teaspoon curry powder
4 cups cooked asparagus *or* broccoli
2 tablespoons slivered almonds

1. In a large saucepan, combine the stew, mayonnaise, lemon juice, and curry powder. Bring to a simmer over low heat. Cook until thoroughly heated.
2. Spoon over the cooked asparagus or broccoli. Sprinkle with the almonds and serve.

Fish

AND

Shellfish

Salmon Fillets Baked in a Pouch with Oriental-Style Vegetables

Salmon Fillets Baked in a Pouch with Oriental-Style Vegetables

SERVES 4

5 tablespoons **I Can't Believe It's Not Butter!**®, melted
2 tablespoons soy sauce
4 salmon fillets (6 to 8 ounces *each*) *or* any firm-fleshed fish such as tuna, swordfish, *or* halibut
4 ounces snow peas, trimmed
2 green onions, trimmed and thinly sliced
4 teaspoons chopped fresh ginger (optional)
Freshly ground pepper to taste

1. Heat the oven to 450° F.

2. In a small bowl, blend I Can't Believe It's Not Butter!® and soy sauce together.

3. Lay each fillet on the bottom half of a 12-inch square of foil.

4. Equally divide the snow peas and arrange on top of each fillet. Repeat with the green onions and ginger. Spoon the sauce evenly over each and top with a grating of pepper to taste.

5. Fold the foil over the fish, crimping the edges to seal well.

6. Place on a baking sheet and bake 15 minutes.

7. Open carefully with the tip of a knife and pull back the foil. Transfer to warm plates. Serve.

Marinated Grouper with Orange-Onion Confit

SERVES 4

¼ cup fresh **Florida Orange Juice**
¼ cup chopped fresh chives
1 teaspoon grated orange zest
1 teaspoon ground cumin
1 garlic clove, crushed
½ teaspoon salt
¼ teaspoon freshly ground pepper
1½ pounds grouper fillets
1½ tablespoons olive oil
1 large onion, cut into ¼-inch slices
12 strips (4×½-inch) orange zest
Fresh chives
Florida Orange Slices

1. In a shallow pie plate, combine the orange juice, chives, grated orange zest, cumin, garlic, salt, and pepper. Add the grouper and coat completely with the marinade.

2. Cover and marinate in the refrigerator for 30 minutes.

3. Heat the oven to 425° F. In the baking pan, combine the oil, onion, and orange zest strips. Roast about 25 minutes or until the onions begin to brown, stirring once.

4. Add the grouper with the marinade, pushing the onion mixture to one side of the pan. Bake 10 to 15 minutes more or until the fish is just cooked through in the center.

5. Remove the fish to a platter and surround with the onion mixture. Garnish with the fresh chives and orange slices and serve.

COURTESEY: FLORIDA DEPARTMENT OF CITRUS

Herb-Baked Fish and Rice

SERVES 3 TO 4

1½ cups hot chicken bouillon
½ cup regular long-grain rice
¼ teaspoon **Durkee® Italian Seasoning**
¼ teaspoon garlic powder
1 package (10 ounces) frozen chopped broccoli, thawed and drained
1 can (4½ ounces) **French's® French Fried Onions**, divided
1 tablespoon grated Parmesan cheese
1 pound fish fillets, thawed if frozen
Durkee® Paprika (optional)
½ cup shredded Cheddar cheese (2 ounces)

1. Heat the oven to 375° F.

2. In an 8×12-inch baking dish, combine the hot bouillon, rice, and seasonings. Bake, covered, 10 minutes.

3. Top with the broccoli, half the can french fried onions, and Parmesan cheese. Place the fish fillets diagonally down the center of the dish. Sprinkle the fish lightly with paprika, if used.

4. Bake, covered, 20 to 25 minutes or until the fish flakes easily with a fork.

5. Loosen the rice by carefully stirring with a fork. Top the fish with the Cheddar cheese and the remaining onions. Bake, uncovered, 3 minutes or until the onions are golden brown.

6. Transfer to warm plates and serve.

Seafood Florentine Bake

SERVES 8

2 pounds fish fillets such as flounder, haddock, *or* pollock
1 teaspoon salt
½ teaspoon onion powder
½ teaspoon pepper
1 can (10¾ to 11 ounces) condensed cream of shrimp *or* Cheddar cheese soup
1 package (10 ounces) frozen chopped spinach, thawed and well drained
2 cups **Bisquick® Original baking mix**
⅓ cup grated Parmesan cheese
1 cup milk
2 eggs

1. Heat the oven to 350° F.

2. Arrange the fish fillets in a greased 13×9-inch baking dish and sprinkle with the salt, onion powder, and pepper.

3. Spoon the soup over the fillets and top with the spinach.

4. Beat the remaining ingredients with a wire whisk or hand beater about 1 minute or until almost smooth. Pour over the spinach.

5. Bake, uncovered, about 40 minutes or until the top is golden brown.

6. Let stand 10 minutes before serving.

❖

Seafood Florentine Bake

Marinated Fish Steaks

SERVES 4

¼ cup (½ stick) **I Can't Believe It's Not Butter!®,** melted
¼ cup Italian dressing
¼ cup soy sauce
½ cup water
⅛ cup lemon juice
1½ pounds thick, firm-fleshed fish such as swordfish, halibut, shark, *or* tuna

1. In a shallow baking dish large enough to hold the fish, blend the melted I Can't Believe It's Not Butter!® with the remaining ingredients *except* fish.

2. Add the fish. Baste and cover. Refrigerate 24 hours.

3. Heat the oven to 350° F.

4. Strain off the marinade and spoon the remaining solids on top of the fish. Bake, uncovered, 20 minutes.

5. Transfer to warm plates and serve.

Spanish-Style Baked Fish

SERVES 8

2 pounds white fish fillets *or* steaks such as orange roughy, cod, halibut, *or* haddock
2 tablespoons butter *or* margarine
Paprika
Salt
2 large cloves garlic, minced
1 tablespoon olive oil
1 quart Freezer Tomato Sauce (4 cups), thawed *(see right)*
¼ cup sliced pitted ripe olives
2 tablespoons drained capers

1. Heat the oven to 400° F.

2. Arrange the fish in a baking pan in a single layer. Dot with the butter and sprinkle lightly with the paprika and salt.

3. Bake, uncovered, 8 to 10 minutes until the fish is tender and flakes with a fork.

4. Meanwhile, in a medium skillet, over low heat, sauté the garlic in the oil until tender. Do not brown. Stir in the tomato sauce, olives, and capers and heat to boiling. Reduce the heat and simmer, uncovered, about 5 minutes.

5. Arrange the fish on a platter, spoon the sauce over, and serve.

Freezer Tomato Sauce

MAKES ABOUT 2 QUARTS

⅔ cup chopped onion
1 tablespoon vegetable oil
6 pounds ripe tomatoes, cored, peeled, seeded (if desired), and coarsely chopped
½ cup finely chopped fresh parsley
2 teaspoons sugar
Salt and pepper to taste
2 **Ziploc® brand Quart Size Freezer Bags**

1. In a large saucepan, over low heat, sauté the chopped onion in the oil until tender. Stir in the tomatoes and parsley.

2. Cook over medium heat, covered, 30 minutes. Simmer, uncovered, until the mixture is the desired sauce consistency, about 20 minutes, stirring occasionally. Stir in the sugar and season to taste with the salt and pepper.

3. Cool to room temperature, then freeze in the two freezer bags.

Cajun Fish

SERVES 4

1 tablespoon vegetable oil
1 small green bell pepper, diced
½ teaspoon dried oregano, crushed
1 can (10¾ ounces) condensed tomato soup
⅓ cup water
⅛ teaspoon garlic powder
⅛ teaspoon pepper
⅛ teaspoon cayenne (red) pepper
1 pound fresh *or* thawed frozen firm-fleshed white fish fillets such as cod, haddock, *or* halibut
4 cups hot cooked rice

1. In a large skillet, over medium heat, heat the oil. Add the bell pepper and oregano and cook until crisp-tender, stirring often. Add the soup, water, garlic powder, pepper, and cayenne pepper. Heat to a boil.

2. Place the fish in the soup mixture. Cover and cook over low heat for 5 minutes or until the fish flakes easily when tested with a fork.

3. Serve with the rice.

Summer Seafood Grill

SERVES 4

1 tablespoon **Mazola Right Blend®**
¼ cup lemon juice
¼ cup minced green onions
2 tablespoons chopped fresh parsley
1 teaspoon salt
½ teaspoon dried thyme
1 clove garlic, minced
1 pound swordfish steaks
Mazola No Stick® Corn Oil Cooking Spray

1. In a shallow baking dish, combine the oil, lemon juice, green onions, parsley, salt, thyme, and garlic.

2. Add the swordfish, turning to coat. Cover, let stand at room temperature no longer than 30 minutes, turning once.

3. Before igniting the grill or broiler, spray the grill or broiler rack with the cooking spray. Grill or broil the swordfish 4 to 5 inches from the heat for 8 to 10 minutes or until opaque, turning once and brushing with the marinade.

4. Remove to a platter and serve.

*F*resh fish should have a pleasant odor with no trace of ammonia. The eyes of a whole fish should be clear and bulging, the gills pink or red, the scales shimmering, the flesh firm and springy. If you're buying fillets or steaks, avoid any with dry, brown edges.

At the fish market or supermarket, whole fish should be presented on a bed of ice; fish fillets and steaks should be set on a tray or freezer paper, not directly on the ice.

Fish spoils easily, so buy it just before you go home. If this is impossible, place the wrapped fish on top of frozen food or in a plastic bag surrounded by ice.

Gingered Fish Kebabs

SERVES 4

⅓ cup lemon juice
3 tablespoons reduced-sodium soy sauce
1 tablespoon **Mazola Right Blend®**
2 tablespoons chopped fresh cilantro
1 tablespoon grated fresh ginger
1 teaspoon sugar
1 large clove garlic, minced
1 pound firm-fleshed fish such as swordfish, halibut, tuna, *or* monkfish, cut into 1-inch cubes
2 cups cubed fresh pineapple
1 medium red *or* green bell pepper, trimmed, seeded, and cut into 1-inch pieces
1 medium red onion, peeled and cut into wedges
Mazola No Stick® Corn Oil Cooking Spray

1. In a large glass bowl, combine the lemon juice, soy sauce, oil, cilantro, ginger, sugar, and garlic.

2. Add the fish, pineapple, bell pepper, and onion. Toss to coat.

3. Cover. Refrigerate several hours or overnight. Stir occasionally.

4. Before igniting the grill or broiler, spray the grill rack or broiling pan with the cooking spray.

5. Spray eight metal skewers with the cooking spray. Alternately thread with fish, pineapple, bell pepper, and onion.

6. Grill or broil 4 to 5 inches from the heat, turning and basting frequently, 8 to 10 minutes or until the fish is firm.

7. Remove to a platter and serve.

Tasty Tuna Tortillas

SERVES 4

⅓ cup fat-free French dressing
¼ cup water
1 stalk celery, sliced
1 small onion, finely chopped
1 medium red *or* green bell pepper, chopped
1 can (6 ounces) tuna packed in water, drained and flaked
1 can (3¼ ounces) tuna packed in water, drained and flaked
8 flour tortillas, warmed

Assorted toppings:

Light sour cream
Low-fat plain yogurt
Low-fat cottage cheese
Hot pepper sauce
Shredded lettuce
Shredded carrots
Bean sprouts
Alfalfa sprouts

1. In a 10-inch skillet, bring the French dressing, water, celery, onion, and bell pepper to the boiling point. Reduce the heat and simmer, stirring occasionally, 5 minutes.

2. Stir in the tuna and heat through.

3. Spoon the mixture in the tortillas and roll up.

4. Serve with assorted toppings.

COURTESY: WISH-BONE®

Tasty Tuna Tortillas

Impossible Tuna and Cheddar Pie

Impossible Tuna and Cheddar Pie

SERVES 6 TO 8

2 cups chopped onion
¼ cup (½ stick) margarine *or* butter
2 cans (6 ounces *each*) solid white tuna in water, drained
2 cups shredded Cheddar cheese, divided (8 ounces)
3 eggs
1¼ cups milk
1 cup **Bisquick® Original baking mix**
⅛ teaspoon pepper
2 tomatoes, thinly sliced

1. Heat the oven to 400° F.

2. Grease a 10×1½-inch glass pie plate, an 8-inch square baking dish, or six 10-ounce custard cups.

3. In a 10-inch skillet, cook the onions and margarine over low heat, stirring occasionally, until the onions are light brown.

4. Sprinkle the tuna, 1 cup cheese, and onions in the pie plate, square dish, or custard cups.

5. Beat the eggs, milk, baking mix, and pepper in a blender on high for 15 seconds (or with a hand beater or wire whisk for 1 minute). Pour into the pie plate, square dish, or custard cups.

6. Bake 25 to 30 minutes (custard cups, 20 to 25 minutes) or until a knife inserted in the center comes out clean. Top with the tomato slices and remaining cheese.

7. Bake 3 to 5 minutes longer or until the cheese is melted.

8. Cool 5 minutes. Cut into wedges and serve.

Impossible Tuna-Tomato Pie

SERVES 8

1 can (6 ounces) tuna in water, drained and flaked
1 medium ripe tomato, seeded, chopped (about ¾ cup)
⅓ cup shredded mozzarella cheese
1 tablespoon chopped fresh basil *or* 1 teaspoon dried basil
1 cup milk
½ cup **Bisquick® Original baking mix**
2 eggs
½ teaspoon salt (optional)
¼ teaspoon pepper

1. Heat the oven to 400° F.

2. In a greased 9-inch pie plate, scatter the tuna, tomato, mozzarella cheese, and basil.

3. In a medium bowl, stir the milk, baking mix, eggs, salt, if using, and pepper with a fork until blended. Pour into the pie plate.

4. Bake about 30 minutes or until a knife inserted in the center comes out clean.

5. Cool 5 minutes. Cut into wedges and serve.

NOTE

High-altitude directions (over 3,500 feet.): Not recommended.

Quick Fixin' Tuna Casserole

SERVES 4

¾ cup milk
2 teaspoons all-purpose flour
1 package (1 pound) **Green Giant® Pasta Accents® Creamy Cheddar Frozen Vegetables and Pasta**
1 can (9 ounces) tuna, drained
⅓ cup croutons, crushed

1. In a small bowl, combine the milk and flour. Blend well.

2. In a large skillet, over medium-high heat, combine the milk mixture with the vegetables and pasta. Bring to a boil. Stir, cover, and reduce the heat.

3. Simmer 3 to 5 minutes until the vegetables are crisp-tender and the sauce is slightly thickened, stirring occasionally.

4. Stir in the tuna. Cover and cook over low heat for 1 minute or until thoroughly heated.

5. Transfer to a serving dish. Sprinkle with the croutons and serve.

Bay Village Shrimp

SERVES 4

1 can (10½ ounces) **Healthy Choice® Recipe Creations™ Cream of Celery with Sautéed Onion and Garlic Condensed Soup**
1 pound shrimp, fresh *or* thawed frozen, shelled and deveined
½ cup asparagus, fresh *or* thawed frozen, cut diagonally into 1-inch pieces
½ cup sliced mushrooms
¼ cup sliced green onions
¼ cup diced red bell pepper
½ teaspoon dried thyme
½ teaspoon salt (optional)
Hot cooked rice (optional)

1. Heat the oven to 375° F.

2. In a large bowl, combine the soup, shrimp, asparagus, mushrooms, green onions, bell pepper, thyme, and salt, if using. Mix well.

3. Place in a 2-quart baking dish sprayed with nonstick cooking spray. Bake, covered, 30 minutes.

4. Serve over rice, if desired.

*B*efore buying frozen fish, be sure that it's frozen solid and check the expiration date on the package. When thawing fish, place it, wrapped, on a plate in the refrigerator—not on a countertop—or put the packaged fish in very cold water to thaw, allowing 30 minutes per pound. You can also thaw fish in the microwave. For precise instructions, consult the manufacturer's manual. Never cook frozen fish in the microwave without defrosting it first. Use thawed fish within a day—do not refreeze it.

Dijon Shrimp Scampi

Dijon Shrimp Scampi

SERVES 4

1 pound large shrimp, shelled and deveined
1 clove garlic, minced
2 tablespoons **Blue Bonnet Margarine**
⅓ cup **Grey Poupon® Country Dijon Mustard**
¼ cup lemon juice
¼ cup chopped fresh parsley
Hot cooked rice (optional)

1. In large skillet, over medium-high heat, cook and stir the shrimp and garlic in the margarine until just pink.

2. Blend in the mustard, lemon juice, and parsley. Heat through.

3. Serve over rice, if desired.

VARIATIONS

Substitute 1 pound skinless, boneless chicken breast, cut into thin strips, for shrimp.

Ginger Shrimp and Scallops Over Rice

Ginger Shrimp and Scallops Over Rice

SERVES 4

1½ cups **UNCLE BEN'S® Brand Instant Rice**
  2 tablespoons butter *or* margarine, divided
  8 ounces medium *or* large shrimp, shelled and deveined
  8 ounces sea *or* bay scallops
  8 ounces snow peas (about 2 cups)
  1 cup chicken broth
  2 teaspoons cornstarch
  1 tablespoon shredded fresh ginger
 ¼ cup thinly sliced green onions with tops

1. Cook the rice according to package directions. Keep warm in a serving dish.

2. While the rice is cooking, in a 10-inch skillet, over medium-high heat, melt 1 tablespoon butter. Add the shrimp and scallops to the skillet. Cook and stir until cooked through, about 3 minutes. Remove to a bowl and reserve.

3. Melt the remaining butter in the same skillet. Add the snow peas. Cook and stir until crisp-tender, about 2 minutes.

4. Add the snow peas to the bowl with the shrimp and scallops.

5. Combine the broth and cornstarch and add to the skillet with the ginger. Cook and stir until very thick, about 1 minute.

6. Return the shrimp mixture to the skillet and heat through. Stir in the green onions and pour the mixture over the warm rice. Serve.

Shrimp in the Pink

SERVES 2

1 tablespoon olive *or* vegetable oil
1 tablespoon **Imperial® Spread**
¼ teaspoon **Lawry's® Garlic Powder with Parsley**
1 pound medium shrimp, shelled and deveined
1¾ cups water
½ cup milk
1 package **Lipton® Noodles & Sauce—Alfredo**
¼ cup chopped green onions

1. In a large skillet, heat the oil, margarine, and garlic powder. Cook the shrimp over medium-high heat, stirring constantly, until the shrimp turn pink. Remove and set aside.

2. Add the water and milk. Bring to the boiling point.

3. Stir in the noodles and sauce. Reduce the heat and simmer, stirring occasionally, 8 minutes or until the noodles are tender.

4. Stir in the shrimp and green onions. Heat through.

5. Transfer to warm plates and serve.

❖ ❖ ❖ ❖ ❖ ❖ ❖ ❖ ❖ ❖ ❖ ❖ ❖ ❖ ❖ ❖ ❖ ❖

Fresh, unfrozen shrimp is usually available only near the areas where it is caught. Most of the raw, unshelled shrimp sold in fish markets and supermarkets has been previously frozen. Even so, thawed shrimp should smell fresh. A "fishy" or ammonia odor indicates age or spoilage. As with other seafood, shrimp is best used on the day of purchase; however, cooked shrimp can be stored in the refrigerator up to 3 days. Do not refreeze thawed uncooked shrimp.

Risotto with Shrimp and Sweet Bell Peppers

SERVES 8

1 red bell pepper, diced
1 yellow bell pepper, diced
2 large cloves garlic, minced
3 tablespoons olive oil, divided
1 jar (27½ ounces) **Ragú® Light Pasta Sauce—Chunky Garden Combination**
3 cans (13¾ ounces *each*) low-salt chicken broth
1½ cups Arborio rice
1 pound large shrimp, shelled and deveined
⅓ cup grated Parmesan cheese

1. In a large skillet, sauté the red and yellow bell peppers and garlic in 2 tablespoons olive oil and set aside.

2. In a large saucepan, combine the pasta sauce with the chicken broth and heat thoroughly.

3. In a Dutch oven or stockpot, lightly sauté the rice in the remaining olive oil. Add about 1 cup heated sauce mixture to the rice. Cook over low to medium heat at a very low simmer, stirring frequently. Continue adding the hot sauce mixture gradually. Stir and cook about 30 to 40 minutes or until the rice is tender.

4. During the last 5 minutes of cooking, add the shrimp to the skillet with the bell peppers. Sauté until the shrimp just turn pink. Stir the Parmesan cheese into the risotto. (The rice should be moist and creamy.)

5. Spoon the hot risotto into a large serving bowl. Top with the shrimp and bell peppers. Serve.

❖

Shrimp and Sausage Jambalaya

SERVES 6

½ cup chopped onion
½ cup chopped green bell pepper
1 can (10½ ounces) **Healthy Choice® Recipe Creations™ Tomato with Garden Herbs Soup**
1 cup water
1 cup cubed **Healthy Choice® Smoked Sausage**
8 ounces large shrimp, cooked, shelled, and deveined
½ teaspoon hot pepper sauce (optional)
4 cups rice cooked according to package directions

1. Spray a large nonstick skillet with cooking spray. Stir-fry the onion and bell pepper in the skillet over medium heat until crisp-tender.

2. Add the soup, water, sausage, shrimp, and hot pepper sauce and mix well.

3. Reduce the heat and simmer 3 minutes. Stir in the rice and cook until thoroughly heated.

4. Transfer to warm plates and serve.

Easy Shrimp Alfredo

SERVES 4

1 tablespoon vegetable oil
1 package (12 ounces) frozen, uncooked large shrimp
1 package (1 pound) **Green Giant® Pasta Accents® Alfredo Frozen Vegetables and Pasta**
⅓ cup white grape juice
¼ cup light sour cream

1. In a large skillet, heat the oil over medium-high heat. Add the frozen shrimp and stir until the shrimp are pink, 2 to 3 minutes.

2. Add the vegetables and pasta and white grape juice. Bring to a boil. Cover, reduce the heat to medium, and simmer 3 to 5 minutes until the vegetables are crisp-tender, stirring occasionally.

3. Stir in the sour cream. Blend well and serve.

To shell and devein shrimp, cut through the shell and a thin layer of flesh down each shrimp's back to the tail with kitchen scissors. Spread open the shell and gently lift out the shrimp. To loosen the tail meat, squeeze the tip of the tail hard and pull the shrimp free. Holding the shrimp under cold water, scrape out the vein with a knife or pull it out with your fingers. To butterfly a shrimp, cut deeply into the flesh along the back without cutting through, so the flesh can be spread open.

Santa Fe Fajitas

SERVES 4 TO 6

3 tablespoons **Kikkoman Lite Soy Sauce**
1 tablespoon lime juice
1 tablespoon chopped fresh cilantro
1 pound medium prawns, shelled and deveined
1 green bell pepper, thinly sliced
1 red bell pepper, thinly sliced
1 red onion, thinly sliced
1 tablespoon vegetable oil
8 to 10 flour tortillas (8 inches), warmed
2 tablespoons tomatillo salsa (optional)

1. Mix together the soy sauce, lime juice, and cilantro. Pour over the prawns in a large resealable plastic bag.
2. Press the air out of the bag and close the top securely. Refrigerate 30 minutes. Turn the bag over once.
3. In a large skillet, cook the bell peppers and onion in hot oil over high heat for 4 minutes, stirring constantly. Remove.
4. Add the prawns and marinade. Cook, stirring, about 2 minutes or until the prawns are pink.
5. Return the vegetables to the pan and heat through.
6. To serve: Wrap the desired amount of filling in a tortilla.

Italian Shrimp with Bow Ties

SERVES 2

1½ cups water
½ cup milk
1 tablespoon margarine *or* butter
1 package **Lipton® Pasta & Sauce—Italian Cheese**
2 cups cooked shrimp *or* 1 can (6 ounces) tuna, drained and flaked
⅓ cup oil-packed sun-dried tomatoes, coarsely chopped *or* 1 medium tomato, coarsely chopped
½ cup frozen green peas, thawed

1. In a medium saucepan, bring the water, milk, and margarine to the boiling point.
2. Stir in the pasta and continue boiling over medium heat for 10 minutes, stirring occasionally.
3. Stir in the shrimp, sun-dried tomatoes, and peas.
4. Lower the heat and simmer 2 minutes or until the pasta is tender and the shrimp are heated through.
5. Transfer to warm plates and serve.

To boil shrimp, half-fill a large saucepan with water. Add salt if you wish, plus whole peppercorns and pickling spices or shrimp boil seasonings, available in the seafood section of most grocery stores. Bring to a boil over high heat, then add the shrimp. If you have shelled the shrimp, add some shells for extra flavor. Return to a boil and simmer for about 3 minutes for medium unshelled shrimp, 5 minutes for jumbo, or just until pink. (If shelled, they may need slightly less time.) Transfer to a colander and rinse with cold water to stop the cooking.

Scallops with Basil
in Lemon Sauce

SERVES 4

¼ cup (½ stick) **I Can't Believe It's Not Butter!®**
1 clove garlic, minced
1½ pounds bay *or* sea scallops, rinsed and well dried
3 tablespoons chopped fresh basil
2 tablespoons fresh lemon juice
Salt and freshly ground pepper to taste

1. In a large heavy skillet, over medium heat, melt I Can't Believe It's Not Butter!® Add the garlic and cook until softened. Do not brown.
2. Add the scallops and basil and sauté over medium-high heat, stirring constantly, 2 minutes.
3. Add the lemon juice and continue cooking, stirring constantly, 2 to 3 minutes longer. Season with the salt and pepper.
4. Serve immediately.

A package of shelled frozen shrimp will keep in the freezer up to a year. Thaw the shrimp in the refrigerator, or cook them frozen as long as they're not being deep-fried. Cook frozen shrimp at a slightly lower temperature than the recipe calls for and about 25 percent longer than thawed shrimp.

All-Time Favorite
BBQ Shrimp Kebabs

SERVES 4

¼ cup **Kikkoman Soy Sauce**
2 tablespoons tomato ketchup
1 tablespoon vinegar
2 teaspoons sugar
½ teaspoon ground ginger
Dash cayenne (red) pepper
1 clove garlic, pressed
1 pound fresh *or* thawed frozen medium shrimp *or* prawns, shelled and deveined
6 metal or bamboo skewers*

1. Prepare the grill.
2. Combine the soy sauce, ketchup, vinegar, sugar, ginger, cayenne pepper, garlic, and 1 tablespoon water in a small saucepan.
3. Bring to a boil, reduce the heat, and simmer, uncovered, 3 minutes.
4. Meanwhile, thread the shrimp onto skewers, leaving space between the pieces.
5. Brush the shrimp thoroughly with the sauce. Place on the grill 4 inches from the hot coals.
6. Cook 2 minutes on each side, or just until the shrimp turn pink. Baste frequently with the remaining sauce.
7. Remove to a platter and serve.

NOTE

*Soak bamboo skewers in water 30 minutes to prevent burning.

Impossible Caesar 'n' Crab Pie

SERVES 8

1 package (10 ounces) frozen sliced asparagus, thawed and drained
1 package (8 ounces) imitation flake-style crabmeat
1 cup shredded mozzarella cheese (4 ounces)
1 cup **Bisquick® Original baking mix**
½ cup milk
½ cup Caesar salad dressing
2 eggs

1. Heat the oven to 400° F.

2. In a greased 9-inch pie plate, scatter the asparagus, crabmeat, and mozzarella cheese.

3. In a medium bowl, stir the baking mix, milk, Caesar salad dressing, and eggs with a fork until well blended. Pour into the prepared pie plate.

4. Bake 30 to 35 minutes or until a knife inserted in the center comes out clean.

5. Cool 5 minutes. Cut into wedges and serve.

NOTE

High-altitude directions (over 3,500 feet): Bake 35 to 40 minutes.

Simple Seafood Risotto

SERVES 2

2 cups water
1 tablespoon margarine *or* butter
1 package **Lipton® Rice & Sauce—Chicken & Parmesan Risotto**
1 package (10 ounces) frozen chopped spinach, thawed and squeezed dry
6 ounces frozen crab meat, thawed *or* 1 can (6½ ounces) crab meat, drained and flaked

1. In a medium saucepan, bring the water, margarine, and rice to a boil. Reduce the heat and simmer, uncovered, stirring occasionally, 8 minutes.

2. Stir in the spinach and crab meat and continue simmering 2 minutes or until the rice is tender and the crab meat is heated through.

3. Transfer to warm plates and serve.

VARIATION

Use 2 cups diced cooked chicken, turkey, or ham.

The lower air pressure of high altitudes affects the condition of ingredients and the process of baking. Because the humidity of the air also tends to be lower at high altitudes, flour dries out more quickly than at sea level and as a result may absorb more liquid. Follow package instructions for adjustments in baking times and ingredient amounts.

$\mathcal{P}$asta

Four-Cheese Lasagna

Four-Cheese Lasagna

SERVES 6 TO 8

- 3 cups **Ricotta Cheese** (30 ounces)
- 1 cup **Mozzarella Cheese,** divided
- ½ cup grated **Parmesan Cheese**
- ½ cup grated **Romano Cheese**
- 2 eggs, lightly beaten
- 2 tablespoons chopped fresh parsley
- 9 lasagna noodles (8 ounces)
- 1 pound ground beef
- 3 cups spaghetti sauce

1. In a large bowl, combine the ricotta, ½ cup mozzarella, Parmesan and Romano cheeses, eggs, and parsley. Set aside.

2. In a large rectangular pan, soak the uncooked lasagna noodles in cold water for 10 minutes to soften slightly, then drain.

3. In a skillet, over medium heat, cook the ground meat until lightly browned and drain.

4. In a large bowl, place the spaghetti sauce and stir the meat into the sauce.

5. Heat the oven to 350° F.

6. In an 12×8-inch glass baking dish, spread ½ cup sauce. Place 3 lasagna noodles side by side over the sauce. Spread ⅓ of the ricotta filling over the noodles. Spread 1 cup sauce over the filling.

7. Repeat the layers with the remaining ingredients, ending with the sauce. Cover tightly with foil and bake 1 hour.

8. Remove the foil, top with the remaining mozzarella cheese, and bake 3 minutes until the cheese has melted.

9. Remove from the oven and allow to stand at least 10 minutes before cutting. Serve.

COURTESY: DAIRY MANAGEMENT, INC.

Mexitalian Lasagna

SERVES 6 TO 9

- 1 can (15 ounces) **HORMEL® Chili No Beans**
- 1 jar (16 ounces) Mexican salsa, drained
- 1 can (4 ounces) sliced mushrooms, drained
- ¾ cup grated Parmesan cheese
- 1½ teaspoons dried Italian seasoning
- 1½ cups cottage cheese
- 1½ teaspoons parsley flakes
- 9 lasagna noodles (8 ounces)
- 2½ cups shredded mozzarella cheese

1. In a large bowl, combine the chili, salsa, mushrooms, Parmesan cheese, and Italian seasoning.

2. In a small bowl, stir together the cottage cheese and parsley flakes.

3. Cook the noodles according to package directions. Do not overcook.

4. Heat the oven to 350° F.

5. In a 9-inch square baking dish coated with cooking spray, layer 3 noodles, ⅓ of the cottage cheese, ⅓ of the chili mixture, and ⅓ of the mozzarella cheese. Repeat to make 3 layers. Cut the noodles to fit if necessary.

6. Bake 25 to 30 minutes or until the lasagna is bubbly and thoroughly heated.

7. Let stand 10 minutes before serving.

Pasta with Chili and Pumpkin Seeds

SERVES 4

5   serrano chilies, stems removed
2   medium onions, chopped
1   can (28 ounces) Italian-style plum tomatoes, crushed
1   can (15 ounces) **HORMEL® Chili No Beans**
8   ounces vermicelli *or* spaghetti
⅓   cup toasted pumpkin seeds
¼   cup chopped fresh cilantro

1. Place the chilies in a stove-top roasting pan. Cover and cook over medium-high heat for 3 to 4 minutes or until the skin chars on all sides.

2. Stir in the onions, tomatoes, and chili. Cook over medium-low heat, stirring occasionally, 15 to 20 minutes.

3. Meanwhile, cook the pasta according to package directions.

4. Serve the chili mixture over the pasta. Top with the pumpkin seeds and cilantro.

Chili Spaghetti Pourover

SERVES 4 TO 6

4   strips bacon, diced
1   medium onion, chopped
1   clove garlic, minced
2   cans (15 ounces *each*) **HORMEL® Chili No Beans**
1   teaspoon sugar
½   teaspoon dried oregano
8   ounces **Creamette® Thin Spaghetti**
Grated Parmesan cheese

1. In a large saucepan, brown the bacon, onion, and garlic. Cook until tender and drain.

2. Stir in the the chili, sugar, and oregano. Bring to a boil. Reduce the heat and simmer 20 minutes.

3. Prepare the spaghetti according to package directions and drain.

4. Pour the sauce over the hot spaghetti. Top with the Parmesan cheese. Serve.

Mexi-Mac Casserole

SERVES 6 TO 8

1   package (7 ounces) **Creamette® Elbow Macaroni** (2 cups uncooked)
1   can (15 ounces) **HORMEL® Chili No Beans**
¼   cup tomato juice
1   can (4 ounces) diced green chilies
¼   cup sliced green onions
1½ cups shredded Cheddar cheese, divided (6 ounces)
2   cups tortilla chips, divided
½   cup sour cream
1   medium tomato, chopped
1   tablespoon chopped fresh cilantro

1. Prepare the macaroni according to package directions and drain.

2. In a medium saucepan, heat the chili, tomato juice, green chilies, and green onions.

3. Combine the macaroni, chili mixture, and ½ cup cheese.

4. Crush 1 cup tortilla chips and spread on the bottom of a 3-quart baking dish. Spoon in the macaroni mixture. Top with the remaining tortilla chips and cheese.

5. Heat the oven to 350° F. Bake 30 minutes.

6. Garnish the top with the sour cream, tomato, and cilantro. Serve.

Mexi-Mac Casserole

Penne with Chicken Strips and Broccoli

Penne with Chicken Strips and Broccoli

SERVES 4 TO 6

½ cup plus 2 tablespoons **I Can't Believe It's Not Butter!**®, softened and divided
3 skinless, boneless chicken breast halves, sliced into strips (about 12 ounces)
¼ cup all-purpose flour
Freshly ground pepper to taste
1 clove garlic, peeled and minced (optional)
12 ounces penne *or* any short tubular pasta such as ziti *or* rigatoni
4 cups broccoli florets and peeled stems, cut into bite-size pieces
1 cup grated Parmesan cheese

1. In a large skillet, over medium heat, melt 2 tablespoons I Can't Believe It's Not Butter!®
2. On a sheet of wax paper, lightly coat the chicken in the flour and pepper and shake off any excess. Immediately place the chicken in the hot skillet and sauté 2 minutes, stirring frequently until just browned on both sides. Stir in the garlic, if using, and cook 1 minute longer. Do not let the garlic brown. Cover and keep warm.
3. In a large pot, bring 5 quarts of water to a rolling boil. Add the pasta and cook, uncovered, 6 minutes. Carefully add the broccoli and continue cooking until the pasta is *al dente*. Reserve 1 cup cooking water before draining the pasta.
4. Meanwhile, in a large serving bowl, blend the cheese with the remaining I Can't Believe It's Not Butter!® until fluffy.
5. Blend with the reserved cooking water to make a sauce. Add the pasta, chicken, and broccoli and gently toss until combined.
6. Serve with additional cheese and add pepper to taste, if desired.

Grilled Chicken and Pasta

SERVES 4

1 envelope **Lipton® Recipe Secrets® Golden Herb with Lemon Soup Mix***
½ cup water
1 pound skinless, boneless chicken breasts
8 ounces bow-tie pasta *or* rotelle
2 cups broccoli florets *and/or* sliced carrots
½ cup sour cream
1 medium tomato, seeded and chopped
Salt and freshly ground pepper (optional)

1. Prepare the grill or broiler.
2. In a shallow bowl, blend the soup mix and water. Reserve half the mixture.
3. Dip the chicken in the remaining mixture to coat. Grill or broil the chicken until done.
4. Cut the chicken into strips and set aside.
5. Meanwhile, cook the pasta according to package directions, adding the broccoli during the last 4 minutes of cooking, and drain.
6. In a large bowl, blend the reserved soup mixture with the sour cream.
7. Stir in the pasta, broccoli, chicken, and tomato until evenly coated. Season, if desired, with salt and ground pepper. Serve.

VARIATION

*Also terrific with **Lipton® Recipe Secrets® Savory Herb with Garlic Soup Mix** or **Lipton® Recipe Secrets® Golden Onion Soup Mix**.

Italian Chicken Pasta

Italian Chicken Pasta

¼ cup all-purpose flour
¼ teaspoon salt
¼ teaspoon pepper
1 pound skinless, boneless chicken, cut into 1-inch cubes
2 tablespoons vegetable oil
1 can (15 ounces) **Hunts® Ready Tomato Sauces Chunky Italian**
8 ounces rotelle, cooked according to package directions

1. In a small bowl, combine the flour and spices. Add the chicken pieces and toss until well coated.

2. In a medium skillet, over medium-high heat, heat the oil, add the chicken, and brown on all sides.

3. Stir in the sauce and heat through.

4. Serve over the hot pasta.

The best dried pastas contain only coarsely ground durum wheat flour called semolina. Perfect pasta is cooked al dente, which, loosely translated, means "firm to the bite." It should never be mushy. Keep testing the pasta, and the moment it becomes flexible and tender—with no hard, uncooked center— remove it from the heat. Drain and toss with sauce immediately. If making pasta salad, rinse under cold water to stop the cooking.

Chicken with Garden Fettuccine

SERVES 6

1½ pounds skinless, boneless chicken breasts, sliced diagonally into thick strips
4 tablespoons olive oil, divided
1 jar (30 ounces) **Ragú® Chunky Gardenstyle Super Mushroom Pasta Sauce**
1½ cups fresh broccoli florets
1½ cups fresh cauliflower florets
1 cup ¾-inch pieces fresh asparagus
1 medium red *or* yellow bell pepper, sliced into thin strips
1 package (12 ounces) fettucine, cooked and drained
Grated Parmesan cheese

1. In a large skillet, lightly brown the chicken in 2 tablespoons olive oil. Drain. Add the pasta sauce. Cover and simmer 20 minutes.
2. In a large skillet, over medium heat, sauté the broccoli, cauliflower, asparagus, and bell pepper in 2 tablespoons olive oil until the vegetables are crisp-tender.
3. Spoon the chicken and sauce over the hot fettucine. Toss to coat well. Spoon the vegetables over the pasta. Sprinkle with the cheese and serve.

Easy Chicken and Pasta

SERVES 4

1 tablespoon vegetable oil
1 pound skinless, boneless chicken breasts, cut up
1 can (10¾ ounces) condensed cream of chicken soup
½ cup water
1 bag (about 16 ounces) frozen seasoned pasta and vegetable combination

1. Heat the oil in a large skillet over medium-high heat. Add the chicken and cook until browned, stirring often. Remove and set the chicken aside.
2. Stir in the soup and water. Mix in the vegetable combination. Heat to a boil.
3. Return the chicken to the skillet. Cover and cook over low heat for 5 minutes or until the chicken is done.
4. Transfer to a warm platter and serve.

Saucy Chicken and Pasta Dinner

SERVES 6

½ cup **Parkay® Spread,** divided
4 skinless, boneless chicken breast halves (about 1¼ pounds), cut into 1-inch pieces
½ teaspoon garlic powder
1 can (4 ounces) mushrooms, undrained
1 cup frozen peas, thawed (optional)
8 ounces wide noodles, cooked and drained
4 ounces **Kraft® Natural Shredded Cheddar Cheese**
Salt and pepper to taste

1. In a large skillet, over medium-high heat, melt ¼ cup spread. Add the chicken and garlic powder and cook, stirring occasionally, 4 minutes.
2. Stir in the remaining spread, mushrooms with liquid, and peas. Cook 2 minutes or until the chicken is cooked through.
3. Stir in the hot cooked noodles and cheese. Toss and cook until the cheese is melted. Season with the salt and pepper. Serve.

Chicken and Crisp Vegetable Toss

Chicken and Crisp Vegetable Toss

SERVES 6 TO 8

1 package (7 ounces) **Creamette® Elbow Macaroni**
  (2 cups uncooked)
½ cup olive *or* vegetable oil
2 tablespoons red wine vinegar
2 tablespoons fresh lemon juice
½ teaspoon dried tarragon
¼ teaspoon dry mustard
¼ teaspoon pepper
2 cups sliced mushrooms
1 cup frozen green peas, thawed and drained

1 cup sliced pitted ripe olives
1 small red bell pepper, cut into small julienne strips
⅓ cup sliced green onions
2 tablespoons chopped fresh parsley
2 cans (5 ounces *each*) **HORMEL® Chunk Chicken,**
  drained and flaked

1. Prepare the macaroni according to package directions and drain.

2. In a large skillet, heat the oil, vinegar, lemon juice, tarragon, dry mustard, and bell pepper. Add the macaroni and remaining ingredients and toss to coat. Heat through. Serve immediately.

Spaghetti with Lean Meatballs

SERVES 6

1 pound ground turkey
1 egg, lightly beaten
½ cup Italian seasoned bread crumbs
2 tablespoons minced fresh parsley
1 small clove garlic, minced (optional)
⅛ teaspoon pepper
1 tablespoon olive oil
1 jar (27½ ounces) **Ragú® Light Pasta Sauce— Tomato & Basil**
12 ounces spaghetti
Grated Parmesan cheese (optional)

1. In a large bowl, thoroughly combine the turkey, egg, bread crumbs, parsley, garlic, if using, and pepper. Shape into 1½-inch meatballs.

2. In a large nonstick skillet, over medium heat, brown the meatballs on all sides in olive oil. Drain.

3. Reduce the heat to low. Add the pasta sauce, cover, and simmer 30 minutes or until the meatballs are completely cooked.

4. Meanwhile, cook the pasta according to package directions and drain.

5. Ladle the sauce and meatballs over the hot spaghetti. Sprinkle with cheese, if desired, and serve.

Turkey Chili Over Pasta

SERVES 6

1 jar (16 ounces) picante sauce
1 can (15 ounces) **HORMEL® Turkey Chili No Beans**
1 onion, chopped
1 jar (4¼ ounces) diced green chilies
1 package (16 ounces) vermicelli *or* spaghetti
¼ cup chopped fresh cilantro

1. In a saucepan, over medium-low heat, combine the picante sauce, chili, onion, and green chilies.

2. Cook, stirring occasionally, 15 minutes.

3. Meanwhile, cook the pasta according to package directions.

4. Pour the sauce over the pasta. Sprinkle with the cilantro. Serve.

Bow Ties Niçoise

SERVES 4

8 ounces bow-tie pasta, cooked and drained
1 can (14½ ounces) **Del Monte® FreshCut™ Diced Tomatoes**
1 can (6 ounces) tuna, undrained
1 can (2 ounces) sliced black olives, drained
Parmesan cheese, grated or shaved

1. In a medium skillet or saucepan, over high heat, bring the tomatoes, tuna, and olives to a boil. Lower the heat and simmer 5 minutes.

2. Place the pasta in a serving bowl and pour the tuna sauce over the pasta. Sprinkle with the Parmesan cheese. Serve.

Spicy Shrimp Pasta

Spicy Shrimp Pasta

SERVES 3 TO 4

1 tablespoon olive oil
1 cup sliced onion
2 teaspoons minced garlic
1 pound large shrimp, shelled and deveined
1 can (15 ounces) **Hunt's® Ready Tomato Sauces Chunky Italian**
⅛ teaspoon red pepper flakes
8 ounces pasta, cooked according to package directions

1. In a large skillet, in hot oil, sauté the onion and minced garlic until tender.

2. Add the shrimp. Cook, stirring constantly, until the shrimp are pink and cooked through.

3. Stir in the remaining ingredients *except* pasta. Heat through.

4. Serve over the pasta.

Creamy Garlic Shrimp and Pasta

SERVES 2

4   slices bacon
8   ounces shrimp, shelled and deveined*
1   cup jarred sliced mushrooms
1   package **Lipton® Pasta & Sauce—Creamy Garlic**
1½ cups water
½   cup milk
½   cup frozen peas, partially thawed

1. In a 12-inch skillet, cook the bacon over medium-high heat until crisp. Remove and crumble. Reserve 2 tablespoons of the drippings.

2. Add the shrimp and mushrooms to the reserved drippings and cook over medium heat for 2 minutes, stirring until the shrimp are done. Remove and keep warm.

3. In the same skillet, stir in the pasta, water, and milk. Bring to the boiling point over high heat.

4. Reduce the heat to medium and cook 3 minutes.

5. Stir in the peas and cook, stirring occasionally, an additional 5 minutes or until the pasta is tender.

6. Stir in the bacon, shrimp, and mushrooms. Heat through.

7. Remove to warm plates and serve.

SUBSTITUTION

*Use 8 ounces frozen, cleaned shrimp, partially thawed, and increase the 2-minute cooking time to 4 minutes or until the shrimp are done. Continue as above.

Linguini with Red Clam Sauce

SERVES 4

8   ounces linguini, cooked and drained
1   can (6½ ounces) chopped clams
1   can (14½ ounces) **Del Monte® FreshCut™ Diced Tomatoes, Garlic & Onion**
Parmesan cheese, grated or shaved

1. Drain the clam juice from the clams. Set the clams aside.

2. In a medium skillet or saucepan, over high heat, bring the clam juice and tomatoes to a boil. Lower the heat and simmer 5 minutes. Add the clams and heat through.

3. Place the pasta in a serving bowl and pour the clam sauce over the pasta. Sprinkle with the Parmesan cheese. Serve.

Parmesan cheese adds a mellow, rich flavor to pasta. To enjoy this cheese at its best, use it freshly grated. When buying Parmesan, look for a wedge that is slightly moist and crumbly, aged at least 2 years, and pale golden beige in color.

Although Parmesan is made partly with skim milk, it is high in fat and sodium. One tablespoon has, on average, 2 grams of fat and 93 milligrams of sodium. Because of its intense flavor, however, a little goes a long way.

Ham, Peas, and Bow Ties

SERVES 6

1 package (16 ounces) bow-tie pasta *or* other pasta
2 tablespoons vegetable oil
1 medium onion, diced
2 cups sliced mushrooms
2 cloves garlic, minced
2 cups **Cure 81® ham,** cut into ½-inch cubes
1 package (10 ounces) frozen peas, thawed
½ cup chicken broth
2 tablespoons lemon juice
½ cup Parmesan cheese

1. Cook the pasta according to package directions. Drain and place in a large bowl.

2. In a large skillet, heat the oil over medium heat. Add the onion, mushrooms, and garlic and cook, stirring, until softened, about 3 minutes.

3. Stir in the ham, peas, chicken broth, and lemon juice. Over high heat, cook several minutes, stirring constantly, until half the liquid has evaporated.

4. Pour the ham mixture over the hot pasta. Add the Parmesan cheese and toss to mix thoroughly.

5. Serve with additional cheese, if desired.

Springtime Ravioli with Lemon Cream Sauce

SERVES 4

1 pound fresh asparagus, cut into 1½-inch pieces
1 package (16 ounces) frozen ravioli
½ cup milk
1 package (3 ounces) cream cheese
¼ cup (½ stick) butter
1 tablespoon freshly grated lemon zest
1 cup **Cure 81® ham,** diced
½ cup grated Parmesan cheese
⅛ teaspoon white pepper

1. Bring a large pot of water to a boil. Add the asparagus and blanch 2 to 3 minutes until crisp-tender. Remove the asparagus from the water with a slotted spoon and place in a colander. Rinse with cold water, drain, and set aside.

2. To the same pot of boiling water, add the ravioli and cook according to package directions.

3. Meanwhile, in a medium saucepan, combine the milk, cream cheese, butter, and lemon zest. Whisk over low heat until smooth and warm, 5 minutes. Stir in the ham, Parmesan cheese, and white pepper. Toss in the ravioli and asparagus.

4. Transfer to a warm serving bowl. Serve immediately.

---

*I*f cooked pasta is to sit for a few minutes after draining while you finish other preparations, toss it with a tablespoon of olive or vegetable oil to keep it from clumping. Leftover pasta that has stuck together can be separated by placing it in a colander and plunging it briefly into boiling water.

Spaghetti with Ham Primavera

SERVES 6

1 package (10 ounces) fresh spaghetti *or* 1 package (16 ounces) dry spaghetti
3 cups broccoli florets
3 tablespoons olive oil
2 cloves garlic, minced
2 cups mushrooms, sliced
1 red bell pepper, cut in chunks
6 ounces **Cure 81® ham,** cut into 1-inch pieces
1 tablespoon cornstarch
1 cup reduced-sodium chicken stock
1 cup grated Parmesan cheese
⅓ cup fresh basil *or* 2 teaspoons dried basil

1. Add the spaghetti to a large pot of boiling water. Cook until tender, 3 to 5 minutes for fresh, 8 to 10 minutes for dry. Drain.
2. Meanwhile, in a smaller saucepan, steam the broccoli until just crisp-tender, about 5 minutes. Drain and set aside.
3. In a nonstick skillet, heat the olive oil over medium heat. Sauté the garlic, mushrooms, and bell pepper until tender. Add the ham and sauté 2 minutes more. Set aside.
4. In a small saucepan, over medium heat, combine the cornstarch and chicken stock. Mix until the cornstarch dissolves.
5. Reduce the heat, stirring constantly until thickened.
6. In a large serving bowl, pour the sauce over the hot pasta. Add the broccoli, vegetable-ham mixture, Parmesan cheese, and basil. Toss to combine thoroughly. Serve.

Peppy Garlic Pasta

SERVES 4

¼ cup olive oil
1 cup **HORMEL® pepperoni** *or* **turkey pepperoni (slices),** cut in half
6 large garlic cloves, very thinly sliced
8 ounces penne *or* other pasta, cooked and drained
¼ cup chopped fresh parsley
¼ cup grated Parmesan cheese

1. In a large skillet, over medium heat, cook the olive oil and pepperoni for several minutes until the pepperoni is crisp.
2. Stir in the garlic and cook until golden.
3. Add the pasta, parsley, and Parmesan cheese. Toss to combine the ingredients and to coat the pasta. Serve with additional Parmesan cheese, if desired.

Peppy Pesto Alfredo

SERVES 4

1 cup **HORMEL® pepperoni (slices),** cut in half
½ cup prepared pesto sauce
¼ cup heavy cream
8 ounces fettuccine, cooked and drained
Parmesan cheese, grated or shaved

1. In a large skillet, over medium heat, cook the pepperoni for several minutes until crisp.
2. In a small bowl, mix together the pesto sauce and cream. Stir into the pepperoni and bring the mixture to a boil. Remove from the heat.
3. Add the fettuccine to the pan and toss to evenly coat the pasta. Serve with the Parmesan cheese.

Peppy Pepper Pasta

SERVES 6

¼ cup olive oil

3 to 4 ounces **HORMEL® pepperoni (slices),** cut in half

2 green bell peppers, cored and cut into ¼-inch strips

2 red bell peppers, cored and cut into ¼-inch strips

1 medium onion, thinly sliced

3 cloves garlic, minced

1 package (16 ounces) linguini, cooked according to package directions

1. In a large skillet, heat the oil over medium heat. Add the pepperoni, bell peppers, and onion. Cook, stirring, until the vegetables are softened, 4 minutes. Stir in the garlic and remove from the heat.

2. Drain the linguini and add to the mixture in the skillet and toss to coat evenly. Serve.

Peppy Penne with Tomato Sauce

SERVES 6

1 tablespoon olive oil

3 to 4 ounces **HORMEL® pepperoni (slices),** cut in half

1 small onion, diced

2 cloves garlic, minced

1 can (15 ounces) tomato sauce

½ cup heavy cream

1 package (16 ounces) penne, cooked according to package directions

1. In a large skillet, heat the oil over medium heat. Add the pepperoni and onion. Cook, stirring, until the onion is softened, 3 minutes. Stir in the garlic.

2. Stir in the tomato sauce and boil 1 minute. Add the cream, mixing thoroughly until the cream begins to boil, 1 minute.

3. Drain the penne and add to the sauce in the skillet. Toss to coat evenly. Serve.

❖

The word pesto comes from the Italian pestare, meaning "to make a paste." The rich, garlicky version made with basil is traditionally served with linguine or spaghetti. But pesto is not just for pasta. It can be a dip for raw vegetables or a sauce for cooked fish or seafood. Brush some on a toasted slice of French bread for an instant appetizer. Spread it over chicken before roasting or on top of broiled pork chops. Toss steamed green beans or thinly sliced summer squash with pesto. Stir a tablespoon or two into an omelet or scrambled eggs. Ready-prepared pesto is available in most supermarkets. It can be frozen up to 3 months, so you can keep some on hand for quick meals.

Penne with Mushrooms and Sausage

SERVES 4

1 tablespoon olive oil
4 links sweet Italian sausage, sliced into ½-inch pieces
2 cloves garlic, minced
2 cups sliced mushrooms
1 can (14½ ounces) **Del Monte® FreshCut™ Diced Tomatoes**
8 ounces penne

1. In a large nonstick skillet, heat the oil over medium-low heat. Add the sausage pieces and garlic. Cook until the sausage begins to brown, about 5 minutes. Drain off excess fat.
2. Stir in the mushrooms and cook 3 minutes.
3. Stir in the tomatoes, reduce the heat to low, and cook, partially covered, 20 minutes.
4. Cook the pasta and drain.
5. Return the pasta to the pot, add the sauce, mix together, and serve.

Sausage Pasta

SERVES 6

1 package (16 ounces) linguini, cooked
1 package (16 ounces) **Hillshire Farm® Smoked Sausage,** any variety
4 green *or* red bell peppers, cut into strips
3 ounces black olives, chopped
4 to 5 large carrots, peeled and sliced into 2-inch julienne sticks
10 ounces frozen peas
½ cup Italian dressing *or* to taste
Garlic and oregano to taste

1. Prepare the linguini according to package directions.
2. Meanwhile, in a large skillet, over medium-high heat, brown the sausage for 3 minutes.
3. Add the peppers, olives, carrots, and peas, stirring often. Cook until the carrots are crisp-tender, approximately 10 minutes.
4. Transfer the pasta and skillet contents into a large serving bowl. Toss well, adding the dressing and herbs.
5. Serve hot or cold.

❖

Garlic has been in use for more than 5,000 years. When buying garlic, choose firm bulbs with unbroken skins. Avoid soft, shriveled, or sprouting garlic bulbs, which will have a bitter flavor. Store it in a cool, dry place, or refrigerate it in a tightly sealed glass container. When sautéing garlic, cook it briefly until soft and translucent and be careful not to scorch it. In soups, stews, and sauces, it can be simmered for hours and will gradually become more mellow.

Cream Cheese Pasta Bake

SERVES 6

4 links sweet Italian sausage, cut in ½-inch slices
8 ounces large pasta shells *or* penne
3 tablespoons butter, divided
1 small onion, chopped
8 ounces mushrooms, wiped clean and thickly sliced
2 cups cooked broccoli florets
1 package (8 ounces) **Cream Cheese**
4 tablespoons sour cream
1 container (8 ounces) cottage cheese
1 cup shredded mozzarella, divided
Salt and freshly ground pepper to taste

1. In a large skillet, cook the sausage, partially covered, over medium-low heat until lightly browned. Remove and drain on paper towels.
2. Cook the pasta according to package directions. Do not overcook. Drain and toss with 1 tablespoon butter to keep from sticking.
3. Heat the oven to 350° F.
4. Wipe out the skillet and add the remaining butter, onion, and mushrooms. Sauté until golden. Remove from the heat, add the broccoli, and gently toss.
5. In a large bowl, beat the cream cheese with the sour cream. Stir in the cottage cheese. Add the pasta, vegetables, sausage, half the mozzarella, salt, and pepper. Gently toss to mix. Spoon into a 3-quart casserole. Sprinkle the remaining mozzarella over the top.
6. Bake 30 minutes or until hot and bubbling.
7. Transfer to warm plates and serve.

COURTESY: DAIRY MANAGEMENT, INC.

Pasta Carbonara

SERVES 4

1 can (10½ ounces) **Healthy Choice® Recipe Creations™ Cream of Roasted Garlic Condensed Soup**
½ cup nonfat milk
1 cup frozen peas, thawed and drained
1 cup frozen diced *or* sliced carrots, thawed and drained
1 cup sliced mushrooms
½ cup chopped onion
4 strips bacon, cooked until crisp, drained, and crumbled
½ teaspoon salt (optional)
8 ounces pasta cooked according to package directions, drained

1. In a small bowl, combine the soup and milk and mix well. Set aside.
2. In a large nonstick skillet sprayed with nonstick cooking spray, sauté the peas, carrots, mushrooms, and onion over medium heat until tender. Add the bacon, soup mixture, and salt. Mix well.
3. Reduce the heat, cover, and simmer 5 minutes or until heated through.
4. Spoon the sauce over the hot pasta and serve.

To freeze freshly minced herbs for use later, place 1 tablespoon in each compartment of an ice cube tray, then add 3 to 4 tablespoons of water and freeze. Pop the frozen cubes into a plastic bag for storage in the freezer and add a label with the date. Frozen herbs will keep about 6 months.

Spaghetti with Bacon, Tomatoes, and Peas

SERVES 4

4 ounces bacon, diced
1 can (14½ ounces) **Del Monte® FreshCut™ Diced Tomatoes, Garlic & Onion**
1 can (8½ ounces) **Del Monte® FreshCut™ Very Young Sweet Peas,** drained
8 ounces spaghetti, cooked and drained
Parmesan cheese, grated or shaved

1. In a medium skillet, over medium heat, cook the diced bacon until crisp. Remove the bacon from the skillet and set aside. Pour the bacon grease from the skillet but do not wash the skillet.
2. Add the tomatoes and peas to the hot skillet and bring to a boil. Lower the heat and simmer 5 minutes.
3. Place the pasta in a serving bowl and pour the sauce over the pasta. Top with the bacon and sprinkle with the Parmesan cheese. Serve.

Guilt-Free Fettuccine

SERVES 6

1 can (14½ ounces) chicken broth
¼ cup all-purpose flour
¼ teaspoon garlic powder
¼ teaspoon pepper
⅓ cup plain yogurt
12 ounces fettuccine, cooked and drained
6 tablespoons grated Parmesan cheese, divided
3 tablespoons chopped fresh parsley

1. In a medium saucepan, gradually mix the broth into the flour, garlic powder, and pepper until smooth. Over medium heat, cook until the mixture boils and thickens, stirring constantly.
2. Remove from the heat. Stir in the yogurt.
3. Pour over and toss with the hot pasta and 4 tablespoons cheese. Sprinkle with the parsley and remaining cheese. Serve.

Fresh Lemon Herbed Pasta

SERVES 4

8 ounces fettuccine *or* other pasta
Juice of 1 medium **Sunkist® Lemon**
2 quarts water
1 large clove garlic, minced
¼ cup chopped fresh basil *or* 2 teaspoons dried basil
2 tablespoons margarine *or* butter
2 tablespoons olive *or* vegetable oil
Grated zest *and* juice of ½ medium **Sunkist® Lemon**
¼ cup chopped fresh parsley
⅔ cup grated Parmesan cheese
Freshly ground pepper to taste

1. Cook the pasta in the juice of 1 lemon and boiling water for 8 to 10 minutes or until tender. Drain well while retaining ¼ cup pasta cooking water.
2. Meanwhile, in a large deep skillet, over medium heat, sauté the garlic with the basil in the butter and oil for 2 to 3 minutes. Stir in the lemon zest and juice.
3. Reduce the heat. Add the pasta with the remaining ¼ cup pasta cooking water, parsley, and ⅓ cup Parmesan cheese. Toss well.
4. Sprinkle with the remaining cheese. Pepper to taste and serve.

Asparagus Fettucine

SERVES 4

1 tablespoon vegetable oil
12 ounces fresh asparagus spears (12 to 15), trimmed and cut into 1-inch pieces (about 1½ cups) *or* 1 package (10 ounces) frozen asparagus cuts, thawed and drained
1 medium red bell pepper, cut into 1-inch-long strips (about 1 cup)
2 cloves garlic, minced
1 can (10¾ ounces) condensed cream of asparagus soup
¾ cup milk
⅓ cup grated Parmesan cheese
⅛ teaspoon pepper
8 ounces fettuccine, cooked according to package directions

1. In a 2-quart saucepan, over medium heat, in hot oil, cook the fresh asparagus (if using frozen asparagus, add with the soup in step 2), bell pepper, and garlic for 3 minutes, stirring constantly. Do not let the garlic brown.
2. Stir in the soup (frozen asparagus, if using), milk, cheese, and pepper. Heat to boiling. Reduce the heat to low. Cover and cook 10 minutes or until the vegetables are tender, stirring often.
3. Serve over the warm fettuccine. Toss to coat. Serve with additional cheese, if desired.

Pasta Primavera

SERVES 4 TO 6

1 cup thinly sliced carrots
1 large clove garlic, minced
¼ cup olive oil
1 can (14½ ounces) **Del Monte® Original Style Stewed Tomatoes**
2 cups sliced mushrooms
2 tablespoons cornstarch
2 teaspoons crushed dried basil
½ teaspoon crushed dried oregano
1 can (14½ ounces) **Del Monte® Blue Lake Cut Green Beans**, drained
8 ounces rigatoni, cooked and drained
¼ cup grated Parmesan cheese
1 tablespoon chopped fresh parsley (optional)

1. In a large skillet, sauté the carrots and garlic in the olive oil over medium-low heat until the carrots are crisp-tender, about 5 minutes.
2. Stir in the tomatoes, mushrooms, cornstarch, and herbs. Cook, stirring constantly, until thickened and translucent. Add the green beans and heat through.
3. Add the pasta to the skillet and toss with the cheese. Garnish with chopped parsley, if desired, and serve.

Pasta Primavera

Creamy Pasta Verde

Creamy Pasta Verde

SERVES 4 TO 6

8 ounces fettucine
1 cup grated Romano cheese
1 cup shredded Monterey Jack cheese
1 carton (4 ounces) frozen pesto, thawed
2 cups sour cream
1 can (14½ ounces) **Del Monte® Blue Lake
    Cut Green Beans**, drained
1 can (15½ ounces) **Del Monte® Sweet Peas**, drained
Chopped fresh parsley (optional)

1. Cook the pasta according to package directions and drain.

2. Return the pasta to the pan. Toss with the cheeses and pesto. Heat gently until the cheeses are melted.

3. Fold in the sour cream and heat through.

4. Add the vegetables. Gently mix and heat thoroughly. Garnish with chopped parsley, if desired. Serve.

The most common variety of imported Romano is pecorino Romano, which is made with sheep's milk. Similar to Parmesan, its flavor is sharper and tangier, and can be substituted for Parmesan, if desired. When selecting a wedge of Romano or Parmesan, make sure the color is even throughout and that there are no cracks, which are sure signs that the cheese is dry.

Spring Vegetable Pasta with Cheeses

SERVES 6

1 large clove garlic, minced
1½ cups fresh broccoli florets
2 tablespoons olive oil
12 ounces fresh asparagus, cut into 1½-inch lengths
1 red bell pepper, diced
1 yellow bell pepper, diced
1 package (9 ounces) frozen snow peas, thawed
1 jar (27½ ounces) **Ragú® Light Pasta Sauce—Chunky Mushroom**
12 ounces long fusilli, cooked and drained
½ cup shredded fontina cheese
¼ cup grated Romano cheese

1. In a large skillet, sauté the garlic and broccoli in the olive oil about 3 minutes. Add the asparagus, red and yellow peppers, and snow peas. Sauté lightly or until the vegetables are crisp-tender. Do not overcook.

2. In a medium saucepan, heat the sauce through.

3. In a large pasta bowl, spoon the sauce over the hot pasta. Sprinkle with the cheeses. Toss to coat well. Top with the sautéed vegetables. Serve immediately.

Fresh Tomato-Basil Pasta Toss

SERVES 4

1 tablespoon **Mazola Right Blend®**
3 cloves garlic, minced
1½ pounds plum tomatoes, coarsely chopped
2 cups loosely packed fresh basil, chopped
2 tablespoons red wine vinegar
½ teaspoon salt
⅛ teaspoon crushed red pepper (optional)
8 ounces linguine, cooked and drained
¼ cup grated Parmesan cheese
Freshly ground pepper, to taste

1. In a large skillet, heat the oil over medium-high heat. Add the garlic and cook, stirring, 1 minute. Stir in the tomatoes and bring to a boil.

2. Reduce the heat, cover, and simmer 5 minutes, stirring occasionally, or until the sauce thickens slightly.

3. Stir in the basil, vinegar, salt, and crushed red pepper. Spoon over the linguine. Sprinkle with the cheese and pepper. Serve.

*I*f you have a microwave oven, you can reheat cooked pasta in minutes. Cook the pasta according to package directions. Drain the cooked pasta and immediately rinse it in cold water to stop the cooking. Drain it again and toss it gently with a little olive oil. Place it in an airtight container and refrigerate it up to 2 days. To reheat the pasta, place it in a microwave-safe covered dish and microwave on high for about 1 minute, stopping halfway through to stir. If the pasta is not hot, continue cooking and testing it at 15-second intervals.

Three-Generations Herbed Spinach Pasta

Three-Generations Herbed Spinach Pasta

SERVES 4

2 cups penne
½ medium onion, sliced
1 clove garlic, minced
¾ teaspoon dried basil, crumbled
1 tablespoon olive oil
1 medium red, yellow, *or* green bell pepper, cut in strips
1 can (13½ ounces) **Del Monte® FreshCut™ Whole Leaf Spinach**, drained
Grated Parmesan cheese (optional)

1. Cook the pasta according to package directions. Drain and keep warm.

2. In a medium skillet, over medium-low heat, cook the onion, garlic, and basil in the oil until the onion is tender.

3. Add the bell pepper strips and cook 3 minutes. Stir in the spinach and heat through. Toss with the pasta.

4. Sprinkle with Parmesan cheese, if desired, and serve.

Penne with Asparagus and Red Peppers

SERVES 4

8 ounces penne
1 tablespoon olive oil
1 red bell pepper, seeded and cut into thin strips
2 cloves garlic, minced
½ cup evaporated skim milk
1 can (12 ounces) **Del Monte® FreshCut™ Slender Whole Asparagus Spears,** drained
¼ cup grated Parmesan cheese (optional)

1. In a large pot, cook the pasta according to package directions.
2. In a large nonstick skillet, heat the oil over medium-high heat. Add the bell pepper and stir-fry until tender, about 4 minutes. Stir in the garlic.
3. Add the milk and cook to reduce the volume by half, about 2 minutes.
4. Cut the asparagus spears into thirds and add to the skillet. Drain the pasta and gently stir into the vegetable mixture to coat.
5. Sprinkle with cheese, if desired. Serve.

Tuscan-Style Fettuccine with Artichokes

SERVES 6

1 package (16 ounces) fettuccine
½ cup (1 stick) **I Can't Believe It's Not Butter!®**
1 can (14 ounces) artichoke hearts, drained and chopped
⅓ cup chopped fresh cilantro
2 tablespoons chopped fresh oregano *or* 1 tablespoon dried oregano
2 tablespoons minced garlic
½ teaspoon pepper
2 to 3 cups freshly grated Parmesan cheese

1. Cook the fettuccine according to package directions and drain. Keep warm and set aside.
2. In a large skillet, over medium-high heat, melt I Can't Believe It's Not Butter!®
3. Add the artichokes, cilantro, oregano, garlic, and pepper.
4. Cook, stirring, several minutes until the ingredients are combined and the mixture is hot. Pour over the warm pasta and toss to coat evenly.
5. Divide onto hot plates, sprinkle generously with the Parmesan cheese, and serve.

Fresh herbs greatly enhance pasta dishes. Most supermarkets carry fresh parsley year round and other herbs in season. To store herbs, rinse and spin or pat them dry. Wrap loosely in paper towels, seal in a plastic food bag, and store in the refrigerator. Or immerse their stems in 2 to 3 inches of water in a jar and cover the bouquet loosely with a plastic bag. To snip fresh herbs, gather them into a small tight bunch. Cut crosswise every ⅛ inch with kitchen scissors.

Confetti Vegetable Pasta

1 jar (28 ounces) **Ragú® Spaghetti Sauce**
1 clove garlic, minced
2 tablespoons olive oil
1 cup chopped fresh broccoli
1 cup shredded carrots
1 small red bell pepper, diced
1 small zucchini, diced
1 small yellow squash, diced
12 ounces twist or ruffle pasta, cooked and drained
1 tablespoon garlic-herb cheese spread
2 tablespoons shredded Parmesan cheese
1 tablespoon chopped fresh parsley

1. In a medium saucepan, thoroughly heat the sauce and set aside.

2. In a large nonstick skillet, over medium heat, sauté the garlic in the olive oil. Add the vegetables. Sauté, stirring frequently, about 5 minutes or until the vegetables are crisp-tender.

3. Toss the hot pasta with the garlic-herb and Parmesan cheeses. Spoon the heated sauce over the pasta. Toss to coat well. Top the pasta with the sautéed vegetables. Sprinkle with parsley and serve.

Three-Cheese Macaroni

3 cups macaroni, cooked in unsalted water and drained
1 can (11 ounces) condensed Cheddar cheese soup
1 cup milk
½ teaspoon **Durkee® Ground Mustard**
¼ teaspoon **Durkee® Seasoned Salt** (optional)
¼ teaspoon **Durkee® Ground Black Pepper**
½ cup shredded Swiss cheese, divided (2 ounces)
½ cup shredded Cheddar cheese, divided (2 ounces)
½ cup grated Parmesan cheese, divided (2 ounces)
1 can (4½ ounces) **French's® French Fried Onions,** divided

1. Heat the oven to 350° F.

2. In a 1½-quart casserole, combine the hot macaroni, soup, milk, seasonings, ¼ cup *each* Swiss, Cheddar, and Parmesan cheeses, and half the can french fried onions.

3. Bake, covered, 25 minutes or until heated through.

4. Top with the remaining cheeses and french fried onions. Bake, uncovered, 5 minutes or until the onions are golden brown.

5. Transfer to warm plates and serve.

O live oil comes in several "grades" that indicate the acidity of the oil—superfine, fine, and virgin or pure. Superfine olive oil has the lowest level of acidity. The low acidity and fruity flavor of both superfine and fine olive oils make them ideal for salad dressing or use as a condiment. Virgin olive oil is excellent for cooking. Even small amounts of olive oil will add a characteristic flavor to food, so use it sparingly. Like all oils, olive oil will eventually turn rancid. It's best to buy in quantities you can use up within a few weeks.

Garden Harvest Pasta Shells

SERVES 6

2 tablespoons vegetable oil
2 cups chopped fresh broccoli
2 medium zucchini, shredded
1 cup chopped mushrooms
1 small onion, chopped
½ cup finely chopped carrots
Pinch ground nutmeg
Salt and pepper to taste
1 pound part-skim ricotta cheese
2 cups shredded part-skim mozzarella cheese (8 ounces)
1 egg, lightly beaten
¼ cup grated Parmesan cheese
3 tablespoons chopped fresh basil *or* 1 tablespoon dried basil
1 jar (27½ ounces) **Ragú® Light Pasta Sauce—Chunky Garden Combination**, divided
1 package (12 ounces) jumbo pasta shells, cooked and drained

1. Heat the oven to 350° F.

2. In a large skillet, heat the oil. Sauté the broccoli, zucchini, mushrooms, onion, and carrots, uncovered, until tender. Season with the nutmeg, salt, and pepper and set aside.

3. In a large bowl, thoroughly combine the ricotta cheese, mozzarella cheese, egg, Parmesan cheese, and basil.

4. Add the vegetables and stir to mix well.

5. Spoon 1 cup pasta sauce evenly in a 13×9-inch baking dish. Fill the shells with the vegetable-cheese mixture. Arrange in the baking dish. Spoon the remaining sauce over the shells.

6. Bake, covered, 45 minutes. Uncover and bake 10 minutes or until bubbly.

7. Transfer to warm plates and serve.

Cheddary Pasta and Vegetables

SERVES 5

1½ cups dry corkscrew pasta
2 medium carrots, sliced
1 cup broccoli florets
1 large red *or* green bell pepper, chopped (optional)
1 can (10¾ ounces) condensed cream of celery soup
½ cup shredded Cheddar cheese
½ cup milk
1 tablespoon prepared mustard

1. In a 4-quart saucepan, prepare the pasta according to package directions. Add the carrots, broccoli, and bell pepper for the last 5 minutes of cooking time. Drain the pasta and vegetables.

2. In the same saucepan, combine the soup, cheese, milk, and mustard. Cook over low heat until the cheese melts, stirring often.

3. Add the pasta and vegetables. Heat through, stirring often.

4. Transfer to a warm large bowl and serve.

Basil, an herb with a minty flavor and clove-like aroma, enlivens tomato-based Italian-style sauces, and dishes made with mozzarella. Fresh basil turns black in the refrigerator. Stand it in a glass of water on the countertop, or strip off the leaves and put them in a jar, cover with olive oil, and store in the refrigerator. They keep up to 6 months. You can use the oil as well as the leaves to flavor soups, stews, and sauces.

Pasta with White Beans, Carrots, and Pesto

SERVES 4

1 cup dried white beans
2 cups vegetable *or* chicken stock
2 cups cold water
2 large carrots, diced
1 bay leaf
8 ounces penne *or* ziti
4 tablespoons pesto sauce
⅛ teaspoon salt
⅛ teaspoon pepper

1. In a large bowl, place the white beans and cover with cold water. Cover the bowl and allow to stand 8 hours. Drain the beans.
2. In a large saucepan, bring the stock and cold water to a boil. Add the carrots, reduce the heat, and simmer until tender. Remove the carrots and set aside.
3. Return the stock and water to a boil. Add the beans and bay leaf. Return to a boil and reduce the heat to low. Cover and simmer 45 minutes to 1 hour until the beans are tender. Discard the bay leaf.
4. Cook the pasta according to package directions and drain.
5. In a large bowl, toss the beans and carrots with the pasta. Toss with the pesto to coat and season with the salt and pepper. Serve.

Pasta and Beans

SERVES 8

1 cup chopped celery
1 small onion, chopped
3 large cloves garlic, minced
1 cup diced ham *or* Canadian bacon
1 can (19 ounces) white kidney beans, drained
1 can (13¾ ounces) reduced-sodium chicken broth
1 jar (27½ ounces) **Ragú® Light Pasta Sauce—Chunky Garden Combination**
⅛ teaspoon crushed red pepper flakes
8 ounces ditalini or elbow macaroni
2 tablespoons minced fresh parsley
Grated Parmesan cheese

1. In a large Dutch oven, over low heat, sauté the celery, onion, and garlic in the olive oil until the vegetables are tender, about 5 minutes. Add the ham and sauté lightly. Add the beans, chicken broth, pasta sauce, and crushed red pepper flakes.
2. Bring to a boil. Reduce the heat to low and simmer 15 minutes.
3. Meanwhile, cook the pasta according to package directions and drain. Add it with the parsley to the sauce. Heat through.
4. Transfer to warm plates and serve with Parmesan cheese.

Penne with Tomatoes and Artichokes

SERVES 4

8 ounces penne, cooked and drained
1 can (14½ ounces) **Del Monte® FreshCut™ Diced Tomatoes, Basil, Garlic & Oregano**
1 jar (6 ounces) marinated artichoke hearts, diced
Parmesan cheese, grated or shaved

1. In a medium saucepan or skillet, over high heat, bring the tomatoes and artichokes, including their marinade, to a boil. Lower the heat and simmer 5 minutes.
2. Place the pasta in a serving bowl and pour the artichoke sauce over the pasta. Sprinkle with the Parmesan cheese. Serve.

Canned beans are convenient to use, but they are often high in salt. You can eliminate about half the salt by draining and rinsing the beans.

You can speed the preparation time when cooking dried beans, which includes a soaking period of at least 8 hours, by doing a quick soak. In a large saucepan or Dutch oven, cover the beans with 2 to 3 inches of cold water. (Some beans require rinsing and picking over before cooking. Check the package instructions.) Bring the water to a boil and cook for 2 minutes, then turn off the heat and let the beans stand for 1 hour. Drain and cover them with fresh water before cooking.

Pasta and Bean Gratin

SERVES 6

8 ounces pasta ruffles
3 cloves garlic, minced
1 small onion, finely chopped
2 tablespoons olive oil
2 tablespoons minced fresh basil
2 tablespoons minced fresh parsley
Salt and pepper to taste
1 can (15 ounces) white kidney beans, drained
1 jar (30 ounces) **Ragú® Light Pasta Sauce—Chunky Mushroom** *or* **Chunky Garden Combination**
¼ cup grated Parmesan cheese
1 cup part-skim ricotta cheese
½ cup bread crumbs

1. Cook the pasta ruffles according to package directions. Drain and set aside.
2. In a large skillet, sauté the garlic and onion in olive oil until soft. Add the seasonings and beans and sauté lightly.
3. In a large bowl, thoroughly combine the pasta sauce, pasta, and Parmesan cheese with the bean mixture. Pour into an 11x7-inch baking dish. Drop the ricotta cheese by the spoonful onto the pasta mixture. Sprinkle with the bread crumbs.
4. Heat the oven to 350° F. Bake 30 minutes or until bubbly.
5. Transfer to warm plates and serve.

Shells Florentine

SERVES 8

2 tablespoons **Fleischmann's® Original Spread**
1 cup coarsely chopped mushrooms (about 4 ounces)
½ cup chopped onion
1 clove garlic, minced
1 teaspoon dried Italian seasoning
¼ teaspoon ground pepper
1 container (16 ounces) low-sodium, low-fat cottage cheese (1% milk fat)
1 package (10 ounces) frozen chopped spinach, thawed, and well drained
½ cup **Egg Beaters® Healthy Real Egg Substitute**
24 jumbo shell macaroni, cooked in unsalted water and drained
1 jar (15¼ ounces) spaghetti sauce, divided

1. Heat the oven to 350° F.

2. In a skillet, over medium-high heat, melt the margarine. Add the mushrooms, onion, garlic, Italian seasoning, and pepper. Cook until tender, about 4 minutes.

3. Remove from the heat. Stir in the cottage cheese, spinach, and Egg Beaters® and mix well. Spoon the mixture into the shells.

4. Spread ½ cup spaghetti sauce in the bottom of a 13×9-inch baking dish. Arrange the shells over the sauce. Top with the remaining sauce and cover. Bake 35 minutes or until hot.

5. Transfer to warm plates and serve.

Vegetable Garden Manicotti

SERVES 7

1 container (16 ounces) nonfat cottage cheese
1 package (10 ounces) frozen chopped spinach, thawed and squeezed dry
2 cups **Healthy Choice® Fat Free Natural Shredded Mozzarella Cheese,** divided
1 cup shredded carrot
1 cup shredded zucchini
¼ cup cholesterol-free egg product
¼ teaspoon garlic powder
⅛ teaspoon pepper
1 package (8 ounces) manicotti shells, cooked and drained
1 jar (26 ounces) **Healthy Choice® Pasta Sauce**
2 tablespoons grated Parmesan cheese

1. In a medium bowl, combine the cottage cheese, spinach, 1 cup mozzarella cheese, carrot, zucchini, egg product, garlic powder, and pepper.

2. Heat the oven to 350° F.

3. Spoon the mixture into the manicotti shells, using a scant ⅓ cup per shell.

4. Cover the bottom of a greased 13×9-inch baking dish with half the pasta sauce. Place the filled manicotti shells in a single layer.

5. Pour the remaining pasta sauce over the shells and sprinkle with the remaining mozzarella and Parmesan cheeses.

6. Bake, covered, 30 to 40 minutes or until hot and bubbly. Remove the cover during the last 10 minutes of baking.

7. Transfer to warm plates and serve.

Baked Ziti with Peppers

Baked Ziti with Peppers

SERVES 8

8 ounces extra lean ground beef
3 cups green, red, *and* yellow bell pepper strips
1 cup sliced onion
1 jar (26 ounces) pasta sauce
¼ cup grated Parmesan cheese (divided)
1 teaspoon dried oregano
2 cups **Healthy Choice® Fat Free Natural Shredded Mozzarella Cheese,** divided
3 cups cooked ziti *or* mostaccioli

1. Heat the oven to 375° F.

2. In a large saucepan sprayed with nonstick cooking spray, brown the ground beef with the bell peppers and onions until the meat is browned and the peppers begin to soften. Drain.

3. Return the pepper mixture to the saucepan and stir in the pasta sauce, 2 tablespoons Parmesan cheese, oregano, 1 cup mozzarella, and pasta. Spoon into a 13x9-inch baking dish. Sprinkle with the remaining mozzarella and Parmesan cheese.

4. Bake, uncovered, 30 minutes or until hot and bubbly. Serve.

Side Dishes

Asparagus with Orange and Pecans

SERVES 8

2½ pounds fresh asparagus spears, trimmed
¼ cup (½ stick) **LAND O LAKES® Butter**
⅓ cup pecan halves
1 teaspoon grated orange zest
1 teaspoon orange juice

1. In a 10-inch skillet, place the asparagus spears and add enough water to cover. Bring to a boil.
2. Cook over medium heat until the asparagus is crisp-tender, 5 to 7 minutes. Drain and set aside.
3. In the same skillet, melt the butter and add the pecans.
4. Cook over medium heat, until the pecans are toasted, 1 to 2 minutes. Stir in the orange zest and juice. Spoon over the cooked asparagus and serve.

Asparagus with Mustard-Dill Dressing

SERVES 4

1 pound asparagus spears, trimmed
2 tablespoons olive oil
1 tablespoon white wine vinegar
1 teaspoon Dijon mustard
1 clove garlic, minced
Pinch *each* sugar, dill, and pepper

1. In a medium saucepan, cook the asparagus in simmering water for 3 to 5 minutes until tender. Drain and rinse in cool water to retain color and drain again. Arrange on a serving plate.
2. In a small bowl, whisk together the remaining ingredients.
3. Drizzle over the asparagus and serve.

COURTESY: NATIONAL PORK PRODUCERS COUNCIL

Creamy Vegetable Medley

SERVES 6
MAKES ABOUT 3 CUPS

1 tablespoon vegetable oil
12 ounces fresh asparagus spears (about 12 to 15), trimmed and cut into 1-inch pieces (about 1½ cups) *or* 1 package (10 ounces) frozen asparagus cuts
2 medium carrots, thinly sliced (about 1 cup)
¼ teaspoon dried basil, crushed
1 cup sliced mushrooms (about 4 ounces)
1 can (10¾ ounces) condensed cream of asparagus soup
2 tablespoons milk

1. In a 3-quart saucepan, over medium heat, in hot oil, cook the asparagus and carrots with the basil until crisp-tender, stirring often.
2. Add the mushrooms and cook until the liquid is evaporated, stirring often.
3. Add the soup and milk. Heat through, stirring occasionally.
4. Transfer to a large bowl and serve.

The most common variety of asparagus is green; however, white and purple varieties exist. Choose firm stalks with closed tips. If you don't plan to use the asparagus on the day you buy it, cut a slice off the bottom of each stalk. Place the bunch, stem ends down, in an inch of water in a tall, quart-size glass or plastic container, cover loosely with a plastic bag, and refrigerate.

Colorful Vegetable Sauté

SERVES 4 TO 6

1 tablespoon olive *or* vegetable oil
1 cup sliced celery *or* red bell pepper
1 can (14½ ounces) **Del Monte® FreshCut™ Green Beans**, drained
1 can (8¼ ounces) **Del Monte® FreshCut™ Sliced Carrots**, drained

1. Heat the oil in a medium skillet over medium heat.

2. Cook the celery until crisp-tender.

3. Add the beans and carrots and heat through.

4. Transfer to a large warm bowl and serve.

Parsley Ginger Carrots

SERVES 4

1 pound young carrots, trimmed and peeled
1 cup water
2 tablespoons **I Can't Believe It's Not Butter!®**, melted
1 teaspoon sugar
½ teaspoon ground ginger
1 tablespoon flat leaf parsley, minced
1 tablespoon lemon juice

1. Cut the carrots lengthwise into quarters, then into 1-inch pieces.

2. In a small saucepan, cook the carrots in water until crisp-tender. Drain.

3. In a small skillet, combine I Can't Believe It's Not Butter!®, sugar, ginger, parsley, and lemon juice. Add the carrots, tossing well to coat.

4. Cook over low heat for 3 to 4 minutes.

5. Toss again and serve.

Carrots Elegante

SERVES 4

1 pound carrots, trimmed, peeled, and thinly sliced
¼ cup golden raisins
¼ cup (½ stick) **I Can't Believe It's Not Butter!®**
3 tablespoons honey
1 tablespoon lemon juice
¼ teaspoon ground ginger
¼ cup sliced, unpeeled almonds

1. Heat the oven to 375° F. Cook the carrots, covered, in ½ inch boiling water for 8 minutes. Drain.

2. Place the carrots in a 1-quart baking dish. Stir in the raisins, I Can't Believe It's Not Butter!®, honey, lemon juice, and ginger.

3. Bake, uncovered, 35 minutes, stirring occasionally.

4. Sprinkle with the almonds before serving.

Carrots have enjoyed a reputation as a healthy food for centuries. Beta carotene, which gives carrots their deep orange color, converts in the body to vitamin A and is thought to reduce the risk of some cancers. While some vegetables are more nutritious when eaten raw, our digestive systems cannot break down the tough cellular walls of carrots sufficiently to get the full benefit of the beta carotene. Fortunately, carrots are delicious cooked about any way you can think of.

Green Beans with Fresh Dill and Scallions

Green Beans with Fresh Dill and Scallions

SERVES 4 TO 6

3 quarts water
1 pound fresh string beans, trimmed and halved
3 tablespoons **I Can't Believe It's Not Butter!**®
5 green onions, trimmed and thickly sliced
3 tablespoons dill, finely chopped
Salt and freshly ground pepper to taste

1. In a large pot, bring the water to a boil.
2. Add the beans and cook over medium heat, covered, 7 minutes and drain.
3. In a large skillet, over medium heat, melt I Can't Believe It's Not Butter!® and sauté the green onions for 3 to 5 minutes or until wilted.
4. Add the beans. Toss with I Can't Believe It's Not Butter!® and green onions. Cook 5 to 7 minutes or until tender.
5. Add the dill, salt, and pepper and toss to completely coat the beans. Serve.

Golden Corn and Broccoli

SERVES 8
MAKES 5 CUPS

1 bunch broccoli (1½ pounds), cut up *or* 1 package (20 ounces) frozen broccoli cuts
1 cup water
1 can (10¾ ounces) condensed corn soup
½ cup shredded Cheddar cheese (2 ounces)
¼ cup milk
Dash pepper

1. In a 3-quart saucepan, combine the broccoli and water. Over high heat, heat to boiling. Reduce the heat to low. Cover and cook 8 minutes or until the broccoli is crisp-tender, stirring occasionally. Drain in a colander.
2. In the same saucepan, combine the soup, cheese, milk, and pepper. Return the broccoli to the saucepan. Over medium heat, heat through, stirring occasionally.
3. Transfer the broccoli to a warm platter, spoon over the sauce, and serve.

orn was unknown beyond the Americas until Columbus carried its seeds back to Spain in 1492. It is available fresh, canned, and frozen and forms the basis of many products— even bourbon. It is naturally sweet, but its sugar content immediately begins to turn into starch once picked. Use fresh corn as soon as possible after purchasing. Never buy fresh corn that has been husked; it deteriorates faster. Husks should be tight and bright green, the silk dry. When boiling corn, don't salt the water; it will toughen the corn.

Chili Corn Pudding

SERVES 4

2 cups fresh corn kernels (8 to 10 ears) *or* 1 can (16 ounces) corn kernels, drained
4 eggs
1 cup milk
½ teaspoon salt
¼ teaspoon ground nutmeg
¼ teaspoon cayenne (red) pepper
1 can (3 ounces) chopped green chilies, drained
½ cup cream
1 tablespoon butter

1. Heat the oven to 350° F.
2. In a large bowl, beat together all the ingredients.
3. Pour into a greased 6-cup soufflé dish or casserole.
4. Bake 40 to 50 minutes or until firm.
5. Serve warm or at room temperature.

COURTESY: NATIONAL PORK PRODUCERS COUNCIL

A ripe eggplant has firm, glossy, purple-black skin that springs back when you touch it. If the eggplant is too ripe, the imprint will remain and the vegetable will be slightly bitter when cooked. When an eggplant is underripe, there is no give at all to the skin and the vegetable doesn't have its full flavor. You can store eggplant in a plastic bag up to 6 days in the refrigerator.

Country Corn Bake

SERVES 4 TO 6

1 can (17 ounces) **Del Monte® Whole Kernel Golden Sweet Corn**
¾ cup milk
¼ cup (½ stick) butter *or* margarine
⅓ cup cornmeal
3 eggs, separated
½ teaspoon baking powder
¼ teaspoon salt
⅛ teaspoon cayenne (red) pepper
⅓ cup sliced green onions

1. Drain the corn and add the milk to the liquid to measure 1½ cups.
2. In a saucepan, combine the milk mixture and butter. Bring to a boil. Slowly stir in the cornmeal. Bring to a boil and cook 3 minutes, stirring constantly. Remove from the heat.
3. Stir in the egg yolks, baking powder, salt, cayenne pepper, green onions, and corn.
4. Beat the egg whites until stiff. Fold into the corn mixture.
5. Pour into a greased 1-quart baking dish.
6. Heat the oven to 375° F. Bake 30 minutes or until golden.
7. Remove from the oven and serve.

Special Eggplant Parmesan

SERVES 4 TO 6

1½ pounds eggplant, cut to ¼-inch-thick slices
2 quarts salted water
½ cup chopped onion
½ teaspoon minced garlic
1 tablespoon **Wesson® Oil**
1 can (14½ ounces) **Hunt's® Ready Tomato Sauces Chunky Special**
¼ teaspoon pepper
2 cups shredded mozzarella cheese
¼ cup grated Parmesan cheese

1. In a large saucepan, cook the eggplant in salted water until just tender and drain. Place on paper towels to absorb any extra moisture.

2. In a medium saucepan, sauté the onion and garlic in hot oil until tender. Stir in the tomato sauce and pepper and simmer for 10 minutes.

3. In a lightly greased 2-quart casserole, layer half the eggplant, half the sauce, 1 cup mozzarella, and 2 tablespoons Parmesan. Repeat the layers.

4. Bake at 350° F for 30 minutes. Remove from the oven and serve.

Dilly Pea Soufflé

SERVES 4 TO 6

1 can (15½ ounces) **Del Monte® Sweet Peas**,
   drained and divided
¼ cup (½ stick) butter *or* margarine
¼ cup all-purpose flour
1 cup milk
6 eggs, separated
¼ cup plus 1 tablespoon grated Parmesan cheese, divided
2 teaspoons Dijon mustard
½ teaspoon dill weed
⅛ teaspoon salt
½ teaspoon cream of tartar

1. Heat the oven to 375° F.

2. Reserve ⅓ cup peas. Purée the remaining peas in a food processor or blender. Set aside.

3. In a medium saucepan, melt the butter over low heat. Blend in the flour and slowly add the milk. Cook, stirring constantly, until thickened. Cool to room temperature.

4. Add the egg yolks and mix well. Stir in all the peas, ¼ cup cheese, mustard, dill weed, and salt. Transfer to a large bowl.

5. In another large bowl, beat the egg whites until frothy. Add the cream of tartar and beat until stiff, but not dry. Fold into the pea mixture.

6. Grease a 1½-quart soufflé dish and dust with the remaining Parmesan cheese. Make a 2-inch foil collar around the soufflé dish.

7. Spoon the mixture into the dish and place in a pan containing 1 inch of hot water.

8. Bake 45 to 50 minutes or until puffed and golden. Remove the collar and serve immediately.

Dilly Pea Soufflé

224 · SIDE DISHES

Gingered Peas and Peppers

SERVES 4

1 tablespoon vegetable oil
½ cup julienne red *or* green bell pepper
½ cup chopped onion
½ teaspoon minced fresh ginger
  or ¼ teaspoon ground ginger
1 can (15½ ounces) **Del Monte® Sweet Peas**, drained
1 tablespoon toasted sesame seeds
Salt and pepper to taste

1. In a saucepan, heat the oil and add the bell pepper, onion, and ginger. Cook over low heat until soft. Do not brown.
2. Add the peas and sesame seeds. Cover and heat through.
3. Season to taste with salt and pepper. Serve.

When buying fresh ginger, choose a firm root that is light brown in color, with no cuts on the skin or withered knobs. Place fresh ginger in a plastic food bag and store in the refrigerator; it will keep up to 1 month. Peel fresh ginger by scraping the blade of a paring knife along the surface. A vegetable peeler removes too much of the juicy, richly flavored layer just beneath the skin. You can also wrap ginger in foil and freeze it up to 4 months. When a recipe calls for ginger, grate or cut as much as you need from the frozen root, then return the balance to the freezer. Thawed ginger will be soft but still flavorful.

Impossible Spinach Pie

SERVES 8

½ cup sliced green onions
2 cloves garlic, minced
1 tablespoon margarine *or* butter
1 package (10 ounces) frozen chopped spinach, thawed and drained
½ cup creamed cottage cheese
½ cup **Bisquick® Original baking mix**
1 cup milk
3 eggs
1 teaspoon lemon juice
¼ teaspoon pepper
3 tablespoons grated Parmesan cheese
¼ teaspoon ground nutmeg

1. Heat the oven to 350° F.
2. In a large skillet, over medium heat, cook the onions and garlic in margarine for 2 to 3 minutes or until the onions are transparent.
3. Stir in the spinach.
4. In a greased 9-inch pie plate, layer the spinach mixture and cottage cheese.
5. In a medium bowl, stir the baking mix, milk, eggs, lemon juice, and pepper with a fork until blended. Pour into the pie plate.
6. Sprinkle with the Parmesan cheese and nutmeg.
7. Bake about 35 minutes or until a knife inserted in the center comes out clean.
8. Cool 5 minutes. Cut into wedges and serve.

Autumn Stuffed Squash

Stuffed Autumn Squash

SERVES 4

2 small acorn squash, halved and seeded
¼ cup (½ stick) **I Can't Believe It's Not Butter!®**, divided
½ cup *each* diced onion, carrots, and red bell pepper
½ cup *each* thickly sliced zucchini and mushrooms
1 small clove garlic, minced

1. Heat the oven to 350° F. Melt 1 tablespoon I Can't Believe It's Not Butter!® and brush on the cut surfaces of the squash. Place cut side down in a large baking dish without crowding. Add enough water to cover the bottom of the pan. Bake 30 minutes.

2. In a medium skillet, melt the remaining I Can't Believe It's Not Butter!® over medium heat. Sauté the remaining ingredients for 5 minutes only, stirring frequently.

3. Spoon the vegetables into the squash halves. Bake 20 to 25 minutes or until the squash is tender. Serve

Italian Tomatoes

SERVES 2

4 mushrooms, sliced
Juice of ½ lemon
2 leaves butter lettuce or curly endive
1 large beefsteak tomato, thickly sliced
1 tablespoon finely chopped fresh chives
⅓ cup **Lawry's® Classic Italian with Aged Parmesan Dressing**

1. Place the mushrooms in a small bowl. Squeeze the fresh lemon juice over them to cover. Marinate ½ hour, then drain.

2. Arrange the lettuce and tomato slices on two plates. Add the mushrooms and chives. Chill.

3. Pour the dressing over the tomatoes just before serving.

Stuffed Tomatoes

SERVES 8

8 medium tomatoes
1 package (10 ounces) frozen chopped spinach, thawed
6 tablespoons **Shedd's® Spread Country Crock® (stick)**, divided
½ cup cheese spread with vegetables
¾ cup fresh bread crumbs, divided
Salt and pepper to taste

1. Slice ¼ inch off the top of each tomato and discard. Using a spoon, gently scoop out the seeds and core. Discard. Turn the tomato shells upside down for 10 minutes to drain.

2. In a medium skillet, melt 4 tablespoons Shedd's® Spread Country Crock®. Add the spinach and sauté 7 minutes. Remove from the heat.

3. Stir in the cheese and fold in ½ cup bread crumbs. Set aside.

4. Heat the oven to 400° F. Grease a 13×9-inch baking dish with 1 tablespoon Shedd's® Spread Country Crock®.

5. Lightly sprinkle the inside of each tomato with the salt and pepper. Place upright in the baking dish.

6. Fill each tomato with the cheese mixture, mounding slightly. Top with the remaining bread crumbs and a dab of Shedd's® Spread Country Crock®.

7. Bake 25 minutes. Remove from the oven and serve immediately.

Light and Saucy Vegetable Medley

Light and Saucy Vegetable Medley

SERVES 6

1⅓ cups **1% Milk**
12 ounces red-skin potatoes, finely chopped
 2 cloves garlic, pressed
 ¼ teaspoon salt
 ⅛ teaspoon pepper
 2 cups fresh chopped vegetables such as broccoli, red bell peppers, onions, and mushrooms (8 ounces)
 ¾ cup finely shredded Asiago *or* Parmesan cheese, divided

1. In a large saucepan, slowly heat the milk, potatoes, garlic, salt, and pepper until small bubbles appear at the edge of the pan. Cook, stirring frequently, about 15 minutes or until tender.

2. Mash just enough potatoes to thicken the mixture.

3. Stir in the vegetables and heat through.

4. Remove from the heat and stir in ½ cup cheese. Top with the remaining cheese.

5. Serve immediately.

COURTESY: DAIRY MANAGEMENT, INC.

Baked Garden Omelette

SERVES 8

 1 package (16 ounces) frozen vegetables such as broccoli, red peppers, onions, and mushrooms, cooked and drained
12 extra large eggs, beaten
 ¾ cup milk
 2 tablespoons chopped fresh basil
 1 cup shredded mozzarella cheese
 1 cup shredded fontina *or* provolone cheese
 1 jar (30 ounces) **Ragú® Chunky Gardenstyle Tomato, Garlic & Onion Pasta Sauce**

1. Heat the oven to 350° F.

2. In a large bowl, thoroughly combine the vegetables, eggs, milk, basil, and cheeses. Add 1 cup sauce and mix thoroughly. Pour the mixture into a buttered 13×9-inch baking dish.

3. Bake 45 to 50 minutes or until the omelette is set.

4. Allow the omelette to cool slightly and cut into squares.

5. Serve with the remaining heated sauce.

Italian Vegetable-Cheese Bake

SERVES 8

 1 pound eggplant, chopped
 2 cups chopped tomatoes
 2 cups sliced zucchini
 1 cup sliced artichoke hearts
 1 cup **Healthy Choice® Fat-Free Natural Shredded Mozzarella Cheese** (4 ounces)
 2 teaspoons olive oil
 ½ cup sliced onion
 2 garlic cloves, minced
 2 cups **Healthy Choice® Pasta Sauce**

1. Heat the oven to 350° F.

2. In a 2-quart covered baking dish, combine the eggplant, tomatoes, zucchini, artichoke hearts, and cheese.

3. In a small nonstick skillet, heat the oil and add the onion and garlic. Cook and stir 2 minutes or until the onion is translucent. Mix in the pasta sauce. Pour the sauce over the vegetables.

4. Cover and bake 45 minutes. Cool slightly and serve.

Oven-Roasted Vegetables

MAKES 4½ CUPS

1 envelope **Lipton® Recipe Secrets® Savory Herb with Garlic Soup Mix**

1½ pounds assorted fresh vegetables such as sliced zucchini, squash, bell peppers, carrots, celery, and mushrooms

2 tablespoons olive *or* vegetable oil

1. Heat the oven to 450° F.

2. In a large bowl, add all the ingredients. Toss in the bowl until the vegetables are evenly coated.

3. In a 13×9-inch baking pan, arrange the vegetables.

4. Bake, uncovered, stirring once, 20 minutes or until the vegetables are tender. Remove from the oven and serve.

Grilled Vegetables

SERVES 8

3 pounds assorted fresh vegetables such as eggplant, zucchini, yellow squash, large mushrooms, red, green, *or* yellow bell peppers, and red onion, thickly sliced

1 cup **Wish-Bone® Italian Dressing**

1. In a large shallow baking dish, toss the fresh vegetables with the Italian dressing. Cover and marinate in the refrigerator, turning once, up to 1 hour.

2. Prepare the grill or broiler.

3. Remove the vegetables, reserving the marinade.

4. Grill or broil the vegetables, turning and basting occasionally with the reserved marinade, until the vegetables are tender. Remove from the heat and serve.

Vegetable Polenta Squares

SERVES 6 TO 8

7 cups chicken broth

2 cups polenta *or* stone-ground cornmeal

1 medium onion, chopped

2 tablespoons olive oil

2 cups chopped eggplant

2 cups thinly sliced mushrooms

1 small zucchini, thinly sliced

1 red bell pepper, seeded and chopped

1 can (15 ounces) **HORMEL® Chili No Beans**

3 cups shredded part-skim mozzarella cheese (12 ounces), divided

1. In large saucepan or Dutch oven, boil the chicken broth. In a steady stream, gradually add the polenta, stirring constantly with a wooden spoon. Reduce the heat to simmer, keep stirring, and cook 15 minutes or until the polenta is thickened and pulls away from the sides of the pan.

2. Pour into a greased 15½×10½-inch jelly-roll pan and spread evenly. Let stand 1 hour or until cool and firm. Cut into 3-inch squares.

3. In a large skillet, sauté the onion in the oil until tender. Add the eggplant, mushrooms, zucchini, and red bell pepper and cook over medium heat for 20 minutes or until the vegetables are soft and the liquid has evaporated, stirring frequently. Stir in the chili.

4. Heat the oven to 400° F.

5. Arrange half the polenta squares in the bottom of a greased 13×9-inch baking pan. Spoon half the vegetable mixture over the polenta, spreading to the edges of the pan. Sprinkle with half the cheese. Repeat the layers.

6. Bake 20 to 25 minutes or until the cheese melts. Let stand 10 minutes before cutting.

❖

Sweet Potatoes à l'Orange

SERVES 6

2 pounds sweet potatoes, cooked and peeled
1 egg
¼ cup firmly packed brown sugar
¼ cup orange juice
2 tablespoons butter *or* margarine
2 tablespoons sour cream
1 teaspoon grated orange zest
½ teaspoon ground cinnamon
¼ cup chopped pecans

1. Heat the oven to 350° F.
2. In a large bowl, whip the potatoes with a mixer. Beat in the egg, brown sugar, orange juice, butter, sour cream, orange zest, and cinnamon until fluffy.
3. Pour the mixture into a 1½-quart buttered casserole dish. Sprinkle the pecans over the top. Bake 20 minutes or until heated through.
4. Serve with **Cure 81® ham**.

*W*hile "sweet potato" and "yam" are often used interchangeably, they are two different vegetables from different species that share many similarities. The sweet potatoes most commonly offered for sale are a light-skinned variety with pale yellow flesh, which isn't at all sweet, and a dark orange-skinned variety with sweet orange flesh. Yams resemble the dark-skinned sweet potato, although their flesh is sweeter and more moist. Neither yams nor sweet potatoes should be refrigerated. Store them in a cool dark place.

Candied Yams

SERVES 8

¼ cup (½ stick) butter *or* margarine
½ cup sugar
1 teaspoon ground cinnamon
1 cup low-fat evaporated milk
1 can (29 ounces) yams *or* sweet potatoes, drained

1. In a large heavy-bottomed skillet, over high heat, melt the butter and add the sugar. Stir rapidly just until the mixture is golden brown, 1 minute. Stir in the cinnamon.
2. Remove the pan from the heat and add the milk. Return to the heat, stirring, until the mixture thickens and looks like caramel, 2 to 3 minutes.
3. Add the yams and spoon the caramel over the yams to coat.
4. Heat through and serve.

COURTESY: HORMEL®

Molly's Marvelous Fat-Free Mashed Potatoes

SERVES 6

6 medium-size potatoes (about 2 pounds)
½ cup skim milk
3 tablespoons plus 1 teaspoon **Molly McButter® Natural Butter Flavor Sprinkles**

1. Peel and cut the potatoes into quarters.
2. Place the potatoes in a large pot and cover with cold water. Bring to a boil and cook until tender, 20 to 25 minutes. Drain and mash.
3. Add the milk to the desired consistency. Mix in Molly McButter®.
4. Transfer to a large warm bowl and serve.

Mashed Potatoes
with Carrots and Onions

SERVES 6

4 all-purpose potatoes (about 1½ pounds), peeled and cut
   into chunks
4 carrots, trimmed, peeled, and cut into 1-inch lengths
1 medium onion, peeled and sliced
Salt and freshly ground pepper to taste
¼ cup (½ stick) **I Can't Believe It's Not Butter!**®, softened
½ cup milk
1 tablespoon minced fresh parsley (optional)

1. Place the potatoes, carrots, and onion in a large saucepan. Add cold water to cover and salt to taste. Bring to a boil and simmer about 20 minutes or until tender. Do not overcook.

2. Drain the vegetables and put them through a food mill or mash them until smooth.

3. Wipe out the saucepan and return the vegetables to it. Add I Can't Believe It's Not Butter!® and blend well. Stir in the salt and pepper to taste. Place over low heat and stir in the milk. Stir until heated through.

4. Spoon into a warm serving dish and sprinkle with parsley. Serve.

Italian Scalloped Potatoes

SERVES 6

4 medium potatoes (about 1¼ pounds), very thinly sliced
   (about 4 cups)
1 medium onion, chopped (about ½ cup)
1 cup shredded mozzarella cheese (4 ounces)
¼ cup grated Parmesan cheese
1 can (10¾ ounces) condensed cream of mushroom soup
¼ cup milk
½ teaspooon dried Italian seasoning, crushed
¼ teaspoon garlic powder

1. In a greased 1½-quart casserole dish, arrange half the potatoes and half the onion. Sprinkle with half the mozzarella cheese and half the Parmesan cheese. Repeat the layers.

2. Heat the oven to 400° F.

3. In a small bowl, combine the soup, milk, Italian seasoning, and garlic powder and spoon over the potato mixture.

4. Cover and bake 1 hour.

5. Uncover and bake 10 minutes more or until the potatoes are tender. Transfer to warm plates and serve.

Broccoli Cheese Scalloped Potatoes

SERVES 4

2 tablespoons butter *or* margarine
1 small onion, sliced
1 can (10¾ ounces) condensed broccoli cheese soup
⅓ cup milk
⅛ teaspoon pepper
4 medium potatoes, cooked and sliced ¼ inch thick
(about 3½ cups)
Chopped fresh parsley

1. In a 10-inch skillet, heat the margarine over medium heat and cook the onion until tender.
2. Add the soup, milk, pepper, and potatoes. Heat to boiling. Reduce the heat to low. Cover and simmer 5 minutes or until hot.
3. Garnish with the parsley and serve.

Curried Potatoes and Green Beans

SERVES 4

1 tablespoon olive oil
1 medium onion, cut in wedges
1 clove garlic, minced
1½ teaspoons curry powder
1 can (14½ ounces) **Del Monte® Original Style Stewed Tomatoes**
¼ cup **Del Monte® Seedless Raisins**
1 can (16 ounces) **Del Monte® Whole New Potatoes**, drained and quartered
1 can (14½ ounces) **Del Monte® Blue Lake Cut Green Beans**, drained
Salt and pepper to taste (optional)

1. In a medium skillet, heat the oil over low heat. Add the onion, garlic, and curry. Cook until tender, stirring frequently.
2. Blend in the tomatoes and raisins. Simmer, uncovered, 10 minutes, stirring occasionally.
3. Mix in the potatoes and green beans, cover, and heat through. Season to taste with salt and pepper, if desired. Serve.

*W*hen selecting potatoes, choose firm ones; avoid any with skins that are cut or wrinkled. If skins have a greenish tint, the potatoes have been overexposed to light and will have a somewhat bitter taste. Store potatoes in a dark, ventilated space that is cold, between 45° and 50° F. Do not refrigerate them because temperatures below 40° F turn their starch to sugar. Also, do not store potatoes loose next to onions; a chemical reaction takes place between the two vegetables that shortens the shelf life of both.

Autumnal Wild Rice Pilaf

Autumnal Wild Rice Pilaf

SERVES 6

1   package (10 ounces) white and wild rice mix
1   large golden apple, unpeeled, cored, and diced
1   carrot, peeled and shredded
1   green onion, minced
¼   cup golden raisins
¼   cup minced fresh parsley
¼   cup sliced almonds
¼   cup (½ stick) **I Can't Believe It's Not Butter!®**, melted
2   teaspoons poppy seeds
1   teaspoon grated lemon zest
½   teaspoon ground cinnamon
1   tablespoon apple juice

1. In a medium covered saucepan, cook the rice according to package directions.

2. In a large bowl, place the apple, carrot, onion, raisins, parsley, and almonds. Add the cooked rice and toss together.

3. In a small bowl, combine I Can't Believe It's Not Butter!® with the remaining ingredients. Add to the rice mixture and toss to combine.

4. Serve immediately.

*W*ild rice, a water grass native to North America, grows most abundantly in the Great Lakes region. The seeds are difficult to harvest and so command a high price. For the sake of economy as well as varied texture, wild rice is often mixed with brown or white rice. It is a good accompaniment for game or poultry.

Brown Rice with Black Beans

SERVES 8

1 tablespoon vegetable oil
1 medium onion, chopped
1 can (14½ ounces) stewed tomatoes with their juice
1 can (16 ounces) black beans with their juice
1 teaspoon dried oregano
½ teaspoon garlic powder *or* 1 clove garlic, crushed
1½ cups **Minute® Instant Brown Rice**

1. In a large deep skillet, heat the oil and stir the onion until tender but not browned.
2. Add the tomatoes, beans, oregano, and garlic powder and bring to a boil.
3. Stir in the rice. Return to a boil, cover, reduce the heat, and simmer 5 minutes.
4. Remove from the heat and let stand 5 minutes or until the rice is tender. Serve.

Cumin-Scented Rice

SERVES 4

⅔ cup instant long-grain rice
1⅓ cups water
½ teaspoon salt
1 tablespoon butter
½ teaspoon cumin seed

1. In a medium saucepan, bring all the ingredients to a boil. Cover, lower the heat, and simmer until tender, 12 to 15 minutes.
2. Remove to a bowl and serve.

COURTESY: NATIONAL PORK PRODUCERS COUNCIL

Broccoli and Cheese Rice Pilaf

SERVES 6

¼ cup minced onion
¼ cup diced red bell pepper
2 cups instant long-grain rice
1⅓ cups water
1 can (10½ ounces) **Healthy Choice® Recipe Creations™ Cream of Broccoli with Cheddar and Onion Condensed Soup**
1 tablespoon minced fresh parsley
½ teaspoon salt (optional)

1. In a medium saucepan sprayed with nonstick cooking spray, sauté the onion and bell pepper until tender. Stir in the rice. Add the water, soup, parsley, and salt, if desired, and mix well.
2. Bring to a boil, cover, reduce the heat, and continue cooking 10 minutes or until the liquid is absorbed and the rice is tender.
3. Remove to a bowl and serve.

To prepare perfect rice, be sure to cook the rice in water that is just simmering. Do not let it boil or too much steam will escape and the rice may burn dry before it is done. Keep the pot covered and don't stir the rice while it is cooking. When rice is left to cook undisturbed, small holes form on the surface that allow steam to flow evenly through the grains, cooking each one to plump perfection. If rice is stirred, the steam is not properly distributed and the grains become gummy rather than light and fluffy.

Ratatouille Rice

Ratatouille Rice

SERVES 4

1 family-size bag **UNCLE BEN'S® Brand Boil-In Bag Rice**
1⅓ cups chopped onion
⅔ cup sliced yellow squash
⅔ cup sliced zucchini
½ cup coarsely chopped red *or* green bell pepper
2 cloves garlic, minced
2 teaspoons dried basil, crushed
½ teaspoon salt (optional)
1 large tomato, diced
1 tablespoon chopped fresh parsley

1. Cook the rice according to package directions.

2. In a 10-inch nonstick skillet, cook the onion, stirring constantly, 1 minute.

3. Stir in the remaining ingredients *except* tomato and parsley. Cover and cook over low heat, stirring occasionally, until the vegetables are tender, about 10 minutes.

4. Stir in the tomato and rice. Cover and simmer 10 minutes, stirring occasionally.

5. Sprinkle with the parsley and serve.

Cheddar Rice and Spinach Bake

SERVES 4 TO 6

1 egg
½ cup cheddar cheese spread
1 package (10 ounces) frozen chopped spinach, thawed and drained
2 cups cooked rice
1 medium onion, chopped (about ½ cup)
¼ teaspoon ground nutmeg
½ teaspoon salt
Freshly ground pepper to taste
¼ cup (½ stick) **Shedd's® Spread Country Crock®,** melted plus 1 tablespoon **Shedd's® Spread Country Crock®,** softened

1. Heat the oven to 350° F.

2. In a medium bowl, beat the egg. Add the cheese, by the spoonful, to the bowl. Do not blend.

3. Add the spinach, rice, onion, seasonings, and melted Shedd's® Spread Country Crock® and mix thoroughly.

4. Coat a 1½-quart baking dish with the additional tablespoon Shedd's® Spread Country Crock®. Spoon in the mixture and smooth the top. Cover.

5. Bake 30 minutes. Remove from the oven and serve.

Apricot Cornbread Stuffin' Muffins

MAKES 12 MUFFINS *OR* 30 MINI MUFFINS

1 package (12 ounces) cornbread muffin mix
1 cup dried apricots (6 ounces), finely sliced
¾ cup water
1 egg
½ cup (1 stick) butter *or* margarine
½ cup chopped celery
½ cup chopped onion
2 tablespoons chopped fresh parsley
¼ teaspoon pepper
1 cup chopped pecans

1. Heat the oven to 400° F.

2. Make the cornbread according to package directions except thinly spread the batter in a well-greased 12×15-inch baking pan.

3. Bake 10 to 15 minutes until golden brown.

4. Cool. Cut the cornbread into 1-inch squares and place in a large bowl.

5. Lower the oven temperature to 350° F.

6. Soak the apricots in the water for 10 minutes.

7. Lightly beat the egg and stir into the apricots.

8. In a medium skillet, heat the butter. Stir in the celery, onion, parsley, and pepper. Cook over medium-low heat until softened but not browned, then stir into the cornbread. Add the apricot mixture and pecans to the stuffing and mix thoroughly.

9. Scoop the stuffing mixture into well-greased muffin pans. Pat down the stuffing to form muffin shapes.

10. Bake 20 minutes or until evenly browned. Serve warm or store in the freezer.

Almond Apple Wheat Bread Stuffing

MAKES 10 CUPS

2 cups chopped Granny Smith apples
1½ cups **Blue Diamond® Natural Sliced Almonds** (5 ounces)
¾ cup chopped onion
¾ cup chopped celery
¼ cup (½ stick) butter *or* margarine
1 teaspoon ground cinnamon
½ teaspoon poultry seasoning
¼ teaspoon salt
8 cups cubed whole wheat bread
1 cup raisins
1 egg, lightly beaten
⅓ to ½ cup apple cider *or* juice

1. In a large skillet, over medium-high heat, sauté the apples, almonds, onion, and celery in the butter for 5 minutes, stirring frequently. Remove from the heat. Stir in the cinnamon, poultry seasoning, and salt.

2. In a large bowl, toss together the bread cubes and raisins. Add the apple mixture.

3. In a small bowl, stir the egg into ⅓ cup apple cider and toss into the bread mixture. Add the additional apple cider if a moister stuffing is desired.

4. Use to stuff a 15- to 20-pound turkey or two large roasting chickens. Spoon any remaining stuffing into a lightly greased 9×5-inch loaf pan. Bake, covered, during the last 30 to 40 minutes of turkey or chicken roasting.

5. Remove from the oven and serve.

NOTE

If the dressing dries out during baking, you can add more apple cider, or spoon some chicken or turkey drippings over the platter before serving.

Apple-Walnut Stuffing

SERVES 8

8   cups homemade-style bread *or* cornbread,
    cut into 1-inch cubes
¼   cup (½ stick) butter *or* margarine
½   cup diced celery
½   cup diced onion
¼   cup chopped fresh parsley
2   eggs, beaten
1   cup chicken broth
¼   teaspoon pepper
2   apples, peeled, cored, and diced
1   cup chopped walnuts

1. Heat the oven to 325° F.

2. Place the bread cubes in a large bowl.

3. In a medium skillet, over medium heat, melt the butter. Add the celery, onion, and parsley. Cook, stirring occasionally, until softened, 3 to 5 minutes. Add to the bread.

4. Combine the eggs, broth, and pepper. Add to the bread mixture and mix thoroughly. Stir in the apples and walnuts.

5. Bake in a greased 2-quart baking dish for 25 minutes or until the desired crispness. Remove from the oven and serve.

Southwest Cornbread Stuffing

MAKES 12 CUPS (3 QUARTS)

2   cups chopped onion
1   cup sliced celery
¼   cup (½ stick) butter
1   can (13¾ ounces) chicken broth
1   can (17 ounces) **Del Monte® Whole Kernel Golden Sweet Corn,** drained
1   can (7 ounces) diced green chilies
3   tablespoons chopped fresh parsley
½   teaspoon poultry seasoning
½   teaspoon salt
Pepper to taste
¼   teaspoon dried oregano
6   cups crumbled cornbread *or* dry cornbread stuffing crumbs
½   cup chopped pecan pieces

1. Heat the oven to 350° F.

2. In a large Dutch oven, cook the onion and celery in butter until tender. Stir in the chicken broth, corn, chilies, parsley, poultry seasoning, salt, pepper, and oregano. Mix well. Add the cornbread crumbs and nuts and toss to moisten evenly.

3. Spoon into a covered casserole and bake 30 minutes or until heated through, or use to stuff a 12- to-15 pound turkey.

❖

*W*hen you freeze a casserole, you can save space—and keep the dish for other uses. Line the dish with overlapping sheets of plastic wrap that are long enough to encase the food when folded over. Add the food, fold and seal the plastic wrap, and cover the dish with foil. When frozen, take the food block out of the dish, wrap it tightly in foil, and label, including the date. To reheat, remove the wrapping. Oil the dish and slip the food block into the dish in which it was frozen. Bake the casserole as instructed.

Breads
AND
Muffins

❖

Souper Cornbread

SERVES 6

1 can (10¾ ounces) condensed corn soup
2 eggs
¼ cup milk
1 package (12 to 14 ounces) corn muffin mix
4 ounces bulk pork sausage, cooked and drained

1. In a medium bowl, combine the soup, eggs, and milk. Stir in the corn muffin mix just until blended. Gently fold in the sausage.

2. In a greased 9-inch square baking pan, pour the corn muffin mixture.

3. Heat the oven to 400° F.

4. Bake 20 minutes or until lightly browned and a toothpick inserted in the center comes out clean. Serve.

Cheese Chili Cornbread

SERVES 8

2 eggs, lightly beaten
1 cup plain yogurt
¼ cup (½ stick) melted butter, cooled
1 cup cornmeal
1 teaspoon salt
1 teaspoon baking powder
½ teaspoon baking soda
1 cup grated **Monterey Jack Cheese**
1 cup canned cream-style corn
½ cup minced green onions (about 4)
1 can (4 ounces) chopped green chilies

1. Heat the oven to 400° F.

2. In a medium bowl, whisk together the eggs, yogurt, and butter. Add the cornmeal, salt, baking powder, and baking soda and mix until just well blended. Add the cheese, corn, green onions, and chilies and mix well. Pour into a greased 10-inch heavy skillet.

3. Bake 40 minutes. Remove from the oven and serve.

COURTESY: DAIRY MANAGEMENT, INC.

To store homemade bread for more than a day, wrap it snugly in foil or seal it in two plastic bags. When frozen, both yeast and quick breads retain their original texture and freshness up to 3 months at 0° F. For convenience, slice yeast bread before freezing; you can then remove a slice or two at a time.

To defrost frozen bread, leave it at room temperature for several hours. Or defrost it in a microwave oven according to the manufacturer's directions—usually for 1 to 4 minutes. Or wrap it in foil and warm in a preheated 400° F oven, 15 to 25 minutes. Whatever the storage method, rewarm bread to restore freshness.

Cheese Chili Cornbread

Pizza Bread

SERVES 16

1 package (16 ounces) hot roll mix
1¼ cups hot water
1 cup **Healthy Choice® Fat-Free Pizza Shreds** (4 ounces)
4 teaspoons olive oil, divided
1 cup sun-dried tomatoes (3 ounces)
1 medium onion, thinly sliced
2 garlic cloves, minced
1 cup artichoke hearts, sliced
2 tablespoons fresh rosemary, minced

1. Combine the hot roll mix, water, pizza shreds, and 2 teaspoons olive oil. Knead about 5 minutes until well blended. Coat a 13×9-inch baking pan with nonstick cooking spray. Press the dough onto the pan. Cover and let rise 15 minutes.
2. Soak the sun-dried tomatoes in very hot water for 15 minutes. Drain and then cut into strips.
3. In a small skillet, cook and stir the onion and garlic in 1 teaspoon olive oil until tender.
4. Brush the dough with the remaining 1 teaspoon olive oil.
5. Sprinkle the tomato, onion mixture, artichokes, and rosemary on top.
6. Bake at 400° F until golden brown, 25 to 30 minutes. Remove from the oven and serve.

Multi-Grain Quick Bread

MAKES 1 LOAF

1½ cups all-purpose flour
⅓ cup wheat germ
½ cup old-fashioned oats
2 teaspoons baking powder
2 teaspoons baking soda
½ teaspoon salt
3 egg whites
⅓ cup **Grandma's Molasses**
½ cup firmly packed brown sugar
½ cup **Mott's® Natural Apple Sauce**
½ cup low-fat buttermilk

1. Heat the oven to 350° F.
2. Spray a 9×5-inch loaf pan with nonstick cooking spray.
3. In a medium bowl, mix the flour, wheat germ, oats, baking powder, baking soda, and salt.
4. In a large bowl, whisk the egg whites, molasses, brown sugar, applesauce, and buttermilk until smooth. Add the flour mixture to the wet ingredients and stir until combined.
5. Pour the batter in the prepared pan. Bake 45 to 50 minutes or until an inserted toothpick comes out clean.
6. Allow the bread to cool in the pan for 3 minutes. Remove to a rack and cool completely. Slice. Serve warm or cold.

Banana Oatmeal Bread

MAKES 1 LOAF

½ cup (1 stick) plus 1 tablespoon **I Can't Believe It's Not Butter!®**, softened, divided

2 cups sifted all-purpose flour

½ teaspoon baking powder

½ teaspoon salt

½ teaspoon baking soda

¼ teaspoon ground nutmeg

½ cup quick-cooking oats

2 eggs

2 tablespoons buttermilk

1 teaspoon lemon juice

1 cup sugar

1½ cups sliced ripe bananas (about 3 medium)

½ cup raisins

¼ cup chopped walnuts

1. Heat the oven to 350° F. Grease a 9×5-inch loaf pan with 1 tablespoon of I Can't Believe It's Not Butter!®

2. In a large bowl, sift together the flour, baking powder, salt, baking soda, and nutmeg. Stir in the oats and set aside.

3. In a blender, combine the eggs, remaining I Can't Believe It's Not Butter!®, buttermilk, lemon juice, and sugar and process until smooth. Add the bananas, raisins, and walnuts and process briefly.

4. Pour the mixture into the dry ingredients and mix until the flour is moistened.

5. Pour into the greased pan and bake 45 to 50 minutes or until a toothpick inserted in the center comes out clean.

6. Cool 15 minutes. Remove from the pan and finish cooling on a rack. Serve or store.

Spicy Sweet Potato Bread

MAKES 1 LOAF

¼ cup old-fashioned oats

2 tablespoons firmly packed brown sugar

1 teaspoon margarine *or* butter, softened

1 package (15⅜ ounces) nut bread mix

½ cup cooked mashed sweet potato

½ cup water

½ cup raisins

¼ cup vegetable oil

1 egg

1 teaspoon ground cinnamon

½ teaspoon ground nutmeg

Reynolds® Crystal Color® Plastic Wrap

1. Heat the oven to 350° F. Grease an 8½×4½-inch loaf pan and set aside.

2. In a small bowl, combine the oats, brown sugar, and margarine and set aside.

3. In a large bowl, combine the nut bread mix, sweet potato, water, raisins, oil, egg, cinnamon, and nutmeg. Stir until blended.

4. Pour into the prepared pan. Sprinkle the oat mixture evenly over the batter.

5. Bake 50 to 60 minutes or until a toothpick inserted in the center comes out clean.

6. Cool 15 minutes. Remove from the pan. Cool completely on a rack. Serve or store.

Banana Macadamia Nut Bread

Banana Macadamia Nut Bread

MAKES 3 5½×3-INCH MINI LOAVES *OR* 1 9×5-INCH LOAF

2 cups all-purpose flour

¾ cup sugar

½ cup (1 stick) **LAND O LAKES® Butter,** softened

2 eggs

1 teaspoon baking soda

½ teaspoon salt

1 tablespoon grated orange zest

1 teaspoon vanilla extract

1 cup mashed ripe bananas (2 medium)

¼ cup orange juice

1 cup flaked coconut

1 jar (3½ ounces) coarsely chopped macadamia nuts *or* walnuts (¾ cup)

1. Heat the oven to 350° F.

2. In a large mixer bowl, combine the flour, sugar, butter, eggs, baking soda, salt, orange zest, and vanilla. Beat at low speed, scraping the bowl often, until well mixed, 2 to 3 minutes. Add the bananas and orange juice. Continue beating, scraping the bowl often, until well mixed, 1 minute. By hand, stir in the coconut and nuts. (Batter will be thick.)

3. Spread into three greased 5½×3-inch mini loaf pans or one greased 9×5-inch loaf pan. Bake the mini loaves for 35 to 45 minutes or the 9×5-inch loaf for 60 to 65 minutes or until a toothpick inserted in the center comes out clean. Cool 10 minutes. Remove from the pans, slice, and serve.

Orange Tea Bread

MAKES 1 LOAF

- 2 cups all-purpose flour
- 1½ teaspoons baking powder
- 1 teaspoon baking soda
- ½ teaspoon salt
- ⅔ cup plain nonfat yogurt
- ⅔ cup sugar
- 2 large eggs *or* egg substitute
- 3 tablespoons unsalted butter *or* margarine, melted
- 1 tablepoon grated orange zest

For syrup:

- 2 **Florida Oranges,** squeezed (½ cup juice)
- ¼ cup sugar

1. Heat the oven to 350° F.
2. In a large bowl, sift the flour, baking powder, baking soda, and salt.
3. In a medium bowl, whisk together the yogurt, ⅔ cup sugar, eggs, butter, and orange zest. Add the wet ingredients to the dry and stir the mixture until the batter is stiff. Transfer to a greased 8½×4½-inch nonstick loaf pan, smoothing the top. Bake 45 to 50 minutes or until a skewer inserted in the middle comes out clean.
4. Meanwhile, make the syrup. Combine the orange juice and ¼ cup sugar in a small saucepan. Over medium-high heat, bring to a boil while stirring and simmer 1 minute. Keep warm.
5. Remove the loaf from the oven. With a thin wooden skewer, poke 20 evenly spaced holes in the top of the bread. Brush with one-third of the syrup. Let stand 10 minutes, then invert onto a rack. Poke more holes into the bottom and sides of the bread and brush with the remaining syrup. Allow to cool standing upright.
6. Wrap the cooled bread in plastic and foil overnight for the best flavor. Slice and serve.

COURTESY: FLORIDA DEPARTMENT OF CITRUS

Orange Cranberry Bread

MAKES 1 9×5-INCH LOAF
OR 3 5½×3-INCH MINI LOAVES

For bread:

- ½ cup (1 stick) **LAND O LAKES® Butter,** softened
- ¾ cup sugar
- 1 egg
- 1 teaspoon grated orange zest
- 2½ cups all-purpose flour
- ⅔ cup orange juice
- ⅓ cup milk
- 2 teaspoons baking powder
- ½ teaspoon salt
- ¾ cup coarsely chopped fresh *or* frozen cranberries
- ⅓ cup chopped pecans

For glaze:

- 1 cup confectioners sugar
- 3 to 4 teaspoons orange juice

1. Heat the oven to 350° F. In a large mixer bowl, combine the butter, sugar, egg, and orange zest. Beat at medium speed, scraping the bowl often, until well mixed, 1 to 2 minutes.
2. Reduce the speed to low. Add all the remaining bread ingredients *except* cranberries and pecans. Continue beating, scraping the bowl often, until well mixed, 1 to 2 minutes. By hand, stir in the cranberries and pecans.
3. Spoon into a greased 9×5-inch loaf pan or three greased 5½×3-inch mini loaf pans. Bake 50 to 60 minutes for the 9×5-inch loaf or 30 to 40 minutes for the mini loaves or until a toothpick inserted in the center comes out clean.
4. Cool 10 minutes and remove from the pan. Cool completely.
5. In a small bowl, stir together the glaze ingredients. Spread over the cooled bread. Serve or store.

❖

Julekage (Fruit Bread)

MAKES 1 LOAF

For bread:

1 package (¼ ounce) active dry yeast
¼ cup warm water (105° F to 115° F)
3¼ to 3¾ cups all-purpose flour, divided
½ cup golden raisins
⅓ cup slivered almonds
⅓ cup chopped mixed candied fruit
¼ cup sugar
¾ cup milk
¼ cup (½ stick) **LAND O LAKES® Butter,** softened plus
    1 tablespoon **LAND O LAKES® Butter,** melted
1 egg
½ teaspoon salt
½ teaspoon ground cardamom
½ teaspoon grated lemon zest

For glaze:

1 cup confectioners sugar
3 to 4 teaspoons milk
Candied cherries (optional)

1. In a large mixer bowl, dissolve the yeast in the warm water.
2. Add 2 cups flour and all the remaining bread ingredients *except* 1 tablespoon melted butter. Beat at medium speed, scraping the bowl often, until smooth, 1 to 2 minutes.
3. By hand, stir in enough remaining flour to make the dough easy to handle. Turn the dough onto a lightly floured surface. Knead until smooth and elastic, about 5 minutes. Place in a greased bowl, then turn the greased side up. Cover and let rise in a warm place until double in size, about 1½ hours. The dough is ready if an indentation remains when touched.
4. Punch down the dough and shape into a round loaf. Place in a greased 9-inch round cake pan. Brush the top of the bread with the 1 tablespoon melted butter. Cover and let rise until double in size, about 1 hour.
5. Heat the oven to 350° F. Bake 35 to 45 minutes or until golden brown.
6. Remove from the pan immediately. Cool completely.
7. In a small bowl, stir together the glaze ingredients and spread over the cooled bread. If desired, garnish with candied cherries. Slice and serve.

Chocolate Chip Scones

MAKES 12 SCONES

1¾ cups all-purpose flour
3 tablespoons sugar
2½ teaspoons baking powder
½ teaspoon salt
⅓ cup (5 tablespoons plus 1 teaspoon) **LAND O LAKES® Butter**
2 eggs, slightly beaten, divided
½ cup semisweet chocolate chips
4 to 6 tablespoons half-and-half

1. Heat the oven to 400° F.
2. In a medium bowl, combine the flour, sugar, baking powder, and salt. Cut the butter into the flour mixture until it resembles fine crumbs. Stir in 1 egg, chocolate chips, and just enough half-and-half so the dough leaves the side of the bowl.
3. Turn the dough onto a lightly floured surface. Knead gently 10 times.
4. Roll the dough into a ½-inch-thick circle and cut into 12 wedges. Place the wedges on an ungreased baking sheet. Brush with the remaining beaten egg.
5. Bake 10 to 12 minutes or until golden brown.
6. Immediately remove from the baking sheet. Serve warm.

❖

Orange Raisin Scones

MAKES 12 SCONES AND ½ CUP ORANGE BUTTER

1¾ cups all-purpose flour

3 tablespoons sugar

2½ teaspoons baking powder

2 teaspoons grated orange zest

⅓ cup (5 tablespoons plus 1 teaspoon) **LAND O LAKES®
Butter,** chilled

2 eggs, beaten, divided

½ cup raisins

4 to 6 tablespoons half-and-half

For orange butter:

½ cup (1 stick) **LAND O LAKES® Butter,** softened

2 tablespoons orange marmalade

1. Heat the oven to 400° F.

2. In a medium bowl, combine the flour, sugar, baking powder, and orange zest.

3. Cut ⅓ cup butter into the flour mixture until it resembles fine crumbs. Stir in 1 egg, raisins, and just enough half-and-half so the dough leaves the sides of the bowl.

4. Turn the dough onto a lightly floured surface and knead gently 10 times. Roll into a 9-inch circle and cut into 12 wedges.

5. Place on an ungreased baking sheet. Brush with the remaining beaten egg.

6. Bake 10 to 12 minutes or until golden brown. Immediately remove from the baking sheet.

7. In a small mixer bowl, beat together ½ cup butter and marmalade at medium speed, scraping the bowl often, until well mixed.

8. Serve the orange butter with the scones.

Apple 'n' Honey Scones

MAKES 10 SCONES

2 cups all-purpose flour

⅔ cup plus 1 tablespoon **Kretschmer® Wheat Germ,**
any flavor

2 teaspoons baking powder

1 teaspoon ground cinnamon

¼ teaspoon ground nutmeg

¼ teaspoon baking soda

¼ teaspoon salt (optional)

⅓ cup (5 tablespoons plus 1 teaspoon) margarine, chilled

1¼ cups finely chopped apple

½ cup skim milk

¼ cup honey

1 tablespoon sugar

¼ teaspoon ground cinnamon

1. Heat the oven to 400° F. Lightly spray a large baking sheet with nonstick cooking spray or grease lightly.

2. In a large bowl, combine the flour, ⅔ cup wheat germ, baking powder, spices, baking soda, and salt, if using. Cut in the margarine until the mixture resembles coarse crumbs. In a medium bowl, combine the apple, milk, and honey. Add to the dry ingredients, mixing just until the dry ingredients are moistened.

3. Turn out the dough onto a lightly floured surface and knead gently 5 to 6 times. Pat the dough into a 9-inch circle.

4. Mix together the remaining 1 tablespoon wheat germ, sugar, and cinnamon. Sprinkle over the dough.

5. Cut the dough into 10 wedges. Place ½ inch apart on the prepared baking sheet.

6. Bake 16 to 18 minutes or until light golden brown.

7. Serve warm with additional honey, if desired.

Crumble-Top Banana Muffins

MAKES 12 MUFFINS

1¼ cups all-purpose flour
1 tablespoon **Calumet® Baking Powder**
⅛ teaspoon salt
1 egg
½ cup milk
⅓ cup firmly packed brown sugar
3 tablespoons vegetable oil
1½ cups **Post® Morning Traditions®Banana Crunch® Cereal**
1 cup finely chopped ripe banana

For crumble-top topping:

½ cup **Post® Morning Traditions®Banana Crunch® Cereal,** lightly crushed
1 tablespoon firmly packed brown sugar
½ teaspoon ground cinnamon
1 teaspoon vegetable oil

1. Heat the oven to 400° F.

2. Beat the egg in a small bowl. Stir in the milk, brown sugar, and oil. In a large bowl, mix the flour, baking powder, and salt.

3. Add the wet ingredients to the flour mixture and stir just until moistened. (Batter will be lumpy.) Stir in the cereal and banana.

4. Spoon the batter into a greased or paper-lined muffin pan, filling each cup ⅔ full.

5. For the topping: Mix the cereal, brown sugar, and cinnamon. Drizzle with the oil and stir until crumbly. Sprinkle evenly over the muffins.

6. Bake 20 minutes or until lightly browned. Serve.

Cinnamon Rhubarb Muffins

MAKES 18 MUFFINS

For muffins:

½ cup firmly packed brown sugar
¼ cup (½ stick) **LAND O LAKES® Butter,** softened
1 cup **LAND O LAKES® Sour Cream, Regular, Light,** *or* **No-Fat** (1 cup)
2 eggs
1½ cups all-purpose flour
¾ teaspoon baking soda
½ teaspoon ground cinnamon
1½ cups sliced ¼-inch fresh *or* frozen rhubarb

For topping:

1 tablespoon sugar
½ teaspoon ground cinnamon

1. Heat the oven to 375° F.

2. In a large mixer bowl, combine the brown sugar and butter.

3. Beat at medium speed, scraping the bowl often, until the mixture is creamy, 1 to 2 minutes. Add the sour cream and eggs and continue beating, scraping the bowl often, until well mixed, 1 to 2 minutes.

4. In a medium bowl, stir together the flour, baking soda, and ½ teaspoon cinnamon.

5. By hand, stir the flour mixture into the sour cream mixture just until moistened. Gently stir in the rhubarb. Spoon into greased or paper-lined muffin pans.

6. In a small bowl, stir together 1 tablespoon sugar and ½ teaspoon cinnamon. Sprinkle about ¼ teaspoon mixture on top of each muffin.

7. Bake 25 to 30 minutes or until lightly browned. Let stand 5 minutes and remove from the pans. Serve or store.

Tangerine Muffins

MAKES 12 MUFFINS

- 2 cups all-purpose flour
- 2 teaspoons baking powder
- 1 teaspoon baking soda
- ½ teaspoon salt
- ½ cup sugar
- 1 cup plain low-fat yogurt
- ¼ cup (½ stick) unsalted margarine, melted
- 1 large egg
- 1 tablespoon grated **Florida Tangerine** zest
- 1 cup finely diced **Florida Tangerine,** seeds and white pith removed

1. Heat the oven to 400° F. In a large bowl, sift the flour, baking powder, baking soda, salt, and sugar.
2. In a medium bowl, whisk together the yogurt, melted margarine, egg, and tangerine zest. Stir in the tangerine.
3. Add the wet ingredients to the dry and stir to combine.
4. Spoon the batter into 12 greased muffin cups, filling each ⅔ full. Bake 18 to 20 minutes or until pale gold.
5. Cool 5 minutes and transfer to a rack to cool completely. Serve.

COURTESY: FLORIDA DEPARTMENT OF CITRUS

Our Best Bran Muffins

MAKES 12 MUFFINS

- 1¼ cups all-purpose flour
- ½ cup sugar
- ¼ teaspoon salt
- 1 tablespoon baking powder
- 1½ cups **Kellogg's® All-Bran® Cereal**
- 1¼ cups milk
- 1 egg
- ¼ cup vegetable oil

1. Stir together the flour, sugar, salt, and baking powder. Set aside.
2. In a large mixing bowl, combine the cereal and milk. Let stand about 3 minutes or until the cereal softens.
3. Add the egg and oil and mix well. Add the flour mixture, stirring only until combined.
4. Portion the batter evenly into 12 lightly greased 2½-inch muffin cups.
5. Bake at 400° F about 20 minutes or until golden brown. Serve warm.

To enjoy freshly baked muffins anytime, store extra muffin batter in the refrigerator and bake just what you need when you want it. The batter will keep about 5 days. Or freeze muffin batter in cupcake liners and bake them frozen, according to recipe directions, allowing about 10 minutes of extra baking time. Or bake more muffins than you need and wrap the extra ones individually in foil and freeze. Warm them in their foil wrappers in the oven 20 minutes at 400° F.

Honey-Pecan Bran Muffins

Honey-Pecan Bran Muffins

MAKES 12 MUFFINS

1 cup **Fiber One® Cereal**, crushed
1 cup milk
¼ cup vegetable oil
1 egg
1¼ cups all-purpose flour
¼ cup sugar
¼ cup honey
½ cup pecans, coarsely chopped
2 teaspoons baking powder
½ teaspoon salt

1. Heat the oven to 400° F. Grease the bottoms only of twelve 2½-inch muffin cups or line with paper baking cups.

2. Combine the cereal and milk. Let stand 5 minutes. Beat in the oil and egg. Stir in the remaining ingredients just until moistened.

3. Divide the batter among the muffin cups. Bake until lightly brown, 20 to 30 minutes. Immediately remove from the pan to cool. Serve warm.

Buttermilk is often used in baking because it makes the texture of biscuits, cakes, muffins, and pancakes more tender while adding a pleasing flavor. Another plus is that when buttermilk is substituted for whole milk, it provides a rich taste with less fat. The name buttermilk is misleading, for it is low in milkfat, containing only 1 percent milkfat when made from skim milk and 1¹/₂ to 2 percent when made from low-fat milk.

Florida Orange Date Nut Bran Muffins

MAKES 12 MUFFINS

2 cups shredded bran cereal
¾ cup boiling water
¼ cup vegetable oil
¾ cup buttermilk
¼ cup **Florida Orange Juice**
2 tablespoons dark molasses
2 tablespoons honey
1 tablespoon grated orange zest
1 egg
¾ cup all-purpose flour
½ cup whole wheat flour
1½ teaspoons baking soda
½ teaspoon salt
1 cup chopped dates
¾ cup chopped walnuts

1. Heat the oven to 400° F.

2. Grease one 12-cup muffin tin.

3. In a large bowl, combine the bran cereal, water, and oil, stirring until the bran softens.

4. In a small bowl, whisk the buttermilk, orange juice, molasses, honey, orange zest, and egg until blended.

5. In another small bowl, combine the flours, baking soda, and salt.

6. Add the buttermilk mixture to the bran, stirring to combine.

7. Add the flour mixture, dates, and walnuts to the bran mixture, stirring just until the flour is moistened.

8. Spoon into the muffin cups. Bake until the tops spring back when lightly pressed, about 18 minutes. Let cool in the pan 5 minutes. Remove to a rack. Serve or store.

COURTESY: FLORIDA DEPARTMENT OF CITRUS

Cinnamon Apple Muffins

MAKES 12 MUFFINS

1¼ cups all-purpose flour
¾ cup **Kretschmer® Original Toasted Wheat Germ**
1 tablespoon baking powder
⅓ cup firmly packed brown sugar
1¼ teaspoons ground cinnamon
¾ cup applesauce
½ cup skim milk
2 egg whites, slightly beaten
3 tablespoons vegetable oil

1. Heat the oven to 400° F. Lightly spray twelve medium muffin cups with nonstick cooking spray or line with paper baking cups.

2. In a medium bowl, combine the flour, wheat germ, baking powder, brown sugar, and cinnamon. Set aside.

3. In a large bowl, combine the remaining ingredients.

4. Add the dry ingredients and mix just until the dry ingredients are moistened. Do not overmix.

5. Fill the muffin cups almost full. Bake 20 to 22 minutes or until golden brown.

6. Serve warm or store tightly wrapped in the freezer. To reheat, microwave on high for 30 seconds per muffin.

Applesauce-Oat Muffins

MAKES 12 MUFFINS

2 cups **Cheerios® Toasted Whole Grain Oat Cereal,** crushed (about 1 cup)
1¼ cups all-purpose flour
⅓ cup firmly packed brown sugar
1 teaspoon ground cinnamon
1 teaspoon baking powder
¾ teaspoon baking soda
1 cup applesauce
⅓ cup skim milk
½ cup raisins
3 tablespoons vegetable oil
1 egg white

1. Heat the oven to 400° F. Spray twelve 2½-inch muffin cups with nonstick cooking spray or grease the bottoms only.

2. In a large bowl, mix the cereal, flour, brown sugar, cinnamon, baking powder, and baking soda.

3. Stir in the remaining ingredients just until moistened.

4. Divide the batter evenly among the muffin cups. Bake 18 to 22 minutes or until golden brown.

5. Remove the muffins and serve warm.

Slightly stale bread, bagels, and muffins can be made fresh-tasting again in less than a minute in the microwave. Just wrap a piece in a slightly damp paper towel and heat on high (100%) for 15 seconds. If you prefer, you can refresh muffins in the oven by wrapping them in foil and warming 10 minutes at 400° F. Loaves of bread can also be refreshed in the oven. Preheat the oven to 325° F. Place the bread loaf in a brown paper bag, sprinkle the outside of the bag with water, and warm 10 to 15 minutes.

Cocoa Banana Muffins

MAKES 12 MUFFINS

1 cup all-purpose flour
2 teaspoons baking powder
½ teaspoon salt
2 tablespoons unsweetened cocoa
½ cup sugar
1½ cups **Kellogg's® All-Bran® Cereal**
¾ cup skim milk
2 egg whites
2 tablespoons vegetable oil
1 cup sliced ripe banana (about 1 medium)

1. In a medium bowl, stir together the flour, baking powder, salt, cocoa, and sugar. Set aside.

2. In a large mixing bowl, combine the cereal and milk. Let stand 2 minutes or until the cereal softens.

3. Add the egg whites and oil. Beat well. Stir in the banana.

4. Add the flour mixture, stirring only until combined.

5. Heat the oven to 400° F.

6. Spoon the batter evenly into 2½-inch muffin cups coated with non-stick cooking spray.

7. Bake about 25 minutes or until the muffins are lightly browned. Serve warm.

Cherry Cordial Muffins

MAKES 12 MUFFINS

2 cups all-purpose flour
1 package (11½ ounces) **Nestlé® Toll House® Milk Chocolate Morsels** (2 cups), divided
¼ cup firmly packed light brown sugar
¼ cup sugar
2 teaspoons baking powder
½ teaspoon baking soda
½ teaspoon salt
½ cup candied cherries, chopped, *or* raisins
¾ cup milk
⅓ cup vegetable oil
1 egg

1. Heat the oven to 375° F. Grease or paper-line 12 muffin cups.

2. In a large bowl, combine the flour, 1¾ cups chocolate morsels, brown sugar, sugar, baking powder, baking soda, and salt. Stir in the candied cherries. Set aside.

3. In a small bowl, combine the milk, vegetable oil, and egg until well blended. Stir into the flour mixture just until the dry ingredients are moistened.

4. Spoon into the prepared muffin cups (muffin cups will be full). Sprinkle with the remaining morsels. Bake 18 to 20 minutes until golden.

5. Cool 5 minutes. Remove the muffins from the cups and serve warm immediately. Or cool completely before serving.

Cheese and Spinach Muffins

MAKES 12 MUFFINS

⅔ cup milk
1 tablespoon vegetable oil
1 egg
½ cup coarsely chopped fresh spinach
½ cup shredded Swiss cheese (2 ounces)
¼ cup grated Parmesan cheese
2 tablespoons chopped green onions
2 cups **Bisquick® Original** *or* **Reduced Fat baking mix**

1. Heat the oven to 400° F. Grease the bottoms and sides of 12 medium muffin cups.
2. In a medium bowl, beat the milk, oil, and egg until blended.
3. Stir in the spinach, cheeses, green onions, and baking mix just until moistened.
4. Divide the batter evenly among the muffin cups. Bake 15 minutes or until golden brown.
5. Cool slightly. Remove from the pan and serve.

To measure a dry ingredient accurately, stir it to smooth out any lumps. (If a recipe calls for sifted flour, there's no need to stir the flour first.) Using a spoon, gently fill a measuring cup, mounding the ingredient above the rim, then slide the thin edge of a knife or spatula across the rim to level off the excess. For butter, margarine, vegetable shortening, or brown sugar, always pack the ingredients into the measuring cup firmly.

Zesty Corn Muffins

MAKES 12 MUFFINS

1 cup whole wheat flour
⅔ cup all-purpose flour
4 teaspoons baking powder
¼ teaspoon salt (optional)
¼ cup sugar
½ teaspoon chili powder
1½ cups **Kellogg's® All-Bran® Cereal**
1 cup skim milk
3 egg whites
3 tablespoons vegetable oil
1 can (8¾ ounces) whole kernel corn, drained
¼ cup chopped pimientos, drained
2 tablespoons chopped onion
1 to 2 tablespoons chopped jalapeño peppers
½ cup shredded mozzarella cheese (2 ounces)

1. Heat the oven to 400° F.
2. In a small bowl, stir together the flours, baking powder, salt, if using, sugar, and chili powder. Set aside.
3. In a large bowl, combine the cereal and milk. Let stand 2 minutes or until the cereal softens. Add the egg whites and oil. Beat well. Stir in the corn, pimientos, onion, peppers, and cheese.
4. Add the flour mixture, stirring only until combined.
5. Portion the batter evenly into twelve 2½-inch muffin cups coated with nonstick cooking spray. Bake 20 minutes or until lightly browned.
6. Allow to cool slightly before removing from the pan. Transfer to a towel-lined basket and serve warm.

Morning Madness Puffs

1½ cups all-purpose flour
¼ teaspoon salt
1½ teaspoons baking powder
¾ teaspoon ground nutmeg, divided
¾ cup sugar, divided
1¾ teaspoons ground cinnamon, divided
⅓ cup plus 3 tablespoons **I Can't Believe It's Not Butter!**®, divided
1 egg
½ cup milk

1. Heat the oven to 350° F.
2. In a medium bowl, stir together the flour, salt, baking powder, and ¼ teaspoon nutmeg.
3. In a food processor, using the blade, cream together ½ cup sugar, ¼ teaspoon cinnamon, and ⅓ cup I Can't Believe It's Not Butter!® until very smooth.
4. Add the egg and process until very creamy, approximately 2 minutes. Add the flour mixture and milk alternately to the mixture. Process until smooth.
5. Fill lightly greased muffin cups ⅔ full.
6. Bake 20 to 25 minutes or until golden brown.
7. In a small bowl, combine the remaining sugar and spices.
8. In a small pan or microwave oven, melt the remaining I Can't Believe It's Not Butter!®
9. Remove the puffs from the pan, brush with the melted I Can't Believe It's Not Butter!®, then dip in the sugar and spice mixture. Serve immediately.

Three-Cheese Biscuits

2¼ cups **Bisquick® Original baking mix**
½ cup milk
¼ cup shredded sharp Cheddar cheese (1 ounce)
¼ cup shredded Monterey Jack cheese (1 ounce)
1 tablespoon margarine *or* butter, melted
Grated Parmesan cheese

1. Heat the oven to 450° F.
2. Mix the baking mix, milk, and cheeses until a stiff dough forms.
3. Turn the dough onto a surface well dusted with baking mix and gently roll in the mix to coat.
4. Shape the dough into a ball and knead 10 times. Roll out ½ inch thick. Cut with a 2-inch biscuit cutter dipped in baking mix.
5. Place on a greased baking sheet. Brush the tops with the margarine and sprinkle with the Parmesan cheese.
6. Bake 8 to 10 minutes or until golden brown.
7. Serve warm.

P atting out biscuit dough with your hands instead of rolling it out is an easy shortcut, although it gives the biscuits a slightly rougher texture on top. To eliminate the re-rolling of scraps and save even more time, you can make square biscuits. Simply pat the dough into a rectangle of the recommended thickness, then cut into 2- to 3-inch squares.

Cakes
AND
Pies

Luscious Lemon Poke Cake

SERVES 12

2 baked 9-inch round white cake layers, cooled
2 cups boiling water
1 package (8-serving size) *or* 2 packages (4-serving size *each*) **Jell-O® Lemon Flavor Gelatin Dessert**
1 tub (8 ounces) **Cool Whip® Whipped Topping,** thawed

1. Place the cake layers, top sides up, in two clean 9-inch round cake pans. Pierce the cake with a large fork at ½-inch intervals.

2. Stir the boiling water into the gelatin in a medium bowl at least 2 minutes until completely dissolved. Carefully pour 1 cup gelatin over 1 cake layer.

3. Pour the remaining gelatin over the second cake layer. Refrigerate 3 hours. Dip one cake pan in warm water for 10 seconds. Unmold onto a serving plate.

4. Spread the layer with about 1 cup whipped topping. Unmold the second cake layer and carefully place on the first cake layer.

5. Frost the top and sides of the cake with the remaining whipped topping. Refrigerate at least 1 hour or until ready to serve.

6. Decorate as desired. Cut into wedges and serve. Store leftover cake in the refrigerator.

Brown sugar is a combination of white sugar and molasses. To retain its moist, soft texture, brown sugar should be stored in an airtight container or in a plastic bag. If it hardens, soften it by microwaving the sugar with a slice of apple in a covered microwave-safe container on low for 1 to 2 minutes.

New England Apple Cake

SERVES 16

½ cup (1 stick) **Shedd's® Spread Country Crock®,** at room temperature
1 cup sugar
1 cup firmly packed brown sugar
3 eggs
2 teaspoons vanilla extract
2¼ cups all-purpose flour
2¼ teaspoons baking soda
1 teaspoon salt
2 teaspoons ground cinnamon
½ teaspoon ground nutmeg
7 cups coarsely chopped cooking apples, loosely packed
¾ cup chopped walnuts
1 tablespoon confectioners sugar

1. Heat the oven to 350° F.

2. In a large bowl, cream together the Shedd's® Spread Country Crock® and both sugars. Beat in the eggs and vanilla until well blended.

3. In a medium bowl, combine the flour, baking soda, salt, and spices. Add to the creamed mixture and stir to combine thoroughly. Stir in the apples and walnuts.

4. Spoon into a greased 10-inch Bundt® or tube pan.

5. Bake 50 to 60 minutes or until an inserted toothpick comes out almost clean. (Because of the apples, the toothpick will be moist.)

6. Cool on a rack for 10 minutes, then turn out onto a serving dish.

7. When completely cooled, dust with the confectioners sugar. Cut into wedges and serve. Refrigerate any leftovers.

Chocolate Cherry Valentine Cake

Chocolate Cherry Valentine Cake

SERVES 8

½ cup (1 stick) **LAND O LAKES® Butter,** softened

1 cup sugar

2 eggs

1 teaspoon vanilla extract

3 squares (1 ounce *each*) unsweetened baking chocolate, melted

1½ cups all-purpose flour

¾ teaspoon baking powder

½ teaspoon baking soda

⅛ teaspoon salt

1 cup **LAND O LAKES® Sour Cream, Regular, Light,** *or* **No-Fat**

2 cups frozen cherries, thawed and drained

2 tablespoons confectioners sugar

1. Heat the oven to 350° F.

2. In a large bowl, beat the butter and sugar until light and fluffy. Beat in the eggs one at a time. Beat in the vanilla and chocolate.

3. In a large bowl, combine the flour, baking powder, baking soda, and salt. Add to the butter mixture alternately with the sour cream, beginning and ending with the flour mixture.

4. Fold in the cherries. Scrape into a lightly greased and floured 9-inch heart-shaped or square baking pan. Bake 45 to 55 minutes or until the cake tester comes out clean.

5. Cool on a rack for 20 minutes. Unmold and cool completely. Decorate by dusting the confectioners sugar over a doily and serve.

Dolce Pane con Zucchini

Dolce Pane con Zucchini

SERVES 12

- 3 cups all-purpose flour
- 1½ cups sugar
- 2 teaspoons ground cinnamon
- 1 teaspoon salt
- 1 teaspoon baking powder
- 1 teaspoon baking soda
- 3 eggs
- 2 teaspoons vanilla extract
- 1 cup **Bertolli® Extra Light Olive Oil**
- 3 cups shredded, unpeeled zucchini
- 1½ cups dark raisins
- 1½ cups golden raisins
- 1 cup chopped walnuts

For lemon icing:

- 1½ cups confectioners sugar
- 1 teaspoon lemon zest
- 3 tablespoons lemon juice
- 1 tablespoon **Bertolli® Extra Light Olive Oil**

1. Heat the oven to 350° F.

2. In a large bowl, whisk together the flour, sugar, cinnamon, salt, baking powder, and baking soda. In another large bowl, beat together the eggs, vanilla, and olive oil. Stir in the remaining ingredients. Pour over the flour mixture and stir until thoroughly mixed.

3. Pour the batter into twelve greased individual Bundt'lette® molds to ⅔ full. Bake 30 to 35 minutes or until a toothpick comes out clean. Or pour the batter into two greased 9×5-inch loaf pans and bake 1 hour or until a toothpick comes out clean. Let the cakes cool. Remove from the pans.

4. In a small bowl, combine all the icing ingredients. Drizzle over the room-temperature cakes.

5. Place the cakes on individual plates and serve.

Carrot Cake

SERVES 16

3 cups all-purpose flour
2 teaspoons baking powder
1 teaspoon baking soda
1 teaspoon ground cinnamon
½ teaspoon salt
1 cup **Mott's® Natural Apple Sauce**
1 cup firmly packed light brown sugar
1 cup sugar
6 egg whites
Zest and juice of 1 orange
3 cups peeled and shredded carrots
1 cup raisins

For orange glaze:

2 cups confectioners sugar
2 tablespoons **Mott's® Natural Apple Sauce**
1 to 2 tablespoons orange juice
1 teaspoon freshly grated orange zest

1. Heat the oven to 350° F.

2. Spray a Bundt® pan with nonstick cooking spray.

3. In a medium bowl, combine the flour, baking powder, baking soda, cinnamon, and salt. Set aside.

4. In a large bowl, using an electric mixer, beat together the applesauce, sugars, egg whites, and zest and juice of the orange. With the mixer on medium speed, blend in the flour mixture, beating until just smooth. Stir in the carrots and raisins.

5. Pour the batter in the prepared pan and bake 60 to 65 minutes or until the cake tester comes out clean.

6. Remove the cake from the pan and place on a rack. Cool completely.

7. To prepare the glaze: Combine the glaze ingredients and spoon over the cooled cake. Cut into wedges and serve.

Maple Pecan Cake

MAKES 1 8-INCH LAYER CAKE

2 cups sifted cake flour
1 tablespoon baking powder
1 teaspoon salt
1 cup **Wesson® Oil**
¾ cup firmly packed light brown sugar
½ cup sugar
3 eggs
¼ cup buttermilk
1½ teaspoons vanilla extract
1¼ teaspoons maple extract *or* pure maple syrup
½ cup finely ground pecans
12 pecan halves

For frosting:

1 box (1 pound) confectioners sugar
½ cup (1 stick) butter *or* margarine, softened
1 teaspoon vanilla *or* maple extract
¼ cup milk

1. In a large bowl, combine the flour, baking powder, and salt.

2. In a medium bowl, beat together the remaining cake ingredients, *except* pecans, until well mixed and thickened.

3. Add the oil mixture to the flour mixture and beat 2 minutes or until smooth and well blended. Stir in the ground pecans. Divide the batter between two greased and floured 8-inch round pans.

4. Heat the oven to 350° F. Bake 30 minutes or until a wooden pick comes out clean when inserted in the cake center. Let stand 10 minutes, then turn out onto racks. Cool completely before frosting.

5. In a medium bowl, beat together the sugar, butter, and vanilla, and slowly add the milk to the desired consistency. Frost the cooled cake on a serving plate. Decorate with the pecan halves. Serve.

Granny's Great Graham Torte

Granny's Great Graham Torte

MAKES 1 8-INCH, 2-LAYER TORTE

1 cup (2 sticks) **I Can't Believe It's Not Butter!®**
1 cup sugar
3 eggs
2 cups fine graham cracker crumbs
½ cup all-purpose flour
1 teaspoon baking powder
½ teaspoon ground cinnamon
¼ teaspoon salt
1 cup milk
2 cups peeled and diced Granny Smith apples
1 cup chopped walnuts, divided
1 cup whipping cream
2 tablespoons confectioners sugar

1. Heat the oven to 350° F.

2. With an electric mixer, in a large mixing bowl, beat I Can't Believe It's Not Butter!® and sugar until fluffy. Beat in the eggs one at a time.

3. In a medium bowl, combine the graham cracker crumbs, flour, baking powder, cinnamon, and salt.

4. Alternately add the dry mixture and the milk to the batter. Stir in the apples and ¾ cup walnuts.

5. Spread the batter into two greased 8-inch round pans.

6. Bake 30 to 35 minutes. Cool in the pans 10 minutes, then turn out onto racks to cool completely.

7. In a medium bowl, whip the cream and sugar until stiff.

8. Place 1 layer on a cake plate. Spread the whipped cream on top. Place the second layer on the first and spread the whipped cream on top of the torte.

9. Finely chop the reserved walnuts. Sprinkle over the top of the torte. Refrigerate at least 2 hours before serving.

Williamsburg Cake

SERVES 12

MAKES ABOUT 1½ CUPS FROSTING

½ cup (1 stick) plus 1 teaspoon
  I Can't Believe It's Not Butter!®, softened, divided

1 cup sugar

4 egg whites

1 tablespoon grated orange zest

1 teaspoon vanilla extract

½ cup seedless golden raisins

½ cup chopped walnuts

2 cups all-purpose flour

1 teaspoon baking soda

1 cup low-fat milk

For orange frosting:

½ cup (1 stick) **I Can't Believe It's Not Butter!**®, softened

2 cups confectioners sugar

2 tablespoons orange juice

1 tablespoon grated orange zest

1. Heat the oven to 350° F.

2. In a large bowl, cream together ½ cup I Can't Believe It's Not Butter!® with the sugar until light and fluffy. Add the egg whites, orange zest, and vanilla. Beat until well combined and slightly frothy. Stir in the raisins and walnuts.

3. Sift the flour and baking soda together and add to the batter alternately with the milk, beginning and ending with the flour.

4. Use the 1 teaspoon I Can't Believe It's Not Butter!® to grease an 8-inch square baking pan. Dust with flour. Pour the batter into the pan.

5. Bake 35 to 40 minutes or until a cake tester comes out clean. Remove to a rack and let cool.

6. In a medium bowl, beat together all the frosting ingredients until smooth and silky. Frost the cooled cake with the orange frosting.

7. Cut into wedges and serve.

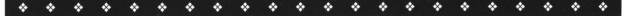

*M*ost cakes will keep at room temperature up to 3 days. It's best to cover a frosted cake with a cake box or a large inverted bowl. If you must use plastic food wrap or foil, insert toothpicks into the top of the cake so that the wrapping does not stick to the frosting. A cake with a cream-based topping or filling should always be refrigerated.

Wrapped in heavy-duty foil, many cakes will keep up to 3 months in the freezer at 0° F. The best way to freeze a cake is to wrap unfrosted layers individually. But if you prefer to frost the cake first, use a frosting made with butter and confectioners sugar; it should not contain egg whites, brown sugar, artificial flavorings, or fresh fruit. First, freeze the cake unwrapped, then protect the frosting with a layer of wax paper before wrapping it in heavy-duty foil. To defrost a cake, unwrap and let it stand at room temperature for 1 to 2 hours.

Chocolate Surprise Cake

Chocolate Surprise Cake

SERVES 12

12 ounces **Cream Cheese,** softened
¼ cup sugar
1 egg
½ teaspoon vanilla extract
1 package (18¼ ounces) chocolate cake mix
½ cup semisweet miniature chocolate chips
Confectioners sugar
Whipped cream (optional)
Raspberries (optional)

1. Heat the oven to 350° F. Butter and flour a 12-cup Bundt® pan.

2. In a small mixing bowl, using an electric mixer, beat the cream cheese and sugar until smooth. Add the egg and vanilla. Beat until blended and set aside.

3. Prepare the cake as label directs and fold in the chocolate chips. Pour the batter into the prepared pan. Evenly cover with the cream cheese mixture. Bake until a wooden pick inserted in the center comes out clean, 45 to 55 minutes. Cool on a rack for 25 minutes. Remove from the pan and cool completely.

4. Dust with the confectioners sugar. Serve with whipped cream and raspberries, if desired.

COURTESY: DAIRY MANAGEMENT, INC.

New York-Style Cheesecake

SERVES 12

1 cup graham cracker crumbs
3 tablespoons margarine, melted
1 cup plus 4 tablespoons sugar, divided
2 tablespoons all-purpose flour
1 tablespoon cornstarch
½ cup low-fat plain *or* lemon yogurt
4 packages (8 ounces *each*) **Healthy Choice® Fat Free Cream Cheese**, softened
4 eggs
2 teaspoons lemon juice
½ teaspoon grated lemon zest
1½ teaspoons vanilla extract
8 ounces reduced-fat sour cream

1. Heat the oven to 375° F.

2. In a medium bowl, combine the graham cracker crumbs, margarine, and 2 tablespoons sugar. Press into the bottom of a 9-inch springform pan. Spray the sides with nonstick cooking spray.

3. In a large bowl, combine the flour, cornstarch, and yogurt. Add the cream cheese and beat well. Beat in the eggs, lemon juice, lemon zest, and vanilla plus 1 cup sugar until smooth. Pour over the crust.

4. Bake 5 minutes. Reduce the oven temperature to 300° F and bake 45 minutes more.

5. Turn off the oven and cool the cake in the oven for 30 minutes.

6. In a small bowl, blend the sour cream with 2 tablespoons sugar. Spread over the top. Return to the oven until set.

7. Chill before serving.

Blueberry Cheesecake

SERVES 8

For crust:

1½ cups cinnamon graham cracker crumbs
¼ cup (½ stick) margarine, melted
2 tablespoons sugar

For filling:

1 package (8 ounces) light cream cheese
¼ cup sugar
2 egg whites
½ teaspoon vanilla extract
Reynolds® Crystal Color® Plastic Wrap
1 cup blueberry pie filling

1. Place the graham crumbs in a medium bowl. Add the margarine and 2 tablespoons sugar. Stir until well blended.

2. Press the crumb mixture evenly into a 9-inch glass pie plate and set aside.

3. Heat the oven to 325° F.

4. In a medium bowl, with an electric mixer, beat the cream cheese and ¼ cup sugar until well blended. Add the egg whites and vanilla. Beat until smooth. Pour into the crust.

5. Bake until the center is set, 25 to 30 minutes. Cool on a rack.

6. Cover with plastic wrap and refrigerate until chilled.

7. Before serving, remove the plastic wrap and spread the blueberry pie filling evenly over the top of the cheesecake.

Chocolate Lover's Cheesecake

Chocolate Lover's Cheesecake

SERVES 10 TO 12

For crust:

1½ cups graham cracker crumbs
⅓ cup sugar
⅓ cup (5 tablespoons plus 1 teaspoon) butter *or* margarine, melted

For filling:

2 packages (8 ounces *each*) cream cheese, softened
¾ cup plus 2 tablespoons sugar, divided
½ cup **Hershey's Cocoa**
2 teaspoons vanilla extract, divided
2 eggs
1 cup **Hershey's Semi-Sweet Chocolate Chips**
1 cup sour cream

1. To prepare the crust: In a medium bowl, blend together the graham cracker crumbs, sugar, and butter. Press the mixture onto the bottom and halfway up the side of a 9-inch springform pan. Set aside.

2. Heat the oven to 375° F.

3. In a large mixer bowl, beat the cream cheese, ¾ cup sugar, cocoa, and 1 teaspoon vanilla until light and fluffy. Add the eggs and beat until smooth. Stir in the chocolate chips. Pour into the crust.

4. Bake 20 minutes. Remove from the oven and cool 15 minutes.

5. Increase the oven temperature to 425° F. Combine the sour cream and the remaining sugar and vanilla. Stir until smooth. Spread evenly over the baked filling.

6. Bake 10 minutes. Loosen the cake from the rim of the pan. Cool.

7. Refrigerate several hours or overnight. Remove the rim of the pan. Cut into wedges and serve.

Praline Cheesecake

SERVES 18

4 cups **Bisquick® Original** *or* **Reduced Fat baking mix**
1¼ cups sugar, divided
½ cup plus ⅓ cup flaked coconut, divided
2 tablespoons unsweetened cocoa
⅓ cup (5 tablespoons plus 1 teaspoon) margarine *or* butter, softened
3 eggs, divided
2 packages (8 ounces *each*) cream cheese, softened
1 tablespoon plus 2 teaspoons vanilla extract, divided
2 cups sour cream
¼ cup firmly packed brown sugar
⅓ cup chopped pecans

1. Heat the oven to 350° F.
2. In a medium bowl, beat together the baking mix, ½ cup sugar, ½ cup coconut, cocoa, margarine, and 1 egg on low speed until crumbly.
3. Press the mixture lightly into an ungreased 13×9-inch pan and set aside.
4. In a medium bowl, beat together the cream cheese, 2 eggs, ¾ cup sugar, and 2 teaspoons vanilla until the mixture is smooth and fluffy. Spread over the crust.
5. Bake about 25 minutes or until set. Remove from the oven and place on a rack.
6. In a small bowl, mix the sour cream, brown sugar, and 1 tablespoon vanilla until smooth. Immediately spread the mixture over the hot cheesecake.
7. In a small bowl, mix together ⅓ cup coconut and pecans. Sprinkle over the cheesecake. Cool 15 minutes.
8. Cover and refrigerate at least 5 hours.
9. Cut into squares and serve.

Black and White Cheesecake

SERVES 10

½ cup marshmallow creme *or* 1 cup miniature marshmallows
1 9-ounce graham cracker crust
1 envelope **Knox® Unflavored Gelatine**
¼ cup cold milk plus ¾ cup milk heated to boiling
2 packages (8 ounces *each*) cream cheese, softened
¾ cup sugar
¼ cup unsweetened cocoa
1 teaspoon vanilla extract (optional)

1. Spread the marshmallow creme or scatter the marshmallows over the bottom of the prepared crust and set aside.
2. In a blender, sprinkle the unflavored gelatin over the cold milk and let stand 2 minutes. Add the hot milk and process at low speed until the gelatin is completely dissolved, about 2 minutes.
3. Add the cream cheese, sugar, cocoa, and vanilla. Process at high speed until blended.
4. Gently pour into the prepared crust and chill until firm, about 2 hours. Cut into wedges and serve.

Lemon-Poppy Seed Coffee Cake

Lemon-Poppy Seed Coffee Cake

SERVES 9

2 cups **Bisquick® Original baking mix**
1 cup milk
¼ cup poppy seeds
¼ cup vegetable oil
2 eggs
1 package (3½ ounces) lemon-flavor instant pudding
  and pie filling

For glaze:

⅔ cup confectioners sugar
3 to 4 teaspoons lemon juice

1. Heat the oven to 350° F.

2. Mix all the ingredients *except* confectioners sugar and lemon juice. Beat 30 seconds. Spread in a greased 9-inch square pan.

3. Bake 35 to 40 minutes or until light golden brown and a toothpick inserted in the center comes out clean. Cool 10 minutes.

4. Mix the confectioners sugar and lemon juice until smooth.

5. Drizzle the glaze on the cake. Cut into squares and serve.

Blueberry-Lemon Coffee Cake

SERVES 6 TO 8

1 egg
2¼ cups **Bisquick® Original** *or* **Reduced Fat baking mix**, reserving ¼ cup
⅓ cup sugar
⅔ cup milk
1 tablespoon grated lemon zest
1 cup frozen blueberries, thawed, rinsed, and well drained

For glaze:

⅔ cup confectioners sugar
3 to 4 teaspoons lemon juice

1. Heat the oven to 400° F. Grease a 9-inch round pan.

2. In a medium bowl, beat the egg slightly. Stir in 2 cups baking mix, sugar, milk, and lemon zest.

3. In a small bowl, mix the blueberries and ¼ cup baking mix and fold into the batter.

4. Spread the batter in the pan. Bake 20 to 25 minutes or until golden brown. Cool 10 minutes.

5. In a small bowl, mix the confectioners sugar and lemon juice until smooth.

6. Drizzle the lemon glaze over the warm cake and serve.

Cinnamon Applesauce Loaf

Cinnamon Applesauce Loaf

MAKES 1 9×5-INCH LOAF

2 cups all-purpose flour
1 teaspoon baking soda
1 teaspoon ground cinnamon
½ teaspoon baking powder
1 cup sweetened applesauce
¾ cup sugar
¾ cup **Egg Beaters® Healthy Real Egg Substitute**
½ cup **Fleischmann's® Original Spread,** melted
½ cup seedless raisins
Confectioners sugar glaze (optional)

1. Heat the oven to 350° F.
2. In a medium bowl, combine the flour, baking soda, cinnamon, and baking powder.
3. In a large bowl, blend the applesauce, sugar, Egg Beaters®, and margarine. Stir into the flour mixture just until blended. The batter will be lumpy. Mix in the raisins.
4. Spoon the batter into a greased 9×5-inch loaf pan.
5. Bake 55 to 60 minutes or until a toothpick inserted in the center comes out clean. Cool.
6. Drizzle with glaze, if desired. Slice and serve.

❖ ❖ ❖ ❖ ❖ ❖ ❖ ❖ ❖ ❖ ❖ ❖ ❖

Baking powder is a combination of dry acidic and alkaline ingredients. Commercial baking powders also contain cornstarch to absorb moisture. To make 1 teaspoon of baking powder, combine ¼ teaspoon baking soda with ½ teaspoon cream of tartar.

Moist and Spicy Prune Cake

SERVES 16

2 cups all-purpose flour
1 teaspoon baking soda
1 teaspoon ground cinnamon
½ teaspoon ground cloves
½ teaspoon ground nutmeg
½ teaspoon ground allspice
¼ teaspoon salt
5 egg whites
1½ cups sugar
1 cup **Mott's® Natural Apple Sauce**
½ cup buttermilk
1 cup stewed pitted prunes, mashed

For icing:

2 cups confectioners sugar
1½ teaspoons lemon juice
¼ teaspoon almond extract
Water, as needed (approximately 2 tablespoons)
⅓ cup toasted, slivered almonds (optional)

1. Sift together the flour, baking soda, spices, and salt. Set aside.
2. In a large mixing bowl, beat together the egg whites and sugar until thoroughly combined. Add the applesauce and mix well. Add the flour mixture alternating with the buttermilk, mixing well between additions. Add the prunes and mix well.
3. Heat the oven to 350° F. Spray a Bundt® pan with cooking spray.
4. Pour the batter into the prepared pan. Bake 50 to 55 minutes or until a cake tester comes out clean.
5. Turn the cake onto a rack and cool completely.
6. To prepare the icing: Combine the sugar, lemon juice, almond extract, and enough water to make the consistency of a thick glaze.
7. Drizzle over the cake and sprinkle with almonds, if desired. Serve.

Orange Grove Poppy Seed Cake

SERVES 14

¼ cup fine dry bread crumbs
3 tablespoons **Florida Orange Juice**
2 tablespoons grated orange zest
3 cups all-purpose flour
2 teaspoons baking powder
1 teaspoon baking soda
½ teaspoon salt
1 cup (2 sticks) unsalted butter *or* margarine
2 cups sugar
3 eggs
1 cup buttermilk
⅓ cup poppy seeds

For glaze:

2 tablespoons **Florida Orange Juice**
1 cup confectioners sugar

1. Butter a 10-inch tube or Bundt® pan. Sprinkle with the bread crumbs, shaking off any excess.

2. In a small bowl, combine the orange juice and orange zest.

3. On a piece of wax paper, sift together the flour, baking powder, baking soda, and salt.

4. Heat the oven to 325° F.

5. In a large mixing bowl, beat the butter until creamy. Add the sugar and beat until light and fluffy. Add the eggs, one at a time, and beat until incorporated. Beat in the flour mixture, alternately with the buttermilk, beginning and ending with the flour mixture until the batter is smooth. Stir in the orange juice with zest and poppy seeds. Turn into the prepared pan.

6. Bake 1 hour or until a cake tester inserted into the cake is dry.

7. Let the cake cool in the pan for 10 minutes, then invert the cake on a rack to cool completely while preparing the glaze.

8. To prepare the glaze: In a small bowl, combine the orange juice and sugar, stirring until smooth.

9. Drizzle over the cooled cake, cut into wedges, and serve.

COURTESY: FLORIDA DEPARTMENT OF CITRUS

Almond Marble Pound Cake

SERVES 24

½ cup sliced almonds, crushed
2 packages (16 ounces *each*) pound cake mix
1⅓ cups water, divided
4 eggs, divided
½ cup (1 stick) margarine, melted and divided
1 cup vanilla chips, melted
1 teaspoon almond extract
1 cup semisweet chocolate chips, melted
1 teaspoon vanilla extract
Reynolds® Crystal Color® Plastic Wrap

1. Grease a 12-cup Bundt® pan with shortening. Sprinkle the almonds in the pan and turn to coat the sides and bottom. Set aside.

2. Pour the pound cake mixes separately into two large bowls. To each mix add ⅔ cup water, 2 eggs, and ¼ cup melted margarine. Beat each mix for 2 minutes.

3. To one mix add the melted vanilla chips and almond extract. Beat 1 minute and set aside. To the other mix add the melted chocolate chips and vanilla extract. Beat 1 minute.

4. Heat the oven to 325° F.

5. Alternating batters, pour into the pan. Using a knife, swirl the batters to marble. Bake until a toothpick inserted in the center comes out clean, 1 hour to 1 hour, 10 minutes.

6. Cool in the pan 5 minutes. Remove from the pan and cool on a rack. When cooled completely, wrap tightly in plastic wrap until ready to serve.

Sweet Potato Pie

SERVES 8

For filling:

4 medium sweet potatoes, peeled and quartered
(approximately 3 cups mashed)
¼ cup sugar
¼ cup firmly packed brown sugar
¼ cup (½ stick) **LAND O LAKES® Butter,** melted
¾ cup half-and-half
3 eggs, slightly beaten
¾ teaspoon ground cinnamon
¼ teaspoon ground allspice
¼ teaspoon ground nutmeg
¼ teaspoon salt
1 teaspoon grated lemon zest

1 prepared single-crust pie pastry

For topping:

1 cup crushed corn flakes
½ cup chopped pecans
⅓ cup firmly packed brown sugar
¼ cup (½ stick) **LAND O LAKES® Butter,** melted

Sweetened whipped cream

1. Place the sweet potatoes in a 4-quart saucepan and cover with water. Cook over high heat until the water comes to a full boil, 6 to 8 minutes. Reduce the heat to medium-high. Continue cooking until the sweet potatoes are fork-tender, 12 to 18 minutes. Drain and mash.

2. Heat the oven to 375° F.

3. In a large mixer bowl, place 3 cups mashed sweet potatoes. Add all the remaining filling ingredients. Beat at low speed, scraping the bowl often, until well mixed, 1 to 2 minutes.

4. Line a 9-inch pie pan with the pastry. Crimp or flute the crust.

5. Pour the filling into the prepared pie shell.

6. In a small bowl, combine all the topping ingredients. Stir with a fork until well mixed.

7. Sprinkle the topping mixture evenly over the filling. Cover the edge of the crust with a 2-inch strip of foil.

8. Bake 30 minutes and remove the foil. Continue baking 35 to 45 minutes or until the filling is set and a knife inserted in the center comes out clean. (If the pecans are browning too quickly, cover the top of the pie with foil.)

9. Cool the pie on a rack at room temperature at least 1 hour before slicing. Cut into wedges and serve with sweetened whipped cream. Store leftovers in the refrigerator.

The more fat a cream contains, the more volume it has when it is whipped. Heavy whipping cream at 36 to 40 percent fat content has greater volume when whipped than light whipping cream (30 to 35 percent fat), which in turn has more volume than light cream (16 to 22 percent), also called coffee cream or table cream. For best results when sweetening or flavoring whipped cream, add confectioners sugar or flavoring near the end of whipping.

Orange Custard Pie

SERVES 10

1¼ cups **Florida Orange Juice**
1 cup skim milk
2 egg yolks
½ cup sugar
3 tablespoons cornstarch
1 envelope unflavored gelatin
1 prepared graham cracker pie crust
2 **Florida Oranges**

1. In a heavy saucepan, combine the orange juice, milk, egg yolks, sugar, cornstarch, and gelatin until blended.

2. Cook, stirring, over medium heat, until the mixture is smooth and begins to boil. Remove from the heat. Allow to cool, then pour into the pie crust.

3. Chill at least 2 hours or until firm.

4. Meanwhile, place the unpeeled oranges on a cutting board. With a sharp knife, slice off the tops and bottoms of the oranges, cutting deep enough so that no white pith shows.

5. Sit the oranges on their bottoms and, working from the top downward, shave off the sides, cutting deep enough to remove all the pith. When the oranges are completely peeled, cut between the membranes that divide the segments and remove the orange sections, seeing that no pith or membrane remains.

6. Lay the orange sections on top of the pie in concentric circles and serve.

COURTESY: FLORIDA DEPARTMENT OF CITRUS

Stouffer's® Caramel Apple Pie

SERVES 8

6 ounces cream cheese, softened
1 egg
1½ teaspoons vanilla extract
3 tablespoons sugar
1 tablespoon all-purpose flour
1 6-ounce graham cracker pie crust
1 package (12 ounces) **Stouffer's® Escalloped Apples,** thawed
⅓ cup caramel topping
½ teaspoon ground cinnamon

1. Heat the oven to 375° F.

2. In a medium mixing bowl, combine the softened cream cheese, egg, vanilla, sugar, and flour. Beat until smooth.

3. Spread the mixture over the pie crust.

4. In a medium bowl, combine the thawed escalloped apples, caramel topping, and cinnamon. Gently spoon over the cream cheese mixture to keep 2 distinct layers.

5. Bake 40 to 45 minutes or until the apples bubble up. Serve at room temperature.

Stouffer's® Caramel Apple Pie

Lemon Berry Pie

SERVES 8

4 ounces **Philadelphia Brand® Cream Cheese,** softened
1 tablespoon milk
1 tablespoon sugar
2 teaspoons grated lemon zest
1 tablespoon lemon juice
1 tub (8 ounces) **Cool Whip® Whipped Topping,** thawed
1 6-ounce **Keebler® Ready-Crust® Graham Cracker Pie Crust**
1 pint strawberries, hulled and halved
2 cups cold milk
2 packages (4-serving size *each*) **Jell-O® Vanilla** *or* **Lemon Flavor Instant Pudding & Pie Filling**

1. Beat the cream cheese, 1 tablespoon milk, and sugar in a medium bowl with a wire whisk until smooth. Stir in the lemon zest and juice. Stir in 1½ cups whipped topping. Spread evenly on the bottom of the prepared crust.

2. Press the strawberries into the cream cheese layer, reserving several for garnish, if desired.

3. Pour 2 cups milk in a large bowl. Add the pudding mixes. Beat with a wire whisk for 1 minute. Let stand 1 minute or until thickened. Gently stir in 1 cup whipped topping. Spoon over the strawberries in the crust. Refrigerate 4 hours or until set.

4. Garnish with the remaining whipped topping and reserved strawberries. Cut into wedges and serve. Store leftover pie in the refrigerator.

Double-Layer Pumpkin Pie

SERVES 8

4 ounces **Philadelphia Brand® Cream Cheese,** softened
1 cup plus 1 tablespoon milk *or* half-and-half
1 tablespoon sugar
1½ cups **Cool Whip® Whipped Topping,** thawed
1 6-ounce **Keebler® Ready-Crust® Graham Cracker Pie Crust**
1 can (16 ounces) pumpkin
2 packages (4-serving size *each*) **Jell-O® Vanilla Flavor Instant Pudding & Pie Filling**
1 teaspoon ground cinnamon
½ teaspoon ground ginger
¼ teaspoon ground cloves

1. Mix the cream cheese, 1 tablespoon milk, and sugar in a large bowl with a wire whisk until smooth. Gently stir in the whipped topping.

2. Spread the mixture on the bottom of the prepared crust.

3. Pour 1 cup cold milk into a bowl. Add the pumpkin, pudding mixes, and spices. Beat with a wire whisk until well mixed. (Mixture will be thick.) Spread over the cream cheese layer. Refrigerate 4 hours or until set. Garnish with additional whipped topping, if desired, and serve. Store leftover pie in the refrigerator.

Chocolate and Peanut Butter Cup Pie

SERVES 8

1 envelope **Knox® Unflavored Gelatine**
¼ cup cold milk plus 1½ cups milk heated to boiling
¾ cup creamy *or* chunky peanut butter
½ cup sugar
1 6-ounce prepared chocolate crumb crust
½ cup miniature semisweet chocolate chips

1. In a blender, sprinkle the unflavored gelatin over the cold milk and let stand 2 minutes.
2. Add the hot milk and process at low speed until the gelatin is completely dissolved, about 2 minutes.
3. Add the peanut butter and sugar. Process until blended.
4. Pour into the prepared crust set on a large plate and sprinkle with the chocolate chips.
5. Transfer the pie to the refrigerator and chill until firm, about 3 hours. Cut into wedges and serve.

Double-Layer Chocolate Pie

SERVES 8

4 ounces **Philadelphia Brand® Cream Cheese,** softened
2 cups plus 1 tablespoon cold milk
1 tablespoon sugar
1 tub (8 ounces) **Cool Whip® Whipped Topping,** thawed
1 6-ounce **Keebler® Ready-Crust® Chocolate Pie Crust**
2 packages (4-serving size *each*) **Jell-O® Chocolate Flavor Instant Pudding & Pie Filling**

1. Mix the cream cheese, 1 tablespoon milk, and sugar in a large bowl with a wire whisk until smooth.
2. Gently stir in 1½ cups whipped topping. Spread on the bottom of the prepared crust.
3. Pour 2 cups milk into a bowl. Add the pudding mixes. Beat with a wire whisk until well mixed. (Mixture will be thick.)
4. Immediately stir in the remaining whipped topping. Spread over the cream cheese layer. Refrigerate 4 hours or until set.
5. Garnish with additional whipped topping, if desired. Cut into wedges and serve. Store leftover pie in the refrigerator.

*W*hile the Aztec Indians of Mexico had used cacao beans for centuries to brew a bitter, strong-flavored beverage, chocolate, as we know it, is a European innovation. Second only to vanilla in popularity as a flavor, chocolate comes in several varieties and many forms. Depending upon the amount of cocoa butter and chocolate liquor, and if vanilla, lecithin, or sugar are added, chocolate is classified as unsweetened or baking chocolate, bittersweet, semisweet, or sweet chocolate. Dry milk added to sweetened chocolate creates milk chocolate.

Praline Pumpkin Pie

SERVES 8

½ cup chopped pecans *or* walnuts
⅓ cup (5 tablespoons plus 1 teaspoon) margarine *or* butter
⅓ cup firmly packed brown sugar
1 6-ounce **Keebler® Ready-Crust® Graham Cracker Pie Crust**
1 cup cold milk
2 packages (4-serving size *each*) **Jell-O® Vanilla Flavor Instant Pudding & Pie Filling**
1 can (16 ounces) pumpkin
1¼ teaspoons pumpkin pie spice
1 tub (8 ounces) **Cool Whip® Whipped Topping,** thawed
Finely chopped nuts (optional)

1. In a small saucepan, heat the nuts, margarine, and sugar until the margarine and sugar are melted and the mixture comes to a boil. Boil 30 seconds. Spread on the bottom of the prepared crust. Cool.

2. In a large bowl, combine the milk and pudding mix. Beat with a wire whisk or mixer for 1 minute (mixture will be thick). Stir in the pumpkin and spice until well mixed. Gently stir in 1½ cups whipped topping. Spread over the nut layer.

3. Refrigerate 4 hours or until set.

4. Garnish with the remaining whipped topping. Sprinkle with finely chopped nuts, if desired, and serve. Store leftover pie in the refrigerator.

Cappuccino Ice Cream Pie

SERVES 8
MAKES 1½ CUPS SAUCE

2 cups **Quaker® Oatmeal Squares™ (Regular** *or* **Cinnamon)**
¼ cup (½ stick) butter *or* margarine, melted
1 quart coffee *or* vanilla ice cream, slightly softened

For cappuccino fudge sauce:

1 teaspoon ground cinnamon
1 tablespoon instant coffee
1 tablespoon water
1 jar (18 ounces) hot fudge topping

1. Heat the oven to 350° F.

2. Place the cereal in a plastic bag and crush with a rolling pin or can.

3. In a medium bowl, stir the crushed cereal and butter together. Press the mixture firmly and evenly onto the bottom and the sides of an 8- or 9-inch pie plate.

4. Bake the crust in the center of the oven for 10 to 12 minutes until evenly browned. Cool completely.

5. Spoon the slightly softened ice cream into the crust and cover the top with plastic wrap. Using your hands, press the ice cream evenly into the crust. Place the covered pie in the freezer until the ice cream is firm, at least several hours.

6. To make the sauce: In a medium bowl, mix the cinnamon, instant coffee, and water until the coffee has dissolved. Stir the mixture into the hot fudge topping. Refrigerate until ready to use.

7. To serve: Remove the pie from the freezer and cut into 8 wedges. Spoon warm cappuccino fudge sauce over each serving of ice cream pie.

Cappuccino Ice Cream Pie

Lite Peach Pear Tart

Lite Peach Pear Tart

1 can (16 ounces) **Del Monte® Lite Pear Halves**
1 can (16 ounces) **Del Monte® Lite Sliced Peaches**
1 envelope unflavored gelatin
1 package (8 ounces) light cream cheese, softened
1 cup (8 ounces) vanilla yogurt
1 teaspoon grated lemon zest
1 teaspoon vanilla extract
Pastry for 9-inch removable-bottom tart or springform pan, baked
Cranberries (optional)
Mint leaves (optional)
Toasted almonds (optional)

1. Drain the fruit, reserving 1 cup liquid in a small saucepan.
2. Sprinkle the gelatin over the reserved liquid to soften. Warm over low heat, stirring until the gelatin is completely dissolved.
3. In a medium bowl, blend the cream cheese, yogurt, lemon zest, and vanilla extract until smooth. Stir in the gelatin mixture. Pour into the baked crust.
4. Cover and chill at least 1 hour or until set.
5. Just before serving, drain the fruit on paper towels. Arrange over the filling. Garnish with cranberries, mint leaves, or toasted almonds, if desired.

Easy Fruit Tart

2 cups **Bisquick® Original baking mix**
⅔ cup sugar, divided
⅓ cup (5 tablespoons plus 1 teaspoon) margarine *or* butter, softened
1 egg
1 package (3 ounces) cream cheese, softened
1 teaspoon vanilla extract
¾ cup heavy whipping cream
Assorted fresh fruit
½ cup apple jelly, melted

1. Heat the oven to 375° F. Grease a baking sheet and dust it with baking mix.
2. In a medium bowl, stir together the baking mix and ⅓ cup sugar. Cut in the margarine until crumbly. Mix in the egg until a soft dough forms.
3. Pat the dough into a 12×10-inch rectangle on the baking sheet. Pinch the edges of the rectangle, forming a ½-inch rim.
4. Bake 10 to 12 minutes or until the edges just begin to brown.
5. Cool the crust on the baking sheet on a rack for 2 minutes. Remove the crust with a spatula onto the rack and cool completely.
6. In a small bowl, beat the cream cheese, ⅓ cup sugar, and vanilla on low speed until smooth. Beat in the whipping cream on medium speed.
7. Spread over the crust to within ¼ inch of the rim. Arrange the fruit on the crust and brush with the jelly.
8. Refrigerate at least 2 hours. Cut into wedges and serve.

Cookies

AND

Confections

❖

Cinnamon 'n' Sugar Shortbread (page 288), Lemon-Butter Snowbars, Old-Fashioned Butter Cookies (Left to right)

Old-Fashioned Butter Cookies

MAKES 30 COOKIES

¾ cup sugar
1 cup (2 sticks) **LAND O LAKES® Butter,** softened
2 egg yolks
1 teaspoon vanilla extract
2 cups all-purpose flour
¼ teaspoon salt
Pecan halves

1. In a large bowl, combine the sugar, butter, egg yolks, and vanilla. With an electric mixer, beat at medium speed, scraping the bowl often, until well combined, 1 to 2 minutes.

2. Add the flour and salt. Beat at low speed, scraping the bowl often, until well mixed.

3. Heat the oven to 350° F.

4. Shape rounded teaspoonfuls of dough into 1-inch balls. Place 2 inches apart on ungreased baking sheets. With the bottom of a glass dipped in sugar, flatten the cookies to ¼-inch thickness. Place a pecan half in the center of each.

5. Bake 10 to 12 minutes or until the edges are lightly browned.

6. Cool slightly. Remove from the baking sheets and serve or store.

Lemon-Butter Snowbars

MAKES 16 BARS

For crust:

1⅓ cups all-purpose flour
¼ cup sugar
½ cup (1 stick) **LAND O LAKES® Butter,** softened

For filling:

¾ cup sugar
2 eggs
2 tablespoons all-purpose flour
¼ teaspoon baking powder
3 tablespoons lemon juice
1 tablespoon confectioners sugar

1. Heat the oven to 350° F.

2. In a medium bowl, combine all the crust ingredients. With an electric mixer, beat at low speed, scraping the bowl often, until the mixture is crumbly, 2 to 3 minutes.

3. Press on the bottom of an 8-inch square baking pan. Bake 15 to 20 minutes or until the edges are lightly browned.

4. Meanwhile, in a medium mixer bowl, combine the filling ingredients. Beat at low speed, scraping the bowl often, until smooth. Pour the filling over the hot crust.

5. Continue baking 18 to 20 minutes or until the filling is set.

6. Sprinkle with the confectioners sugar. Cool, cut into bars, and serve or store.

Cinnamon 'n' Sugar Shortbread

(PHOTO PAGE 286)
MAKES 16 COOKIES

For shortbread:

1¾ cups all-purpose flour
¾ cup confectioners sugar
½ cup cake flour
1 cup (2 sticks) **LAND O LAKES® Butter,** softened
½ teaspoon ground cinnamon

For topping:

1 tablespoon sugar
⅛ teaspoon ground cinnamon

1. Heat the oven to 350° F.

2. In a large bowl, combine the shortbread ingredients. With a fork, stir the mixture until a soft dough forms. Divide the dough in half. Press evenly on the bottom of two 9-inch pie pans.

3. In a small bowl, combine the topping ingredients and sprinkle over the shortbread.

4. Score each pan of dough into 8 wedges. Prick all over with a fork. Bake 20 to 30 minutes or until light golden brown.

5. Cool on a rack. Cut into wedges and serve or store.

Confectioners, or powdered, sugar is granulated sugar that has been pulverized. It dissolves quickly and is ideal for icings and candy-making. You can substitute 1¾ cup packed confectioners sugar for 1 cup granulated sugar.

Lemon Tea Cakes

MAKES 36 COOKIES

For cookies:

⅔ cup sugar
1 cup (2 sticks) **LAND O LAKES® Butter,** softened
1 egg
½ teaspoon salt
1 teaspoon vanilla extract
2¼ cups all-purpose flour
1½ teaspoons grated lemon zest
1 to 2 drops yellow food coloring, if desired

For glaze:

1½ cups confectioners sugar
3 to 4 tablespoons milk
1 drop yellow food coloring, if desired

Candied violets or tiny frosting flowers

1. Heat the oven to 350° F.

2. In a large mixer bowl, combine the sugar, butter, egg, salt, and vanilla. Beat at medium speed, scraping the bowl often, until creamy, 2 to 3 minutes. By hand, stir in the flour until well mixed.

3. In a small bowl, place ¾ cup dough. By hand, stir in the lemon zest and food coloring. Shape the dough into thirty-six ½-inch balls.

4. Divide the remaining dough into 36 pieces. Place 1 lemon dough ball in the center of each piece of dough. Shape into 1-inch balls, making sure the lemon dough is covered.

5. Place 2 inches apart on baking sheets. Bake 15 to 18 minutes or until the edges are lightly browned. Cool completely.

6. In a medium bowl, stir together the glaze ingredients. Dip the top of each cookie into the glaze and let excess drip off. Place on a rack over wax paper. Garnish with candied violets before the glaze sets.

7. Serve or store in an airtight container.

Holiday Cutout Cookies

2½ cups all-purpose flour
1 cup sugar
1 cup (2 sticks) **LAND O LAKES® Butter,** softened
1 egg
1 teaspoon baking powder
2 tablespoons milk
2 teaspoons almond extract
Colored sugars (optional)
Frosting (optional)
Decorator candies (optional)

1. Heat the oven to 400° F.

2. In a large mixer bowl, combine the flour, sugar, butter, egg, baking powder, milk, and almond extract.

3. Beat at low speed, scraping the bowl often, until well mixed, 1 to 2 minutes.

4. Divide the dough into thirds and wrap in plastic food wrap. Refrigerate overnight or until firm, at least 2 hours.

5. On a lightly floured surface, roll out the dough, one-third at a time (keeping the remaining dough refrigerated), to ¼-inch thickness.

6. Cut with 3-inch cookie cutters. If the dough becomes too soft, return it to the refrigerator to firm up.

7. Place 1 inch apart on ungreased baking sheets. Sprinkle the cookies with colored sugar, if desired, or bake plain.

8. Bake 6 to 10 minutes or until the edges are lightly browned.

9. Cool completely. Decorate or frost the cookies, if desired, and serve.

Triple Almond Cookies

½ cup (1 stick) butter, softened
½ cup vegetable shortening
1 cup sugar
2 eggs
½ teaspoon almond extract
1 teaspoon vanilla extract
¾ cup **Blue Diamond® Chopped Almonds**
3 cups sifted all-purpose flour
½ teaspoon salt
Red and green sugar crystals
½ cup **Blue Diamond® Sliced Almonds**

1. In a large bowl, cream the butter and shortening with the sugar until smooth and creamy. Add the eggs and extracts and combine well. Fold in the chopped almonds.

2. In a medium bowl, combine the flour and salt. Fold into the butter mixture until a stiff dough is formed.

3. Shape the dough into 2 logs, each with a diameter of 2 to 3 inches. Wrap tightly in wax paper or plastic wrap and freeze at least 2 hours.

4. Heat the oven to 350° F.

5. Remove the logs from the freezer. Cut the dough into ¼-inch discs and place on ungreased baking sheets. Sprinkle with the sugar crystals and top with 3 almond slices in a cloverleaf pattern.

6. Bake 10 to 12 minutes.

7. Allow to cool for 2 minutes on the baking sheet, then transfer to a rack. Cool completely. Serve or store.

Lemon Oat Lacies

MAKE ABOUT 54 COOKIES

2 cups (4 sticks) margarine, softened
1 cup sugar
2 cups all-purpose flour
3 cups **Quaker® Oats** (quick *or* old-fashioned)
1 tablespoon grated lemon zest
1 teaspoon vanilla extract
Confectioners sugar

1. In a medium bowl, beat the margarine and sugar until creamy. Add the flour, oats, lemon zest, and vanilla. Mix well. Cover and chill 30 minutes.
2. Heat the oven to 350° F.
3. Shape the dough into 1-inch balls. Place on an ungreased baking sheet and flatten with the bottom of a glass dipped in the confectioners sugar.
4. Bake 12 to 15 minutes or until the edges are light golden brown.
5. Cool 1 minute. Remove the cookies to a rack. Cool completely.
6. Sprinkle with confectioners sugar, if desired. Serve or store.

To keep cookies fresh after baking, store them at room temperature in a tightly covered container. Most types will keep this way for 2 weeks. Keep chewy cookies soft by placing a piece of bread in the cookie jar. Refresh crisp cookies by briefly heating them at 300° F in an oven. If you wish to freeze cookies, cover them tightly and store in the freezer up to 3 months.

Choc-Oat Chip Cookies

MAKES ABOUT 60 COOKIES

1 cup (2 sticks) margarine *or* butter, softened
1¼ cups firmly packed brown sugar
½ cup sugar
2 eggs
2 tablespoons milk
2 teaspoons vanilla extract
1¾ cups all-purpose flour
1 teaspoon baking soda
½ teaspoon salt (optional)
2½ cups **Quaker® Oats** (quick *or* old fashioned)
1 package (12 ounces) semisweet chocolate chips (2 cups)
1 cup coarsely chopped nuts (optional)

1. Heat the oven to 375° F.
2. In a large bowl, beat the margarine and sugars until creamy. Add the eggs, milk, and vanilla and beat well. Add the flour, baking soda, and salt, if using. Mix well. Stir in the oats, chocolate chips, and nuts, if using. Mix well.
3. Drop by rounded measuring tablespoonfuls onto an ungreased baking sheet. Bake 9 to 10 minutes for a chewy cookie or 12 to 13 minutes for a crisp cookie.
4. Cool 1 minute on the baking sheet. Remove the cookies to a rack. Cool completely. Serve or store.

Cream Cheese Cookies

MAKES 36 3½-INCH COOKIES

2 squares (1 ounce *each*) semisweet chocolate
2 cups all-purpose flour
½ teaspoon baking powder
¼ teaspoon salt
½ cup (1 stick) butter
1 package (3 ounces) **Cream Cheese**
1 cup sugar
1 egg
1 teaspoon vanilla extract

1. In a small saucepan, melt and cool the chocolate.

2. Combine the flour, baking powder, and salt.

3. With an electric mixer, combine the butter and cream cheese.

4. Add the sugar and continue beating until fluffy. Add the chocolate, egg, and vanilla, beating well. Add the flour mixture and beat until thoroughly blended.

5. Cover and refrigerate overnight.

6. On a lightly floured surface, roll half the dough to a ⅛-inch thickness, keeping the remainder refrigerated.

7. Cut with a cookie cutter and place on a greased baking sheet. Return the dough scraps from the cutting board to the refrigerator to cool before rolling out. Continue in this fashion until all the dough is used.

8. Heat the oven to 375° F. Bake approximately 8 minutes.

9. Let cool. Serve or store in an airtight container.

COURTESY: DAIRY MANAGEMENT, INC.

Sensibly Delicious Chocolate Crinkle-Top Cookies

MAKES ABOUT 36 COOKIES

1½ cups all-purpose flour
1½ teaspoons baking powder
¼ teaspoon salt
1 package (12 ounces) **Nestlé® Toll House® Semi-Sweet Chocolate Morsels** (2 cups), divided
1 cup sugar
2 tablespoons margarine, softened
1½ teaspoons vanilla extract
2 egg whites
¼ cup water
½ cup confectioners sugar

1. In a small bowl, combine the flour, baking powder, and salt.

2. In a small, heavy saucepan, over low heat, melt 1 cup morsels and stir until smooth.

3. In a large mixer bowl, beat the sugar, margarine, and vanilla. Beat in the melted chocolate. Beat in the egg whites. Gradually beat in the dry ingredients alternately with the water. Stir in the remaining morsels. Cover and chill until firm.

4. Heat the oven to 350° F.

5. Shape the dough into 1½-inch balls and roll in confectioners sugar to coat generously. Place on greased baking sheets. Bake 10 to 15 minutes or until the sides are set but the centers are still slightly soft.

6. Cool 2 minutes. Remove to racks to cool completely. Serve or store in an airtight container.

Santa's Favorite Chocolate Chip Pecan Cookies

MAKES ABOUT 54 COOKIES

2¾ cups all-purpose flour
1¼ teaspoons baking soda
 1 teaspoon salt
1½ cups (3 sticks) butter, softened
1½ cups firmly packed brown sugar
 1 teaspoon vanilla extract
 2 eggs
 2 packages (12 ounces *each*) **Nestlé® Toll House® Semi-Sweet Chocolate Morsels** (4 cups)
 1 cup chopped pecans

1. Heat the oven to 375° F.

2. In a small bowl, combine the flour, baking soda, and salt.

3. In a large bowl, beat the butter, sugar, and vanilla until creamy.

4. Add the eggs one at a time, beating well after each. Gradually beat in the flour mixture. Stir in the morsels and pecans.

5. Drop by well-rounded tablespoonfuls onto ungreased baking sheets. Bake 10 to 12 minutes.

6. Let stand 2 minutes. Remove to a rack to cool completely before serving.

Crunchy Peanut Butter Cookies

MAKES ABOUT 36 COOKIES

1¼ cups all-purpose flour
 ½ teaspoon baking soda
 ½ teaspoon ground cinnamon
 ½ teaspoon salt
 ¾ cup (1½ sticks) butter, softened
 ½ cup firmly packed brown sugar
 ½ cup sugar
 ½ cup creamy peanut butter
 1 egg
 1 teaspoon vanilla extract
 1 package (12 ounces) **Nestlé® Toll House® Semi-Sweet Chocolate Morsels** (2 cups)
 ½ cup coarsely chopped unsalted peanuts

1. Heat the oven to 375° F.

2. In a small bowl, combine the flour, baking soda, cinnamon, and salt. Set aside.

3. In a large mixer bowl, beat the butter, brown sugar, sugar, and peanut butter until creamy. Beat in the egg and vanilla. Gradually beat in the flour mixture. Stir in the morsels and peanuts.

4. Drop the dough by rounded tablespoonfuls onto ungreased baking sheets. Press down slightly to flatten into 2-inch circles. Bake 7 to 10 minutes or until the edges are set but the centers are still soft.

5. Let stand 2 minutes. Remove to racks to cool completely. Serve or store in an airtight container.

Giant Pizzazz Cookie

2 cups all-purpose flour
1 teaspoon baking soda
1 cup (2 sticks) butter *or* margarine
½ cup firmly packed light brown sugar
1 teaspoon vanilla extract
1 cup **"M&M's"® Semi-Sweet** *or* **Milk Chocolate Mini Baking Bits**
¾ cup shredded coconut
½ cup dry roasted peanuts
½ cup caramel topping

1. Heat the oven to 350° F.
2. In a large bowl, combine the flour and baking soda. Set aside.
3. Cream the butter, sugar, and vanilla until light and fluffy. Add the flour mixture, just blending. The dough will be crumbly.
4. Pat the dough evenly into a greased 12-inch round pizza pan or a 13×9-inch baking pan. Prick the crust with a fork. Bake 15 to 16 minutes or until firm.
5. Combine the "M&M's"® Mini Baking Bits, coconut, and peanuts.
6. Spread the warm crust evenly with the caramel topping. Sprinkle evenly with the combined chocolate, coconut, and nut mixture. Pat lightly. Bake 5 minutes or until the coconut begins to turn golden.
7. Cool completely. Cut into wedges or bars and serve.

"M&M's" is a registered trademark of Mars, Incorporated.

Chocolate Coconut Snowballs

½ cup (1 stick) butter
1 package (3 ounces) cream cheese, softened
¾ cup sugar
1 egg yolk
2 teaspoons almond extract
2 teaspoons orange juice
1¼ cups all-purpose flour
2 teaspoons baking powder
¼ teaspoon salt
1 package (14 ounces) coconut (about 5 cups), divided
1 package (12 ounces) **"M&M's"® Semi-Sweet Mini Chocolate Baking Bits** (1¾ cups)

1. In a large bowl, cream the butter, cream cheese, and sugar. Add the egg yolk, almond extract, and orange juice and beat well.
2. In another large bowl, combine the flour, baking powder, and salt. Gradually add to the creamed mixture. Stir in 3 cups coconut, cover tightly, and chill at least 1 hour.
3. Heat the oven to 350° F.
4. Mix "M&M's"® Semi-Sweet Mini Chocolate Baking Bits into the chilled dough. Shape the dough into 1-inch balls. On a sheet of wax paper, roll the balls in the remaining 2 cups coconut. Place on ungreased baking sheets.
5. Bake 10 to 12 minutes or until light brown.
6. Cool, then serve. Store in an airtight container.

"M&M's" is a registered trademark of Mars, Incorporated.

Fudge Revel Cookies

MAKES 42 COOKIES

¾ cup firmly packed brown sugar
½ cup sugar
1 cup (2 sticks) **LAND O LAKES® Butter,** softened
2 eggs
1 teaspoon vanilla extract
2⅓ cups all-purpose flour
1 teaspoon baking soda
½ teaspoon salt
2 squares (1 ounce *each*) semisweet baking chocolate, melted and cooled

1. Heat the oven to 350° F.

2. In a large mixer bowl, combine the brown sugar, sugar, and butter. Beat at medium speed, scraping the bowl often, until creamy, 1 to 2 minutes. Add the eggs and vanilla. Continue beating until well mixed, 1 to 2 minutes.

3. Reduce speed to low. Add the flour, baking soda, and salt. Beat, scraping the bowl often, until well mixed, 1 to 2 minutes.

4. Pour the cooled chocolate over the cookie dough and swirl with a knife just enough to create a marbled effect. Do not overmix.

5. Drop by rounded teaspoonfuls 2 inches apart onto ungreased baking sheets. Bake 11 to 13 minutes or until lightly browned.

6. Let stand 1 minute. Remove from the baking sheets.

7. Serve or store in an airtight container.

Chocolate Almond Crinkles

MAKES 36 COOKIES

¼ cup almond *or* vegetable oil
1 cup sugar
2 eggs
1 teaspoon vanilla extract
¼ teaspoon almond extract
2 squares (1 ounce *each*) unsweetened chocolate, melted and cooled
1 cup cake flour
1 teaspoon baking powder
¼ teaspoon salt
½ cup sifted confectioners sugar
½ cup **Blue Diamond® Natural Sliced Almonds,** toasted

1. In a medium bowl, blend the almond oil with the sugar, eggs, vanilla, almond extract, and chocolate. Mix well.

2. In a small bowl, combine the flour, baking powder, and salt. Blend into the creamed mixture. Cover with plastic wrap and chill thoroughly for several hours.

3. Heat the oven to 350° F.

4. Lightly dust a flat surface with flour and roll the dough into thirty-six 1-inch balls. Roll in the confectioners sugar and place on a non-stick baking sheet 1 inch apart. Press several almonds (crisscross pattern) in the center of each cookie.

5. Bake 8 to 10 minutes. Do not overbake.

6. Cool on a rack. Store in an airtight container.

Peanut Butter 'n' Milk Chocolate Chip Cookies

MAKES ABOUT 48 COOKIES

¾ cup (1½ sticks) **Parkay® Stick,** softened
1 cup sugar
1 cup firmly packed brown sugar
½ cup peanut butter
2 eggs
2 teaspoons vanilla extract
2½ cups all-purpose flour
1 teaspoon baking soda
½ teaspoon salt
1 package (11½ ounces) **Baker's® Milk Chocolate Chips**
  (2 cups)

1. Heat the oven to 350° F.
2. In a large bowl, with an electric mixer on medium speed, beat the spread, sugars, and peanut butter until light and fluffy. Blend in the eggs and vanilla. Mix in the flour, baking soda, and salt. Stir in the chips.
3. Drop by rounded tablespoonfuls onto ungreased baking sheets. Bake 10 to 12 minutes or until lightly browned.
4. Cool 2 minutes. Remove from the baking sheets onto racks to cool completely. Serve or store in an airtight container.

Butterscotch Fruit Drops

(PHOTO PAGE 296)
MAKES ABOUT 72 DROPS

2 cups all-purpose flour
1 teaspoon baking soda
½ teaspoon salt
½ cup (1 stick) butter *or* margarine, softened
¾ cup firmly packed brown sugar
1 egg
2 tablespoons milk
1 teaspoon grated lemon zest (optional)
1 package (12 ounces) **Nestlé® Toll House® Butterscotch Flavored Morsels** (2 cups)
1 cup mixed dried fruit, chopped *or* raisins

1. Heat the oven to 350° F. In a small bowl, combine the flour, baking soda, and salt. Set aside.
2. In large mixer bowl, beat the butter and brown sugar until creamy. Beat in the egg, milk, and lemon zest. Gradually beat in the flour mixture. Stir in the butterscotch morsels and fruit.
3. Drop by rounded measuring teaspoonfuls onto ungreased baking sheets. Bake 9 to 11 minutes until golden brown.
4. Let stand 2 minutes. Remove from the baking sheets and cool. Serve or store in an airtight container.

*M*elting chocolate in the microwave is a quick and convenient way to avoid using a double-boiler. Place 1 ounce of chocolate in a small microwave-safe bowl. Heat it on high just until shiny, 1 to 2 minutes. As it melts, the chocolate will hold its shape, so stop once during cooking and stir. Remove from the microwave and continue to stir the chocolate until it is completely melted and smooth.

Sensibly Delicious Chocolate Chip Brownies

MAKES 24 BROWNIES

1 package (12 ounces) **Nestlé® Toll House® Semi-Sweet Chocolate Morsels** (2 cups), divided
1 cup sugar
½ cup unsweetened applesauce
2 tablespoons margarine
3 egg whites
1¼ cups all-purpose flour
¼ teaspoon baking soda
¼ teaspoon salt
1 teaspoon vanilla extract
⅓ cup chopped nuts

1. Heat the oven to 350° F.

2. In a large heavy saucepan, over low heat, melt 1 cup morsels, sugar, applesauce, and margarine, stirring until smooth. Remove from the heat.

3. Add the egg whites and stir well. Stir in the flour, baking soda, salt, and vanilla. Stir in the remaining morsels and nuts.

4. Spread into a greased 13×9-inch baking pan. Bake 16 to 20 minutes or just until set.

5. Remove from the oven and cool completely. Cut into 2-inch squares and serve.

Sensibly Delicious Chocolate Chip Brownies (top), Butterscotch Fruit Drops (page 295)

Frosted Brownies

1 cup all-purpose flour
⅔ cup sugar
¼ cup unsweetened cocoa
2 tablespoons cornstarch
1 teaspoon baking powder
½ teaspoon baking soda
¾ teaspoon salt
2 egg whites, lightly beaten
½ cup evaporated skim milk
½ cup **Mott's® Natural Apple Sauce**
⅓ cup corn syrup
1 teaspoon vanilla extract

For cocoa icing:

1 cup confectioners sugar
1 tablespoon unsweetened cocoa
½ teaspoon vanilla extract
1 tablespoon skim milk

1. In a medium bowl, mix together the flour, sugar, cocoa, cornstarch, baking powder, baking soda, and salt until blended.

2. In a separate bowl, stir together the egg whites, evaporated skim milk, applesauce, corn syrup, and vanilla. Add the dry mixture to the wet and stir until just blended.

3. Heat the oven to 350° F. Spray an 8-inch square baking pan with nonstick cooking spray.

4. Pour the batter into the baking pan. Bake 30 to 35 minutes or until a cake tester comes out clean. Remove from the oven and cool.

5. To prepare the icing: In a medium bowl, blend all the icing ingredients. Beat with a wire whisk until smooth.

6. Spread the icing on the brownies and serve.

Brownies

½ cup (1 stick) butter, melted
½ cup sugar
½ cup firmly packed brown sugar
½ cup unsweetened cocoa
2 eggs
½ cup all-purpose flour
1 teaspoon baking powder
1 teaspoon vanilla extract
½ cup chopped pecans *or* walnuts

1. Heat the oven to 350° F.

2. In a mixing bowl, beat the butter, sugars, and cocoa until well blended. Beat in the eggs, one at a time.

3. In a small bowl, mix the flour and baking powder together. Stir into the cocoa mixture. Stir in the vanilla and nuts.

4. Pour the mixture into a greased or foil-lined 8-inch square baking pan. Bake 25 to 30 minutes or until a cake tester or toothpick inserted in the center comes out clean.

5. Cool completely. Cut into 2-inch squares and serve.

A quick alternative to chopping walnuts is to put the nuts in a plastic bag, seal it tightly, then roll it lightly with a rolling pin. Nuts are high in fat and therefore prone to becoming rancid. Buy nuts in small quantities and store in airtight containers in a cool place. Shelled nuts can be refrigerated up to 4 months.

Cream Cheese Brownies

- 4 squares (1 ounce *each*) German sweet chocolate
- 2 tablespoons butter
- 3 eggs, divided
- 1½ teaspoons vanilla extract, divided
- 1 cup sugar, divided
- ½ cup all-purpose flour
- ½ teaspoon baking powder
- ¼ teaspoon salt
- 1 package (3 ounces) **Cream Cheese,** at room temperature

1. In a small saucepan, melt the chocolate and butter, stirring together.

2. In a large bowl, combine 2 eggs and 1 teaspoon vanilla. Gradually add ¾ cup sugar and beat until thick.

3. In a medium bowl, combine the flour, baking powder, and salt. Add to the egg mixture, beating well. Blend in the chocolate mixture. Heat the oven to 350° F.

4. In a separate bowl, beat the cream cheese and remaining sugar until fluffy. Add the remaining egg and vanilla and blend well.

5. Pour half the chocolate mixture into a greased and floured 8-inch square baking dish. Spread the cheese mixture on top and dot with spoonfuls of the chocolate mixture. With a knife, swirl all the layers for a marbled effect.

6. Bake 40 minutes or until a cake tester comes out clean.

7. Serve or store in an airtight container.

COURTESY: DAIRY MANAGEMENT, INC.

Pecan Pie Bars

- 1½ cups all-purpose flour
- ½ cup plus 2 tablespoons firmly packed dark brown sugar, divided
- ½ cup (1 stick) **I Can't Believe It's Not Butter!®,** chilled plus 2 tablespoons **I Can't Believe It's Not Butter!®,** melted
- 2 eggs, beaten
- 1 cup chopped pecans or walnuts
- 1 teaspoon vanilla extract
- ¼ teaspoon salt

1. Heat the oven to 350° F.

2. In a medium bowl, mix together the flour and 2 tablespoons brown sugar. With a fork or pastry blender, cut in ½ cup I Can't Believe It's Not Butter!® until it resembles coarse crumbs. Pat into an ungreased 8-inch square baking dish.

3. Bake 15 minutes.

4. In a medium bowl, combine the ½ cup brown sugar, 2 tablespoons melted I Can't Believe It's Not Butter!®, eggs, nuts, vanilla, and salt. Pour over the baked layer. Bake 20 to 25 minutes.

5. Let cool. Cut into 2×1½-inch bars and serve.

Pecan Pie Bars

Czechoslovakian Pastry Bars

MAKES ABOUT 48 BARS

1½ cups (3 sticks) **I Can't Believe It's Not Butter!**®, softened
1¼ cups sugar
2 eggs
1 teaspoon vanilla extract
1 teaspoon salt
3¾ cups all-purpose flour, divided
1 cup chopped walnuts
1 jar (12 ounces) raspberry preserves *or* jam

1. Heat the oven to 350° F.

2. In a large bowl, cream together I Can't Believe It's Not Butter!® and sugar until light and fluffy. Beat in the eggs and vanilla until well combined.

3. In a medium bowl, mix the salt with 3½ cups flour. Gradually add to I Can't Believe It's Not Butter!® mixture to form a thick batter.

4. Spread ¾ of the batter evenly over the surface of an 17×11-inch jelly-roll pan or baking sheet with a rim. Spread the jam in an even layer on top. Sprinkle the nuts evenly over all. Blend the remaining flour with the rest of the dough. Crumble on top.

5. Bake 35 minutes or until the crust is golden brown. Cool completely and cut into bars. Serve.

Oatmeal Extravaganzas

MAKES 36 SQUARES

1 cup all-purpose flour
1½ teaspoons baking powder
½ teaspoon salt
1 cup firmly packed brown sugar
¾ cup (1½ sticks) butter, softened
1 teaspoon vanilla extract
1 egg
2 tablespoons water
2 cups quick-cooking oats
1 package (12 ounces) **Nestlé® Toll House® Semi-Sweet Chocolate Morsels** (2 cups)

1. Heat the oven to 375° F.
2. In a small bowl, combine the flour, baking powder, and salt.
3. In a large mixer bowl, beat the brown sugar, butter, and vanilla until creamy. Beat in the egg. Gradually blend in the flour mixture, then the water. Stir in the oats and morsels.
4. Spread in a greased 9-inch square pan. Bake 30 to 35 minutes.
5. Cool. Cut into 1½-inch squares and serve.

Butterscotch Cream Cheese Bars

MAKES 36 BARS

1 package (10 ounces) butterscotch chips
½ cup (1 stick) butter
2 cups graham cracker crumbs
1 package (8 ounces) **Cream Cheese**
1 can (14 ounces) sweetened condensed milk
1 teaspoon vanilla extract
1 egg
1 cup chopped pecans

1. In a medium saucepan, melt the butterscotch chips and butter over low heat. Remove from the heat. Stir in the cracker crumbs and mix well. Reserve ⅔ cup mixture.
2. Press the remainder firmly into the bottom of a buttered 13×9-inch ovenproof glass baking dish, making a uniform layer.
3. Heat the oven to 325° F.
4. In a large bowl, beat the cream cheese until light and fluffy. Beat in the condensed milk, vanilla, and egg and fold in the nuts. Pour into the prepared pan. Scatter the reserved crumb mixture evenly over the top.
5. Bake 25 to 30 minutes or until the cake tester comes out clean. Cool to room temperature, then chill.
6. Cut into 1½×2-inch bars and serve.

COURTESY: DAIRY MANAGEMENT, INC.

Cheesecake Squares

Cheesecake Squares

MAKES 16 SQUARES

1 cup sugar, divided
⅓ cup (5 tablespoons plus 1 teaspoon) butter
1½ cups graham cracker crumbs
3 packages (8 ounces *each*) **Cream Cheese**, at room temperature
4 eggs
1 teaspoon vanilla extract
1 can (21 ounces) blueberry filling *or* topping
16 large ripe strawberries, hulled

1. Heat the oven to 325° F. In a medium saucepan, heat ¼ cup sugar and the butter on low heat until the butter is melted, stirring occasionally. Stir in the graham cracker crumbs. Press the mixture evenly over the bottom of a 13×9-inch baking pan.

2. In a large bowl, with an electric mixer, beat the cream cheese until smooth. Gradually beat in the remaining sugar. Beat in the eggs, one at a time, and the vanilla until well blended.

3. Spoon the blueberry filling evenly over the crust. Pour the cream cheese mixture over the blueberries. Bake just until set, 45 to 50 minutes. Cool. Chill until cold, about 2 hours or longer.

4. Cut into 16 squares. Garnish with the strawberries and serve.

COURTESY: DAIRY MANAGEMENT, INC.

Double-Chocolate Fantasy Bars

MAKES 32 BARS

⅓ cup (5 tablespoons plus 1 teaspoon) butter *or* margarine (not spread), melted

2 cups chocolate cookie crumbs

1 can (14 ounces) sweetened condensed milk

1 package (12 ounces) **"M&M's"® Semi-Sweet Chocolate Mini Baking Bits** (1¾ cups)

1 cup shredded coconut

1 cup chopped walnuts *or* pecans

1. Heat the oven to 350° F (325° F for a glass pan).

2. In a bowl, combine the butter and cookie crumbs. Press the mixture into the bottom of a 13×9-inch baking pan.

3. Pour the sweetened condensed milk evenly over the crumbs.

4. Combine "M&M's"® Semi-Sweet Chocolate Mini Baking Bits, coconut, and nuts. Sprinkle the mixture evenly over the condensed milk. Press in lightly.

5. Bake 25 to 30 minutes or until set. Cool completely before cutting.

6. Serve or store in an airtight container.

"M&M's" is a registered trademark of Mars, Incorporated.

Candy Bar Squares

MAKES 24 SQUARES

1 container (8 ounces) **Parkay® Soft Margarine**

1 cup sugar

½ cup firmly packed brown sugar

2 eggs

3 cups all-purpose flour

1 teaspoon baking soda

1 teaspoon salt

6 chocolate-covered nut *or* nougat-filled candy bars (about 1¾ ounces *each*), chopped, divided

1. Heat the oven to 350° F.

2. In a large bowl, with an electric mixer on medium speed, beat the margarine and sugars together until light and fluffy. Blend in eggs.

3. Mix in the flour, baking soda, and salt.

4. Reserve ½ cup chopped candy bars for the topping. Stir the remaining candy into the batter.

5. Spread the mixture into an ungreased 13×9-inch baking pan. Scatter the reserved ½ cup candy evenly over the top.

6. Bake 25 to 30 minutes or until lightly browned.

7. Cool in the pan on a rack. Cut into squares and serve.

Cream Cheese Mints

Cream Cheese Mints

MAKES 36 1-INCH MINTS

1 package (3 ounces) **Cream Cheese,** softened
½ teaspoon peppermint extract
3 cups confectioners sugar, sifted
Rainbow sugar (optional)

1. In a large bowl, with an electric mixer, beat together the cream cheese and peppermint extract. Add the confectioners sugar gradually and beat until smooth, kneading the last of the sugar in with your hands.
2. Form the mixture into balls the size of a cherry and roll in rainbow sugar, if desired. Place on wax paper and flatten with a fork. Let stand overnight.
3. Serve or store in an airtight container.

COURTESY: DAIRY MANAGEMENT, INC.

Fudgemallow Candy

MAKES ABOUT 16 SQUARES

1 package (12 ounces) **Baker's® Semi-Sweet Real Chocolate Chips** (2 cups)
1 cup chunky peanut butter
1 bag (6¼ ounces) miniature marshmallows (3½ cups)

1. Microwave the chocolate chips and peanut butter in a microwave-safe 2-quart bowl on medium (50%) for 2 to 3 minutes or until melted, stirring after each minute.
2. Fold in the marshmallows. Pour into a greased 9-inch square pan. Smooth over the top. Chill until firm.
3. Cut into squares. Serve or store in an airtight container.

Fantasy Fudge

MAKES 3 POUNDS

¾ cup (1½ sticks) **Parkay® Soft Margarine**
3 cups sugar
⅔ cup evaporated milk
1 package (12 ounces) **Baker's® Semi-Sweet Real Chocolate Chips** (2 cups)
1 jar (7 ounces) **Kraft® Marshmallow Cream**
1 cup chopped nuts
1 teaspoon vanilla extract

1. In a 4-quart bowl or casserole, microwave the margarine on high for 1 minute or until melted. Add the sugar and milk. Mix well.
2. Microwave 5 minutes or until the mixture begins to boil, stirring after 3 minutes. Mix well and scrape the bowl. Continue microwaving 5½ minutes. Stir after 3 minutes.
3. Gradually stir in the chips until melted. Add the remaining ingredients and mix well.
4. Pour into a lightly greased 9-inch square or 13×9-inch baking pan.
5. Cool at room temperature. Cut into squares. Serve or store.

*I*f you do not have the type of chocolate called for in a recipe, you can use these substitutions. For 1 ounce of unsweetened chocolate, use 3 tablespoons cocoa plus 1 tablespoon shortening. For 1⅔ ounces of semisweet chocolate, use 1 ounce unsweetened chocolate plus 4 teaspoons sugar. Bittersweet and semisweet chocolate can be used interchangeably.

Mocha Walnut Truffles

MAKES 24 TRUFFLES

1 package (8 ounces) bittersweet *or* semisweet chocolate, finely chopped
½ cup heavy whipping cream
1 tablespoon instant coffee powder
2 tablespoons vanilla extract
1½ cups ground walnuts
Reynolds® Plastic Wrap

1. Place the chocolate in a medium bowl.

2. Heat the cream in a small saucepan, over medium heat, just until it boils. Add the coffee powder and stir until dissolved.

3. Pour over the chocolate and let stand 30 seconds. Whisk until smooth. Stir in the vanilla.

4. Place a sheet of plastic wrap over the surface of the chocolate mixture. Refrigerate 6 hours or overnight.

5. Place the walnuts on a plastic wrap–lined baking sheet. Roll rounded teaspoons of the truffle mixture into balls. Roll in the nuts until evenly coated.

6. Refrigerate covered with plastic wrap. Serve.

*E*vaporated milk is canned, unsweetened, homogenized milk which has had 60% of its water content removed. Sweetened condensed milk consists of whole milk and sugar. It too has had 60% of its water content removed. The result is a very sweet and sticky mixture. Evaporated milk and sweetened condensed milk cannot be substituted for each other.

Easy "Toffee" Candy

MAKES ABOUT 50 PIECES

1¼ cups (2½ sticks) butter (not margarine), divided
35 to 40 soda crackers
1 cup firmly packed dark brown sugar
1 can (14 ounces) **Carnation® Sweetened Condensed Milk** (1¼ cups)
1½ cups **Nestlé® Toll House® Semi-Sweet Chocolate Morsels**
¾ cup finely chopped walnuts

1. Heat the oven to 425° F.

2. In a medium saucepan, melt ¼ cup butter. Pour evenly into a heavy-duty foil-lined 15½×10½-inch jelly-roll pan. Arrange the crackers over the butter. Cut the crackers to fill any empty spaces.

3. Melt the remaining butter in the same saucepan and stir in the sugar. Bring to a boil over medium heat. Reduce the heat and cook 2 minutes, stirring occasionally.

4. Remove from the heat and stir in the sweetened condensed milk. Spread evenly over the crackers.

5. Bake 10 to 12 minutes until the mixture is bubbly and slightly darkened. Carefully remove from the oven. Cool 1 minute.

6. Sprinkle with the chocolate morsels and let stand 5 minutes until melted. Spread the chocolate. Sprinkle with the nuts and press into the chocolate.

7. Cool. Chill until the chocolate is set. Invert the jelly-roll pan and dislodge the candy. Remove the foil and cut the candy into pieces. Serve or store in an airtight container.

Topsy-Turvy Delights

MAKES 36 PIECES

2 cups **Wheat Chex® brand cereal,** crushed to 1¼ cups
1 cup flaked coconut
½ cup golden raisins
½ cup all-purpose flour
½ teaspoon baking powder
½ teaspoon ground cinnamon
½ cup (1 stick) butter *or* margarine
½ cup firmly packed brown sugar
¼ cup honey
½ cup semisweet chocolate chips
½ teaspoon vegetable shortening
Almonds (optional)
Pecans (optional)
Confectioners sugar (optional)
Chocolate drizzle (optional)

1. Heat the oven to 350° F. Grease 36 miniature muffin cups.

2. In a medium bowl, combine the cereal, coconut, raisins, flour, baking powder, and cinnamon. Mix well and set aside.

3. In a saucepan, combine the butter, sugar, and honey. Cook over medium heat, stirring until the butter melts and the sugar is dissolved. Pour over the cereal mixture, stirring until well combined.

4. Place 1 tablespoon mixture into each prepared muffin cup. Press firmly onto the bottom and sides.

5. Bake 12 to 14 minutes or until golden brown. Cool in the pan for 10 minutes. Loosen the edges and remove. Cool completely.

6. In a small saucepan, over low heat, melt the chocolate chips and shortening. Stir until smooth. Remove from the heat.

7. Dip the bottoms of the baked cups into the chocolate. Allow excess chocolate to drip off. Cool chocolate-side-up.

8. Decorate, if desired, with almonds, pecans, sugar, or chocolate drizzle. Serve.

®Chex cereal brands are registered trademarks of General Mills, Inc.

Chocolate Walnut Toffee Candy

MAKES ABOUT 36 PIECES

1 cup (2 sticks) butter *or* margarine
1 cup sugar
1 package (12 ounces) **Nestlé® Toll House® Semi-Sweet Chocolate Morsels** (2 cups), divided
1 cup finely chopped walnuts, divided

1. Over medium heat, in a medium heavy saucepan, heat the butter and sugar to boiling, stirring constantly. Boil 6 minutes or until golden colored, stirring constantly.

2. Pour into a buttered 9-inch square baking pan. Let stand 3 minutes or until the top begins to firm.

3. Sprinkle 1 cup morsels over the toffee. Let stand 5 minutes or until the morsels are shiny. Spread the chocolate over the surface. Sprinkle ½ cup walnuts over the chocolate and press down slightly.

4. Chill 15 minutes or until the chocolate is firm. Invert the toffee onto a wax paper–lined tray.

5. Microwave the remaining morsels in a small microwave-safe bowl on high for 1 minute. Stir. Microwave at additional 10- to 20-second intervals, stirring until smooth.

6. Dry off any excess moisture from the cooled toffee surface. Spread the chocolate over the toffee. Sprinkle with the remaining walnuts and press down slightly.

7. Chill until firm. Break into bite-size pieces with a sharp knife. Serve or store in an airtight container.

Desserts

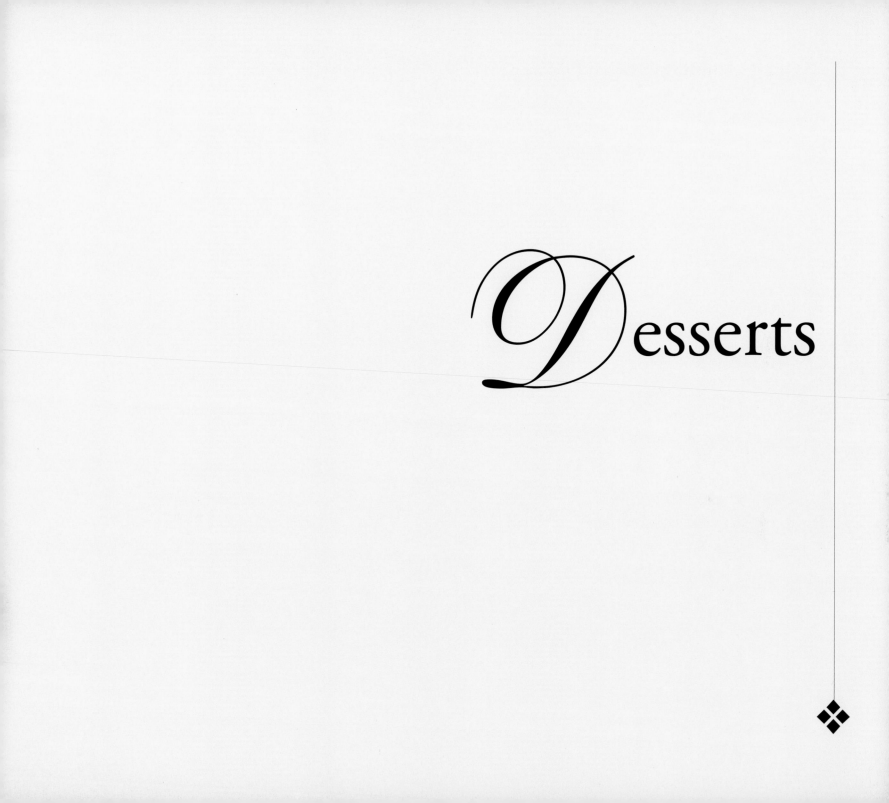

Orange and Raisin Bread Pudding

SERVES 8

3 eggs
⅓ cup sugar
2 cups milk
½ cup **Florida Orange Juice**
1 tablespoon grated orange zest
1 teaspoon vanilla extract
1 teaspoon ground cinnamon
½ teaspoon freshly grated nutmeg
½ teaspoon grated lemon zest
12 slices firm-textured white bread, lightly toasted with crusts removed, divided
3 **Florida Oranges,** peels, pith, and membranes removed, cut into small pieces (2 cups), divided
½ cup raisins, divided
3 tablespoons orange marmalade
Sifted confectioners sugar

1. In a large bowl, beat the eggs with an electric mixer until combined. Add the sugar, a little at a time. Beat the mixture until it ribbons when the beater is lifted, 8 to 10 minutes. Add the milk, orange juice and zest, vanilla, spices, and lemon zest and beat until combined.

2. Line a buttered 8-inch square baking dish with 4 slices of bread. Top the bread with half the orange pieces and half the raisins.

3. Spoon one-third of the custard over the mixture. Add another layer of bread, top with the remaining orange pieces and raisins.

4. Spoon half the remaining custard over the mixture. Top with the remaining bread slices. Spoon the rest of the custard over the bread, carefully pressing down on the top layer so that it is covered with the custard.

5. Cover the pudding with plastic wrap and chill 1 hour or overnight.

6. Heat the oven to 350° F.

7. Spread the orange marmalade on top of the pudding.

8. Set the baking dish in a larger baking pan, adding enough hot water to the larger pan to reach halfway up the sides of the dish. Bake 1 hour or until puffed, golden brown, and a toothpick inserted in the center comes out clean.

9. Let cool to warm. Sprinkle with confectioners sugar before serving.

COURTESY: FLORIDA DEPARTMENT OF CITRUS

Banana Split Pudding Cup

SERVES 6

2 cups low-fat milk
1 package (3⅝ ounces) vanilla-flavor instant pudding and pie filling
2 medium bananas, sliced
1 cup miniature marshmallows
1 cup chocolate bear-shaped graham snacks
1 cup frozen whipped topping, thawed
Reynolds® Crystal Color® Plastic Wrap
6 maraschino cherries
Colored sprinkles

1. In a large bowl, beat the milk and pudding mix with a wire whisk until well blended, 1 to 2 minutes.

2. Stir in the banana slices, marshmallows, and graham snacks.

3. Spoon evenly into six dessert dishes. Top each with the whipped topping. Cover with plastic wrap and refrigerate until ready to serve.

4. Before serving, garnish each dessert with a cherry, colored sprinkles, and a graham snack.

Peach Melba Bread Pudding

SERVES 8

4 cups low-sodium white bread cubes

1 can (16 ounces) sliced peaches in their own juice, drained and chopped; reserve ¼ cup juice

½ cup seedless raisins

1¼ cups skim milk

1 carton (8 ounces) **Egg Beaters® Healthy Real Egg Substitute**

½ cup sugar

2 tablespoons **Fleischmann's® Original Spread,** melted

1 teaspoon vanilla extract

¼ teaspoon ground cinnamon

½ cup seedless raspberry preserves, warmed

1. Heat the oven to 350° F.

2. In a greased 2-quart casserole, combine the bread cubes, peaches, and raisins. Set aside.

3. In a medium bowl, combine the reserved peach juice, milk, egg product, sugar, margarine, vanilla, and cinnamon. Pour over the bread mixture.

4. Bake 45 to 50 minutes or until a knife inserted in the center comes out clean. Serve warm topped with the preserves.

Applesauce Bread Pudding

SERVES 8 TO 10

1 loaf (16 ounces) light-style white bread

1 cup raisins

2 teaspoons ground cinnamon

2 cups skim milk

1 cup **Mott's® Natural Apple Sauce**

8 egg whites

½ cup firmly packed brown sugar

1½ teaspoons vanilla extract

1. Cut the sliced bread into ½-inch cubes. Toss with the raisins and cinnamon in a large bowl.

2. Beat together the milk, applesauce, egg whites, sugar, and vanilla. Pour the mixture over the bread cubes and let stand 25 minutes.

3. Heat the oven to 350° F.

4. Spray an 8-inch square baking pan with nonstick cooking spray.

5. Pour the bread mixture into the prepared pan and bake 35 to 40 minutes or until a knife inserted in the center comes out clean.

6. Remove from the oven. Let cool 15 to 20 minutes and serve.

❖

Instead of whipping heavy cream for desserts, you can make a lighter topping with milk. In a medium freezer-safe bowl, pour 1 cup whole milk or evaporated skim milk. Place in the freezer until very cold and ice crystals appear. Using an electric mixer on high, beat until thick and foamy. Beat in 1 tablespoon superfine or confectioners sugar and ½ teaspoon vanilla extract. Serve immediately.

Citrus Mousse

SERVES 4

1 package (3 ounces) vanilla-flavor pudding and pie filling (not instant)

1½ cups cold milk

1 egg, lightly beaten

2 teaspoons grated lemon, lime, *or* orange zest

¼ cup fresh lemon *or* lime juice, *or* frozen orange juice concentrate, undiluted

1 cup frozen whipped topping, thawed

1. In a medium saucepan, whisk together pudding, milk, and egg. Over medium-high heat, bring to a boil, stirring constantly. Boil 1 minute. Remove from the heat and stir in the zest and juice.

2. Transfer to a medium bowl. Place plastic wrap directly over the surface and refrigerate until cool, about 1 hour. Fold in the topping.

3. Spoon into serving bowls or use a pastry bag to fill hollowed-out citrus shells. Chill thoroughly before serving.

COURTESY: DAIRY MANAGEMENT, INC.

Rhubarb Custard Dessert

SERVES 12

For crust:

- 2 cups all-purpose flour
- ½ cup (1 stick) **LAND O LAKES® Butter,** softened
- 2 tablespoons sugar

For filling:

- 2 cups sugar
- ¼ cup all-purpose flour
- 1 cup whipping cream
- 6 egg yolks, reserve egg whites
- ¼ teaspoon salt
- 5 cups chopped rhubarb *or* 2 packages (16 ounces *each*) frozen chopped rhubarb, thawed and drained

For meringue:

- 6 reserved egg whites
- ¼ teaspoon salt
- 1 teaspoon vanilla extract
- ¾ cup sugar

1. Heat the oven to 350° F.
2. In a small mixer bowl, combine all the crust ingredients. Beat at low speed, scraping the bowl often, until crumbly, 1 to 2 minutes. Press on the bottom of a 13×9-inch baking pan.
3. Bake 15 minutes.
4. Meanwhile, in a large mixer bowl, combine all the filling ingredients *except* rhubarb. Beat at medium speed, scraping the bowl often, until smooth, 1 to 2 minutes. By hand, stir in the rhubarb. Pour over the hot crust.
5. Continue baking 45 to 55 minutes or until firm to the touch.
6. Increase the oven temperature to 400° F.
7. In a clean large mixer bowl with clean beaters, whip the egg whites at high speed, scraping the bowl often, until soft peaks form, 1 to 2 minutes. Add the salt and vanilla. Continue beating, gradually adding the sugar, until stiff peaks form, 2 to 4 minutes.
8. Spread the meringue over the filling, sealing around the edges. Continue baking 6 to 8 minutes or until the meringue is lightly browned.
9. Cool completely. Store refrigerated until ready to serve.

Eggnog Pudding

SERVES 4

- 2 cups milk
- 1 package (4-serving size) **Jell-O® Vanilla Flavor Instant Pudding & Pie Filling**
- ½ teaspoon rum extract
- ¼ teaspoon ground nutmeg

1. Pour the milk into a medium bowl. Add the pudding mix, rum extract, and nutmeg. Beat with a wire whisk for 2 minutes. Transfer to dessert glasses. Refrigerate until ready to serve.

When separating egg yolks from whites, make sure the eggs are cold. However, when beating egg whites, they should be at room temperature for the greatest volume. Beat egg whites with grease-free beaters in a clean glass or metal — not plastic — bowl with a pinch of cream of tartar to help stabilize them. Freeze egg whites in an ice cube tray, then transfer them to a freezer bag. They'll keep for a month.

Cranberry Steamed Pudding

SERVES 12

For pudding:

  2 cups all-purpose flour
  1 cup sugar
  1 cup milk
  1 egg
  2 tablespoons **LAND O LAKES® Butter,** softened
  1 teaspoon baking soda
  1 teaspoon ground cinnamon
  1 teaspoon ground nutmeg
  ¼ cup all-purpose flour
  2 cups fresh *or* frozen whole cranberries

For sauce:

  ½ cup sugar
  ½ cup firmly packed brown sugar
  ½ cup (1 stick) **LAND O LAKES® Butter**
  ½ cup whipping cream
  1 teaspoon vanilla extract

1. In a large mixer bowl, combine all the pudding ingredients *except* ¼ cup flour and cranberries. Beat at medium speed, scraping the bowl often, until well mixed, 1 to 2 minutes.

2. In a small bowl, toss together ¼ cup flour and cranberries.

3. Fold the cranberry mixture into the batter by hand. Pour into a greased 1½-quart metal mold. Cover tightly with foil.

4. Place a rack in a Dutch oven. Add boiling water to just below the rack. Place the mold on the rack and cover.

5. Cook over medium heat at a low boil for 2 hours or until a wooden pick inserted in the center comes out clean. Add boiling water occasionally to keep the water level just below the rack.

6. Remove from the Dutch oven and let stand 2 to 3 minutes. Remove foil and unmold. Serve warm or cold with warm sauce.

7. To make the sauce: In a 1-quart saucepan, combine all the sauce ingredients *except* vanilla. Cook over medium heat, stirring occasionally, until the mixture thickens and comes to a full boil, 4 to 5 minutes. Boil 1 minute. Stir in the vanilla. Store the sauce in the refrigerator.

Holiday Cranberry Mold

SERVES 10

  2 cups boiling water
  1 package (8-serving size) *or* 2 packages (4-serving size *each*) **Jell-O® Cranberry Flavor Gelatin***
  1½ cups cold ginger ale *or* water
  2 cups halved green *and/or* red seedless grapes
  1 can (11 ounces) mandarin orange segments, drained

1. In a large bowl, stir the boiling water into the gelatin for 2 minutes or until completely dissolved. Stir in the cold ginger ale.

2. Refrigerate about 1½ hours or until thickened (a spoon drawn through leaves an impression).

3. Stir in the fruit. Spoon into a 5-cup mold. Refrigerate 4 hours or until firm.

4. In a bowl slightly larger than the mold, filled halfway with warm water, dip the mold in the water about 15 seconds. Gently pull the gelatin from around the edges with moist fingers. Place a moistened serving plate on top of the mold. Invert the mold and plate. Holding the mold and plate together, shake slightly to loosen. Gently remove the mold and center the gelatin on the plate. Serve.

VARIATION

*Or use **Jell-O® Cranberry Flavor Sugar Free Low Calorie Gelatin Dessert** and diet ginger ale.

Lite Fruit Whip

2 cans (16 ounces *each*) **Del Monte® Lite Fruit Cocktail**, drained; reserve ⅔ cup liquid
1 cup orange juice, chilled and divided
1 package (3 ounces) orange *or* lemon flavor gelatin
Zest of 1 lemon, grated
2 tablespoons lemon juice
1 teaspoon vanilla extract
2 egg whites, at room temperature

1. In a medium saucepan, combine the reserved fruit liquid and ½ cup orange juice. Heat to boiling. Add the gelatin and dissolve completely. Stir in the remaining orange juice, lemon zest, lemon juice, and vanilla.
2. Chill until partially set, 60 to 70 minutes.
3. Add the egg whites and beat with an electric mixer until double in size and creamy, 5 to 7 minutes.
4. In a serving bowl, spread half the fruit cocktail. Top with the gelatin mixture and chill until firm.
5. Top with the remaining fruit and serve.

Hot Caramel Apples

¼ cup (½ stick) butter *or* margarine
½ cup sugar
1 teaspoon ground cinnamon
1 cup regular *or* low-fat evaporated milk
4 large Granny Smith or Golden Delicious apples, peeled, cored, and cut into ½-inch slices

1. In a large heavy-bottomed skillet, over medium-high heat, melt the butter and add the sugar. Stir rapidly just until the mixture is golden brown, 1 to 2 minutes. Stir in the cinnamon.
2. Remove the pan from the heat and add the milk. Return to the heat, stirring, until the hardened sugar dissolves and the mixture looks like caramel, 2 to 3 minutes.
3. Add the apples and coat with caramel. Cover the skillet, reduce the heat, and simmer until the apples are just tender, about 5 minutes.
4. With a slotted spoon, transfer the apples to a serving bowl. Over high heat, bring the caramel to a boil until thickened, 1 to 2 minutes. Pour over the apples. Serve.

Apples are available year-round, but are at their best during the harvest season of late summer through fall. This is the period when you can find a wider selection, especially of local types. Although thousands of apple varieties exist, only a few are produced in sufficient quantity for supermarket distribution. Apples in the United States were once sprayed with the chemical protective agent alar, but the practice was stopped in 1989. For this reason, some apple varieties may appear more blemished than in the past. At room temperature, apples ripen quickly. To keep them fresh longer, store them in a plastic bag in the refrigerator.

Peach Pear Parfait

Peach Pear Parfait

SERVES 8

1 can (16 ounces) **Del Monte® Yellow Cling Sliced Peaches,** drained
1 can (16 ounces) **Del Monte® Bartlett Sliced Pears,** drained
⅓ cup apple cider
3 egg yolks
¾ cup sifted confectioners sugar
½ teaspoon ground allspice
Dash salt
1 cup whipping cream
Raspberries (optional)

1. In a bowl, combine the fruit. Sprinkle with 2 tablespoons apple cider and toss. Cover and chill.

2. In the top of a double boiler, blend the egg yolks, sugar, allspice, and salt until smooth. Blend in the remaining apple cider.

3. Cook over hot water, stirring constantly until thickened, about 10 to 12 minutes. Chill.

4. Whip the cream until stiff peaks form and fold into the egg mixture. Spoon over the fruit. Garnish with raspberries, if desired, and serve.

❖ ❖ ❖ ❖ ❖ ❖ ❖ ❖ ❖ ❖ ❖ ❖ ❖ ❖ ❖

For best results when whipping cream, the cream and utensils should be cold. Chill the beaters and mixing bowl in the freezer about 30 minutes before whipping to allow the cream to whip to its greatest volume and best consistency.

Peaches and Cream

SERVES 6 TO 8

½ cup frozen whipped topping, thawed
1 cup peach yogurt
½ teaspoon vanilla extract
¼ teaspoon almond extract
2 cans (16 ounces *each*) **Del Monte® Yellow Cling Sliced Peaches,** drained and chilled
Toasted sliced almonds (optional)

1. In a medium bowl, combine the whipped topping, yogurt, and flavorings and chill.

2. In individual small glass dishes, arrange the peach slices and top with the yogurt mixture.

3. Garnish with toasted sliced almonds, if desired, and serve.

Crisp Fruit Medley

SERVES 4 TO 6

1 cup pineapple chunks, fresh, frozen, *or* canned
1 cup orange segments *or* canned mandarin oranges
1 cup red *or* green seedless grapes
1 banana, sliced
1 cup shredded coconut
1 cup miniature marshmallows
1 carton (8 ounces) plain *or* flavored yogurt
1 cup **Quaker® Oatmeal Squares™ (Regular *or* Cinnamon)**

1. In a large bowl, gently stir together all the ingredients *except* cereal. Chill at least 1 hour.

2. Just before serving, fold in or sprinkle on the cereal.

Strawberry Parfaits

SERVES 4

4 slices low-fat pound cake, cut into cubes
¼ cup corn syrup
¼ cup plus 2 tablespoons lime juice, divided
2 teaspoons grated lime zest, divided
2 packages (10 ounces *each*) frozen sliced strawberries, thawed and drained
1 envelope unflavored gelatin
2 cartons (8 ounces *each*) **2% Low-fat Strawberry Yogurt**
2 egg whites

1. Divide the cake among four goblets.

2. In a small bowl, mix the corn syrup, ¼ cup lime juice, and 1 teaspoon lime zest. Drizzle over the cake.

3. In a large bowl, toss the strawberries with the remaining lime juice and lime zest. Reserve.

4. In a small saucepan, sprinkle the gelatin over ¼ cup water and let sit 1 minute. Dissolve over very low heat and stir.

5. If the fruit is on the bottom of the yogurt, blend, then add to the strawberries. Stir in the gelatin.

6. In a medium bowl, beat the egg whites until stiff. Fold into the strawberry yogurt mixture. Spoon into the goblets over the cake. Refrigerate at least 2 hours and serve.

COURTESY: DAIRY MANAGEMENT, INC.

Chocolate Sack

Chocolate Sack

SERVES 6

1 sheet frozen puff pastry
1 package (8 ounces) semisweet chocolate
⅓ cup chopped walnuts
2 tablespoons butter *or* margarine
Confectioners sugar

1. Thaw the pastry for 20 minutes.
2. Heat the oven to 425° F.
3. On a floured board, roll the pastry sheet to a 14-inch square. In the center of the square, place the chocolate, walnuts, and butter. Pull the pastry edges together, twist, and turn.
4. Place on an ungreased baking sheet and bake 20 minutes. Let stand at least 10 minutes.
5. Sprinkle with the confectioners sugar and serve.

Fresh coconuts are available year-round, but the convenience of packaged coconut has made it the more popular choice for cooking and baking. It comes in a variety of forms: sweetened and unsweetened, flaked or shredded, and dried, moist, or frozen. Coconut is high in fat and should be refrigerated after opening.

Cherry Snowflake Trifle

SERVES 14

1 fat-free pound cake (12 to 16 ounces)
½ cup strawberry jam
2 teaspoons almond extract, divided
3 packages (3½ ounces *each*) coconut cream–flavor instant pudding and pie filling
3 cups skim milk
1 quart nonfat frozen vanilla yogurt, slightly softened
1 can (20 ounces) light cherry pie filling
¼ cup flaked coconut
Reynolds® Plastic Wrap

1. Cut the top from the pound cake to make an even rectangle. Slice the cake horizontally into layers.
2. In a small bowl, combine the jam and 1 teaspoon almond extract. Brush the cut sides of the layers and the cake top with the mixture. Set the top aside.
3. Stack the layers and cut crosswise into ½-inch slices. Place the cake slices vertically around the side and along the bottom of a 3-quart straight-sided bowl. Reserve the leftover slices.
4. In a large bowl, beat together the pudding mix and milk until thickened. Add the softened yogurt and beat well.
5. Pour the pudding into the cake-lined bowl until even with the top of the cake slices. Reserve the remaining pudding.
6. Combine the pie filling and remaining 1 teaspoon almond extract.
7. Spoon a ring of pie filling around the edge of the bowl. Cube all the remaining cake and place in the center of the cherry ring. Top with the remaining pudding and pie filling. Sprinkle the coconut in the center.
8. Cover the bowl with plastic wrap. Refrigerate over-night before serving.

Strawberry Angel Trifle

SERVES 14

1 8-inch purchased angel food cake
½ cup strawberry fruit spread, melted and divided
1 can (22 ounces) lemon pie filling
1 carton (12 ounces) frozen whipped topping, thawed
1 can (20 ounces) pineapple chunks, drained
   or 2½ cups fresh pineapple chunks, drained
4 kiwi fruit, peeled and sliced
2 pints strawberries, hulled and sliced
Reynolds® Plastic Wrap

1. Cut the angel food cake in half. Tear half the cake into bite-size pieces.

2. Place the cake pieces in the bottom of a 3-quart glass bowl or trifle dish. Drizzle with half the melted fruit spread.

3. In a large bowl, combine the pie filling and whipped topping. Spread half the filling mixture over the cake pieces.

4. Layer half the pineapple, kiwi fruit, and strawberries over the filling mixture. Tear the remaining half cake into bite-size pieces. Place the cake pieces over the filling. Repeat the layers with the remaining ingredients.

5. Cover with plastic wrap and refrigerate at least 4 hours or overnight before serving.

Shortcake Biscuits

MAKES 9 BISCUITS

3 cups all-purpose flour
2½ tablespoons sugar
4½ teaspoons baking powder
¾ teaspoon cream of tartar
¾ teaspoon salt
¾ cup (1½ sticks) **I Can't Believe It's Not Butter!®**, chilled and diced
¾ cup milk
1 egg, beaten
Fresh *or* frozen strawberries, *or* other berries
Frozen whipped topping, thawed (optional)

1. Sift together the flour, sugar, baking powder, cream of tartar, and salt, or mix with a fork. Cut in the chilled I Can't Believe It's Not Butter!® Stir in the milk and egg. Mix to form a dough. Knead the dough once or twice on a floured surface. Shape into a ½-inch-thick square.

2. Cut into nine 3-inch biscuits. Place on a baking sheet. Heat the oven to 400° F. Bake 15 minutes.

3. Split the warm biscuits and top with your favorite fresh or frozen berries. Whipped topping may be added, if desired.

Shortcake Biscuits

Chocolate Cherry Dessert

SERVES 8 TO 10

⅔ cup confectioners sugar
1 package (3 ounces) cream cheese, softened
½ teaspoon almond extract
1 egg
1¾ cups **Bisquick® Original** *or* **Reduced Fat baking mix**
⅔ cup miniature semisweet chocolate chips
1 can (21 ounces) cherry pie filling
¼ cup vanilla chips
2 teaspoons vegetable shortening

1. Heat the oven to 400° F.

2. In a medium bowl, with an electric mixer, beat the confectioners sugar, cream cheese, almond extract, and egg. Stir in the baking mix until well blended.

3. Pat the dough into a 12-inch circle on an ungreased baking sheet. Bake 8 to 10 minutes or until light golden brown.

4. Sprinkle the chocolate chips over the hot crust. Bake 1 minute longer or until the chips are melted. Spread evenly.

5. Cool 5 minutes. Gently loosen and transfer to a serving plate. Spread the pie filling over the crust.

6. In a small saucepan, over low heat, melt the vanilla chips and shortening until smooth. Drizzle over the pie filling.

7. Cut into wedges and serve.

Apple Cobbler

SERVES 6 TO 8

¾ cup (1½ sticks) **I Can't Believe It's Not Butter!®,** divided
4 cups peeled and sliced tart apples such as Granny Smith
1 cup sugar, divided
2 teaspoons ground cinnamon
1 cup low-fat milk
1 egg
1½ cups all-purpose flour
2 teaspoons baking powder
½ teaspoon salt

1. In a small saucepan, melt ¼ cup (½ stick) I Can't Believe It's Not Butter!® and pour into an 8-inch square baking pan.

2. In a medium bowl, toss the apples with ½ cup sugar and the cinnamon. Spread evenly on the bottom of the prepared pan.

3. In a small saucepan, melt the remaining I Can't Believe It's Not Butter!® Add the milk and egg and beat well.

4. Heat the oven to 375° F.

5. In a large bowl, stir together the remaining ingredients. Add the milk and egg mixture and beat until smooth. Spread the batter evenly over the apples. Bake 40 to 45 minutes or until nicely browned on top.

6. While still warm, spoon onto plates, fruit side up, and serve.

Peachy Berry Crisp

SERVES 9

½ cup **Kretschmer® Wheat Germ,** any flavor
½ cup **Quaker Oats®** (quick *or* old-fashioned)
⅓ cup firmly packed brown sugar
¼ cup all-purpose flour
¼ cup (½ stick) margarine, melted
1 teaspoon ground cinnamon
2 bags (16 ounces *each*) frozen sliced peaches, thawed
2 cups fresh *or* frozen blueberries, unthawed
1 tablespoon all-purpose flour
Vanilla low-fat yogurt (optional)

1. Heat the oven to 375° F.
2. Combine the wheat germ, oats, brown sugar, ¼ cup flour, margarine, and cinnamon. Mix well. Set aside.
3. Combine the fruit and 1 tablespoon flour, tossing to coat. Spoon into an 8-inch square glass baking dish.
4. Top evenly with the wheat germ mixture. Bake 30 to 35 minutes or until the peaches are tender.
5. Serve topped with yogurt, if desired.

Quick-cooking and old-fashioned oats are both rolled oats, which means they have been formed by rolling the groats after the hulls are removed. The quick-cooking variety is a little thinner and therefore requires less cooking time. In baked goods for which the baking time is very brief, quick-cooking oats are preferable. It's best to use whichever type is called for in a recipe.

Georgia Peach Crumble

SERVES 8 TO 10

2 cans (16 ounces *each*) **Del Monte® Yellow Cling Sliced Peaches**
1 can (12 ounces) peach nectar
3 tablespoons cornstarch
1 tablespoon sugar
1 teaspoon ground cinnamon
½ teaspoon ground nutmeg
1 cup quick-cooking *or* old-fashioned oats
½ cup all-purpose flour
½ cup firmly packed brown sugar
½ teaspoon baking soda
¼ teaspoon salt
½ cup (1 stick) butter, softened
½ cup unsalted peanuts
Vanilla ice cream (optional)

1. Drain the peaches, reserving the syrup. Add the nectar to measure 2½ cups total liquid.
2. In a small saucepan, combine the reserved syrup mixture, cornstarch, sugar, cinnamon, and nutmeg. Stir to dissolve the cornstarch. Cook, stirring constantly, until thickened.
3. Heat the oven to 350° F.
4. In a large bowl, combine the oats, flour, brown sugar, baking soda, and salt. With a pastry cutter, cut the butter into the dry ingredients until well blended. Stir in the peanuts.
5. Place the peaches in a greased 13×9-inch baking dish. Top with syrup mixture. Sprinkle with the crumb topping. Bake 30 minutes.
6. Serve warm, and, if desired, with vanilla ice cream.

Three-Berry Kuchen

Three-Berry Kuchen

SERVES 8

1¾ cups all-purpose flour, divided
2 teaspoons baking powder
½ teaspoon baking soda
½ teaspoon salt
4 egg whites
2 tablespoons sugar
⅔ cup **Mott's® Natural Apple Sauce**
¼ cup plain nonfat yogurt
1 teaspoon lemon zest
2 cups assorted berries such as blueberries, raspberries, and blackberries, frozen, fresh, *or* canned
¼ cup firmly packed brown sugar
2 tablespoons cold margarine

1. Heat the oven to 350° F. Spray a 10-inch springform pan with nonstick cooking spray.
2. In a medium bowl, combine 1½ cups flour, baking powder, baking soda, and salt. In a large bowl, whisk the egg whites, sugar, applesauce, yogurt, and lemon zest until smooth. Add the flour mixture all at once to the wet ingredients. Stir until blended.
3. Place in the prepared pan. Place the berries on top of the batter.
4. In a small bowl, combine the remaining flour and brown sugar. Cut in the cold margarine and mix until evenly blended. Put the topping on the batter.
5. Bake 50 to 55 minutes. Cool 20 minutes before serving.

Classic Fruit Crisp

SERVES 9

For topping:

½ cup **Kretschmer® Wheat Germ**, any flavor
½ cup **Quaker® Oats** (quick *or* old-fashioned)
¼ cup all-purpose flour
¼ cup firmly packed brown sugar
¼ cup (½ stick) margarine, melted
½ teaspoon ground cinnamon

For filling:

6 cups peeled and thinly sliced apples, peaches, *or* pears
¼ cup water
¼ cup firmly packed brown sugar
2 tablespoons all-purpose flour
½ teaspoon ground cinnamon

Vanilla frozen yogurt (optional)

1. Heat the oven to 375° F.
2. In a small bowl, combine the topping ingredients and mix well. Set aside.
3. In a large bowl, combine the filling ingredients, *except* frozen yogurt, tossing to coat. Spoon into an 8-inch square glass baking dish. Sprinkle the wheat germ mixture evenly over the top.
4. Bake 30 to 35 minutes or until the fruit is tender.
5. Serve warm, topped with frozen yogurt, if desired.

Chocolate Meringue Cups with Chocolate Sauce

Chocolate Meringue Cups with Chocolate Sauce

MAKES 12 MERINGUE CUPS

For chocolate meringue cups:

3 egg whites
⅛ teaspoon cream of tartar
⅛ teaspoon salt
1 cup sifted confectioners sugar
1 teaspoon vanilla extract
1 cup **Nestlé® Toll House® Semi-Sweet Chocolate Mini Morsels**
Ice cream

For sauce:

1 cup **Nestlé® Toll House® Semi-Sweet Chocolate Mini Morsels**
½ cup whipping cream
2 tablespoons butter
¼ cup raspberry-flavored liqueur

1. Draw twelve 2-inch circles 1 inch apart on a parchment paper–lined baking sheet. Set aside. Heat the oven to 300° F.
2. In a large bowl, combine the egg whites, cream of tartar, and salt. Beat until soft peaks form.
3. Gradually add the confectioners sugar and vanilla. Beat until stiff peaks form. Fold in the chocolate morsels.
4. Spoon the meringue into the circles, making a well in the center.
5. Bake 25 minutes, then turn off the oven and let stand in the oven with the door ajar for 30 minutes.
6. To prepare the sauce: In a double boiler, over hot, not boiling, water, combine the chocolate, whipping cream, and butter.
7. Stir until the morsels are melted and the mixture is smooth. Stir in the liqueur. Serve warm or chilled.
8. To serve: Remove the meringue cups from the paper. Top each cup with a scoop of ice cream and the chocolate sauce.

Chocolate-Dipped Strawberries

MAKES 16 PIECES

½ cup semisweet chocolate chips
2 teaspoons whipping cream *or* butter
1 pint fresh strawberries (about 16) *or* 2 medium apples, cut into wedges
Fresh mint leaves (optional)

1. In a small double boiler, melt the chocolate chips over low heat.
2. Whisk the cream into the melted chocolate until smooth.
3. Dip the fruit in the warm sauce.
4. Lay the fruit on a plate lined with wax paper. Cool. Transfer to the refrigerator and allow the chocolate to harden.
5. When ready to serve, peel the fruit away from the wax paper and arrange on a serving plate. Garnish with mint leaves, if desired.

COURTESY: NATIONAL PORK PRODUCERS COUNCIL

Creamsicle Crunch

Creamsicle Crunch

SERVES 6

1 cup coarsely crushed chocolate wafer cookies
 (about 20 cookies)
1 envelope **Knox® Unflavored Gelatine**
⅓ cup orange juice
1 cup milk, heated to boiling
1 package (8 ounces) cream cheese, softened
½ cup sugar
1 teaspoon vanilla extract
½ teaspoon grated orange zest (optional)
1 cup frozen whipped topping, thawed

1. Divide ½ cup crushed cookies into six parfait glasses. Set aside.

2. In a blender, sprinkle the gelatin over the juice and let stand
 1 minute. Add the hot milk and process at low speed until the
 gelatin is completely dissolved, about 2 minutes.

3. Add the cream cheese, sugar, vanilla, and, if desired, orange zest.
 Process at high speed until blended. Add the whipped topping and
 pulse until just blended.

4. Pour into the parfait glasses and top with the remaining crushed
 cookies. Chill until firm, about 2 hours, and serve.

*W*hipped cream can be prepared ahead. For 8
 ounces of cream put 1 tablespoon cold water
in a cup, add ¹/₂ teaspoon unflavored gelatin, and set in a
pan of simmering water. Stir until the gelatin dissolves;
cool. In a bowl, whip the cream until soft peaks form; add
the dissolved gelatin. Whip until stiff. Cover and refrigerate up to 24 hours. Whisk the cream before serving.

Raspberry Surprise

SERVES 10

36 ladyfingers, cut in half
1 can (16 ounces) sliced peaches, drained
1 envelope **Knox® Unflavored Gelatine**
¼ cup cold water
½ cup sugar
2 bags (12 ounces *each*) frozen raspberries, thawed, puréed, and, if desired, strained
¾ cup heavy whipping cream

1. Line the sides and bottom of a 9-inch springform pan with ladyfingers, overlapping, if necessary, to cover completely. Spread the peaches in a single layer over the bottom. Set aside.
2. In a medium saucepan, sprinkle the gelatin over the water and let stand 1 minute. Stir over low heat until the gelatin is completely dissolved, about 3 minutes. Stir in the sugar until dissolved.
3. Remove from the heat and gradually whisk in the raspberry purée and cream. Pour into the prepared pan and chill until firm, about 4 hours.
4. Release the springform pan and serve.

Blueberry Bombe

SERVES 8

1 envelope **Knox® Unflavored Gelatine**
½ cup cold milk plus 1 cup milk heated to boiling
1 package (12 ounces) frozen unsweetened blueberries *or* strawberries, rinsed
¼ cup sugar
2 cups frozen whipped topping, thawed
Grated lemon zest (optional)

1. In a blender, sprinkle the unflavored gelatin over the cold milk and let stand 2 minutes. Add the hot milk. Process at low speed until the gelatin is completely dissolved, about 2 minutes. Add the blueberries and sugar. Process until blended, about 1 minute.
2. Pour into a large bowl, then, with a wire whisk, blend in the whipped topping.
3. Pour into eight dessert cups and chill until firm, about 3 hours.
4. Garnish, if desired, with additional whipped topping and grated lemon zest and serve.

Dessert Cheese Spread

SERVES 8

8 ounces **Sharp Cheddar Cheese**, cut into 1-inch pieces
1 package (8 ounces) **Cream Cheese**, softened and cut into 1-inch pieces
1 teaspoon ground nutmeg
3 tablespoons vanilla extract
⅔ cup pitted dates, chopped
⅔ cup walnuts, chopped

1. In a food processor with the knife blade, blend the Cheddar cheese, cream cheese, nutmeg, vanilla, and dates for 1 minute.
2. Press the mixture firmly into a shallow 7-inch container lined with plastic wrap.
3. Close the sides of the plastic wrap over the cheese mixture and chill 4 hours.
4. Unmold the cheese and remove the plastic wrap.
5. Press the walnuts onto the top and sides of the cheese.
6. Serve with fruit and plain cookies.

COURTESY: DAIRY MANAGEMENT, INC.

Choco-Orange Dessert Log

SERVES 32

1 package (8 ounces) cream cheese, slightly softened
½ cup confectioners sugar
2 teaspoons grated orange zest
Reynolds® Crystal Color® Plastic Wrap
⅓ cup miniature semisweet chocolate chips
⅓ cup chopped pecans
Chocolate wafers, ginger snaps, *or* other crisp cookies

1. In a medium bowl, combine the cream cheese, confectioners sugar, and orange zest.
2. Place the mixture on a sheet of plastic wrap. Overlap the sides of the plastic wrap over the mixture. Using the plastic wrap, roll and shape the mixture into an 8-inch log. Fold the ends of the plastic wrap under the log. Chill at least 2 hours.
3. Before serving, sprinkle the chocolate chips and pecans on another sheet of plastic wrap. Unwrap the chilled log and roll in the chocolate chips and pecans to coat.
4. Serve as a spread with crisp cookies.

Strawberry Ice

SERVES 6 TO 8

4 cups strawberries (about 2 pints), halved
1 bag (10½ ounces) miniature marshmallows
1 tablespoon milk
1 tablespoon lemon juice
1 teaspoon grated lemon zest

1. Place the strawberries in a blender or food processor fitted with a steel blade and cover. Blend until smooth.
2. In a large microwave-safe bowl, microwave the marshmallows and milk on high for 1 to 2 minutes or until smooth when stirred. (Or, in a large saucepan, over low heat, stir together the marshmallows and milk until smooth.) Cool slightly and pour the marshmallow mixture into a large mixing bowl.
3. Gradually add the strawberries to the marshmallow mixture, beating until well blended. Blend in the lemon juice and zest.
4. Pour into a 9-inch square baking pan and freeze 2 hours or until almost firm.
5. Coarsely chop the mixture and spoon into a chilled mixing bowl. Beat with an electric mixer until smooth. Freeze 4 to 6 hours or until firm.
6. Spoon into dessert glasses and serve.

To grate lemon, orange, or lime rind for zest, lay a piece of parchment paper, wax paper, or plastic wrap under the fine-hole side of a metal grater. Grate a few strokes with the fruit, just until the pith, the bitter white part, begins to appear. Move to a new spot on the fruit and grate. The zest, the colored part of the rind, will collect on the paper. Grated zest from oranges and lemons freezes well. Before using the fruit, first grate the rind and store it in the freezer for later use.

Ultimate Fudge Sundae

SERVES 4

1 tablespoon **I Can't Believe It's Not Butter!**®
1 cup chopped pecans
¼ teaspoon salt
1 pint vanilla ice cream *or* frozen yogurt
Chocolate Fudge Sauce
Caramel Sauce

1. In a medium skillet, over medium heat, melt I Can't Believe It's Not Butter!® Stir in the pecans and toast 3 to 5 minutes, stirring occasionally until golden brown. Sprinkle the salt over the nuts and mix well. Spread the nuts onto wax paper to cool.
2. On another piece of wax paper drop a 2- to 3-inch-diameter scoop of ice cream. Gather the wax paper around the ice cream and quickly form into a ball. Drop onto the pecans and quickly roll to cover with pecans.
3. Transfer the pecan ball to a piece of plastic wrap. Wrap securely and place in the freezer until firm or ready to serve.
4. Repeat with the remaining ice cream.
5. Into individual serving bowls, spoon about 2 tablespoons *each* fudge sauce and caramel sauce. Remove the ice cream from the freezer. Unwrap and place in the bowls over the sauces.

Chocolate Fudge Sauce

MAKES 2½ CUPS

½ cup (1 stick) **I Can't Believe It's Not Butter!**®
1 cup semisweet chocolate chips (6 ounces)
1 can (12 ounces) evaporated milk
1½ cups confectioners sugar
1 teaspoon vanilla extract

1. In a medium saucepan, over low heat, melt I Can't Believe It's Not Butter!® and chocolate, stirring until smooth.
2. Stir in the milk and sugar. On high heat bring to a boil, stirring constantly. Lower the heat, boil and stir 3 minutes until the sauce thickens. Remove from the heat and add the vanilla.
3. When cool, transfer the sauce to a covered container. Store in the refrigerator. (It will stay fresh for 1 week.)
4. Serve hot or cold.

Caramel Sauce

MAKES 1½ CUPS

½ cup (1 stick) **I Can't Believe It's Not Butter!**®
½ cup sugar
1 can (12 ounces) evaporated milk
1 teaspoon vanilla extract

1. In a medium saucepan, over high heat, melt I Can't Believe It's Not Butter!®
2. Add the sugar, stirring constantly, until the mixture turns golden brown, 3 to 5 minutes.
3. Remove from the heat and stir in the milk. Return to the heat and bring the mixture to a boil.
4. Lower the heat. Boil and stir 10 to 12 minutes until the sauce thickens. Remove from the heat and add the vanilla.
5. When cool, transfer the sauce to a covered container. Store in the refrigerator. (It will stay fresh for 1 week.)
6. Serve hot or cold.

❖

Beverages

Key West Kooler, Orange Fantasia, and Grapefruit Spritzer

Grapefruit Spritzer

SERVES 4

1 can (6 ounces) **Florida Frozen Concentrated Grapefruit Juice,** thawed, undiluted
2¼ cups chilled club soda *or* seltzer
4 teaspoons grenadine

1. Pour the juice into the pitcher. Slowly pour in the club soda and mix well.

2. Pour 1 teaspoon grenadine into each glass and fill with the grapefruit mixture.

3. Serve.

COURTESY: FLORIDA DEPARTMENT OF CITRUS

Orange Fantasia

SERVES 2

1½ cups **Florida Orange Juice**
1 cup orange sherbet (½ pint)
2 sprigs fresh mint leaves

1. In a blender, blend the juice and sherbet on medium speed until smooth.

2. Pour over cracked ice. Garnish with the mint and serve.

COURTESY: FLORIDA DEPARTMENT OF CITRUS

Key West Koolers

SERVES 2

1½ cups **Florida Grapefruit Juice**
1 small ripe banana, cut into chunks
1 ripe kiwi fruit, peeled and sliced
1 tablespoon honey
1 cup ice cubes
Orange julienne (optional)

1. In a blender, blend all the ingredients on high speed until smooth and frothy.
2. Pour into glasses, garnish with orange julienne, if desired, and serve.

COURTESY: FLORIDA DEPARTMENT OF CITRUS

Orange Tea Quencher

SERVES 4

4 rounded teaspoons unsweetened instant tea mix
2 cups cold water
½ cup orange juice
¼ cup lime juice
4 tablespoons **SugarTwin®**
1¼ cups club soda *or* sparkling water
Lime slices

1. In a 2-quart pitcher, combine the tea, water, orange juice, lime juice, and SugarTwin®. Mix well. Add the club soda.
2. Pour into ice-filled tall glasses. Garnish each with a slice of lime before serving.

Tropical Mockalada

SERVES 1

⅓ cup brewed **Lipton® Regular** *or* **Decaffeinated Tea,** chilled
⅓ cup crushed pineapple in natural juice, chilled
¼ cup light cream *or* half-and-half
⅓ large ripe banana
3 tablespoons cream of coconut
1 teaspoon lime juice
½ cup ice cubes (about 3 or 4)
Pineapple chunks (optional)

1. In a blender, combine all the ingredients *except* ice cubes and process at high speed until blended.
2. Add the ice cubes one at a time and process until the ice cubes are blended.
3. Garnish, if desired, with pineapple chunks threaded on a small paper parasol. Serve.

Boston Breeze

SERVES 1

½ cup brewed **Lipton® Regular** *or* **Decaffeinated Tea,** chilled
½ cup cranberry juice cocktail
½ cup orange juice
Seltzer

1. In a shaker, combine all the ingredients *except* seltzer and shake until blended.
2. Just before serving, add a splash of seltzer. Pour into an ice-filled glass and serve.

Tea Sparkler

Tea Sparkler

SERVES 5

3 cups brewed **Lipton® Regular** *or* **Decaffeinated Tea**, chilled

2 cups chilled grape juice

⅓ cup sugar

Few drops angostura bitters (optional)

Chilled club soda

1 medium orange, 1 medium lemon, and 1 medium lime, sliced (optional)

1. In a large pitcher, combine all the ingredients *except* club soda and fruit. Chill at least 2 hours.

2. Just before serving, add a splash of soda. Pour into ice-filled glasses and garnish, if desired, with orange, lemon, and lime slices.

Coffee Yogurt Refresher

SERVES 2

½ cup skim milk
4 teaspoons **Taster's Choice® Gourmet Roast™ freeze-dried coffee**
1 pint vanilla-flavored low-fat yogurt, frozen

1. In a blender, combine the skim milk and coffee. Cover and blend at high speed until the coffee is dissolved.
2. Add the frozen yogurt. Cover and blend at high speed just until blended. Serve immediately. Garnish as desired.

Peach Melba Tea Shake

SERVES 9

4½ cups boiling water
7 **Lipton® Flo-Thru Tea Bags**
⅓ cup sugar
6 cups vanilla ice cream (3 pints)
3 medium ripe peaches, halved
1½ cups raspberries (about ½ pint)
Fresh mint leaves (optional)

1. In a teapot, pour the boiling water over the tea bags. Cover and brew 5 minutes.
2. Remove the tea bags. Stir in the sugar and cool. For every three servings, combine in a 5-cup blender, 1½ cups tea mixture, 2 cups ice cream, 2 peach halves, and ½ cup raspberries. Process at high speed until well blended.
3. Garnish, if desired, with additional raspberries and mint. Serve.

Southwest Refresher

SERVES 3

1½ cups vegetable juice, chilled
½ cup peeled, chopped, and seeded cucumber
1 tablespoon lime juice
¼ teaspoon chili powder
1 cup ice cubes
4 cucumber slices (optional)

1. In a blender, combine the vegetable juice, chopped cucumber, lime juice, and chili powder. Blend until smooth.
2. Add the ice cubes, one at a time, blending until the ice is finely crushed.
3. Pour immediately into chilled glasses. Garnish with cucumber slices, if desired. Serve.

Tangy Twister

SERVES 3

2 cups vegetable juice
⅓ cup orange juice
¼ cup grapefruit juice
2 teaspoons honey
3 orange slices

1. In a 1-quart pitcher, combine the vegetable juice, orange juice, grapefruit juice, and honey.
2. Serve over ice. Garnish with the orange slices.

Fruit Shakes

SERVES 2

1 cup plain low-fat yogurt
½ cup **Low-fat Milk**
2 tablespoons honey
1 cup sliced fruit such as bananas, strawberries, *or* peaches

1. Place the ingredients in the container of an electric blender. Cover and whirl until smooth, 1 to 2 minutes.

2. Pour into glasses and serve.

COURTESY: DAIRY MANAGEMENT, INC.

Pink Passion Frappé

SERVES 2

2 ounces **Martinelli's® Gold Medal™ Sparkling Cider**
2 ounces pineapple juice
2 ounces cranberry juice
2 ice cubes
Whipped cream
Lime slices
Maraschino cherries

1. Blend together the cider, pineapple juice, cranberry juice, and ice cubes in a blender until frothy.

2. Serve in champagne glasses. Garnish with a dollop of whipped cream, a slice of lime, and a cherry.

Fruit Shakes

Warming Cran-Herbal Punch

SERVES 10

3½ cups water
2½ cups cranberry juice cocktail
8 **Lipton® Gentle Orange® Herbal Tea Bags**
¼ cup firmly packed brown sugar
Whole cranberries (optional)
Orange slices (optional)

1. In a large saucepan, bring the water and cranberry juice to a boil.
2. Add the tea bags. Cover and brew 5 minutes. Remove the tea bags.
3. Stir in the sugar. Garnish, if desired, with cranberry-skewered orange slices.
4. Ladle into cups or transfer to a punch bowl and serve.

Tangy Mulled Cider

SERVES 10

4 whole cloves
1 medium apple, cored and cut into 4 wedges
6 cups vegetable juice
2 cups apple cider
1 cinnamon stick (3 inches long)

1. Insert 1 clove into each apple wedge.
2. In a 3-quart saucepan, over medium heat, combine the vegetable juice, cider, cinnamon stick, and apple wedges. Heat 15 minutes.
3. Discard the apple wedges and cinnamon stick before serving.

Sparkling Rose Tea Punch

MAKES 8 CUPS (2 QUARTS)

4 cups water
8 **Lipton® Honey & Lemon Flavored Tea Bags**
16 ounces frozen strawberries, partially thawed
¼ cup sugar
5 ice cubes
1 cup seltzer, chilled
Thinly sliced lemons and oranges (optional)
Fresh mint leaves (optional)

1. In a medium saucepan, bring the water to a boil.
2. Add the tea bags, cover, and brew 5 minutes. Remove the tea bags. Chill the tea until very cold.
3. In a blender or food processor, process the strawberries, sugar, and ice cubes until smooth.
4. With a wire whisk or spoon, stir the fruit mixture into the chilled tea. Strain, if desired. Pour the punch into a serving bowl.
5. Just before serving, stir in the seltzer. Garnish, if desired, with thinly sliced lemons or oranges or fresh mint leaves.
6. Ladle into cups and serve.

When you have a party, you can decorate the punch bowl. Hang frosted red or green grapes in clusters around the rim or arrange a ring of delicate flowers along the base of the punch bowl.